Indus Fire Worship Cult

And

Vedic Yajna

A Comparative Study

Indus Fire Worship Cult
And
Vedic Yajna

A Comparative Study

Dipan Bhattacharya

A Translation By

Bibekananda Chatterjee

HORNBILL
PRESS

Indus Fire Worship Cult And Vedic Yajna
A Comparative Study by Dipan Bhattacharya
Translated By Bibekananda Chatterjee
ISBN: 978-81-965620-0-7
Cover & Illustration © Rajesh Deb
First Published in 2023 by
Hornbill Press
Price: INR 599 / $7.99 / €6.99

A Unit of Atmajaa Media Ventures Pvt. Ltd.
2/6, B. L. Ghosh Road, Kolkata – 700057
Phone: +91-9432718042, +91-6289457589
E-mail: presshornbill@gmail.com; info@hornbillbooks.co
Website: www.hornbillbooks.com
Copyright © 2023 Dipan Bhattacharya

Typeset in Garamond by Atmajaa Digital
Printed in India & Overseas at
Atmajaa Media Ventures Pvt. Ltd.
90/6A, Mahatma Gandhi Road, Kolkata - 07

To

My beloved Father

Late S.P. Bhattacharya

Ravindra Singh Bisht
P.G.D.A., Ph.D., Sahityaratna
Jt. Director General, ASI (retd.)
Padma Shri Awardee

9/19, Rajendranagar-3,
Sahibabad, Ghaziabad
Pin : 201005
Tel # 0120-3260196

Date: 06.06.2022

Harappan Civilisation opened a new dimension of the history of Indian sub-continent. Initially, excavations of Harappa and Mohenjo-daro brought the perspective of Indian antiquity into a new era. Most of the Harappan sites (excavated then) went to Pakistan at the time of partition but subsequently a large number of Indus sites have been found on Indian soil as a result of extensive diligence of Indian archeologists mostly belonging to the ASI. The exploration is still going on and new sites are being added into the list regularly.

The author Sandipani Bhattacharya is an avid independent researcher in this field. I know him for long and noticed his hard work and updated knowledge on the subject along with regular field work. He has done a good job by analyzing Harappan fire-places (usually containing a central column found in some sites) which still require more researches about their probable use. Many eminent archaeologists believe in their being fire altars. Apart from it, Mr. Bhattacharya has raised a very useful collection of antiquities from various Harappan sites of eastern zone. I am happy that he has gifted many of them to educational institutions for research purpose. Recently, his contribution to universities in Purulia and Bankura in West Bengal has widely welcomed by educationists and general public including students.

Publication of this book on the centenary year of Mohenjo-daro excavation is a remarkable incident and I wish overall success of the book.

TRANSLATOR'S NOTE

Knowing very little about the Vedic Yajnas and fire worship traditions of the Pre-Harappan and Indus valley civilization (that the author of this book considered my advantage), the translation of this book was a learning process. The author openhandedly suggested that I need not strictly follow his narratives. I should try to understand andinterpret, rather than simply translatecase-scenarios. Having my responsibilities clearly defined, I found satisfaction in attempting to make this book a valuable resource for a broader range of readers. This is particularly true for those individuals who, despite having limited knowledge of Vedic principles or the historical context of the Harappan culture, hold a keen interest in ancient religions.

I need to admit that only after reading the original book a number of times I was able to grasp the essence of fire worship, fertility cult and the inherent suggestion connecting to the eternal dynamics of the *"Purusha"* and *"Prakriti"* in the manifestation of an entire civilization with its cross-cultural interactions, fusion of beliefs and traditions, crafts and artistry as well as rites and rituals.

In Vedic context, the concept of "Kunda" meant fire-pit, with a religious connotation, hence the term was avoided in many cases where the fire was not the Vedic "Agni", but instrumental in fueling Harappan industry and craftwork.

I express my sincere gratitude to my family members, friends and especially my daughter Ananya who helped completing the task.

Bibekananda Chatterjee

AUTHOR'S NOTE

This marked my debut as an author, my first foray into writing. The book, titled "*Sindhu Sobhyotar Agnipuja o Boidik Yajna: Ekti Tulonamulok Alochona*," was written in Bengali. It received high acclaim within academic circles, earning me the prestigious "Rakhaldas Memorial Award" from the esteemed organization Bangiya Sahitya Parishad. My fascination with the Indus Valley Civilization (IVC) has been long-standing, stemming from my profound interest in archaeology and ancient history. The enigmatic facets of the Indus Valley Civilization transcended mere intellectual curiosity for me, evolving into an obsession. In India, remnants of this grand civilization are scattered across vast expanses, predominantly in the states of Rajasthan, Haryana, and Gujarat. While protected archaeological sites exist, numerous smaller sites are gradually succumbing to human activities. I've taken it upon myself to discover and salvage these sites' artifacts, striving to ensure their preservation. Initially, everything seemed fine until I shared a few write-ups on social media, never anticipating the overwhelming appreciation for my explorations into this wandering history. Research based works on the IVC in Bengali are scarce, motivating me to share my research with you. If the readers find merit in it, I'll feel that my painstaking efforts have not been in vain.

The decision to embark on writing a book naturally prompts the question of 'what to write about.' The expansive domain of the Indus Valley Civilization (IVC) is adorned with a myriad of facts and artifacts, intertwined with my own profound interests. Initially,

I found myself a bit perplexed. There's a scarcity of material available on the religious practices of the Harappan civilization. Moreover, it's crucial to note a marked distinction between the concept of religion during that era and present-day religious perceptions. Any attempt to elucidate their religious customs by solely referencing established theories would render it substantially incomplete. While we can draw upon various aspects from contemporary civilizations and cultures for insight, it would be unjust to assert that the evolution of thoughts and faith in the IVC followed identical paths. Making such an inference would be rather unfair.

Consider, for instance, the depictions of horned deities uncovered in the IVC. It would be an error to equate these representations with contemporary shamans who don horned headgear in various cultures. Similarly, assuming that identifying four animals alongside one of these figures signifies 'Pashupati Mahadev' would lead to a similar misinterpretation. The joint burials discovered in the IVC often evoke connections to the concept of *Sati*, albeit lacking concrete evidence, thus mirroring a comparable flaw. The burial practices within the IVC remain a subject ripe for investigation. A meticulous examination of the interred bodies, their adornments, vessels, and other funerary items could unveil numerous hitherto unknown details. However, our theories must be substantiated methodically through these artifacts; otherwise, our discoveries will linger as mere conjectures, devoid of conclusive findings.

In the Harappan civilization, akin to the horned deities, various symbols of mythical creatures emerge, amalgamating different animals. Yet, discerning the social or religious significance of these symbols remains uncertain; perhaps they possess both connotations. Different clans often adopt animals as their totems, representing their distinct identities. Nations, too, bear symbols; for instance, our State Emblem derives from the Lion Capital of Asoka at Sarnath, featuring not just lions but several other animal carvings. Hence, a multifaceted analysis of diverse materials becomes imperative.

Likewise, the Peepal tree and its leaves held significant prominence in the IVC. Numerous seals and tablets depict humans beneath or beside these trees. Certain artifacts indicate their use in religious rites, possibly tied to the ancient practice of tree worship. At Mahenjodaro, within a house, a peculiar construction with fenced flooring enclosing an elevated area was unearthed. Staircases ascended from two sides to this platform, with opposing staircases descending from it into a series of rooms, connected in a way that allowed circumambulation of the raised floor. Within these enigmatic rooms lay fragments of stone figurines. The enclosed space mirrors the railings encircling a tree. Could this have been a temple housing a revered tree? Trees were linked to Yaksha, a spirit, during the later Vedic period. Was this then a remnant of that ancient belief?

Consider the grand bath at Mahenjodaro: the adjoining chambers resemble changing rooms, while the significant hall appears akin to a temple's prayer hall. It's plausible that the people of the Indus Valley gathered for worship after cleansing themselves and changing attire. Are we, therefore, following customs rooted in the IVC? Unfortunately, the absence of documented customs leaves us bereft of definitive answers.

When I opted to delve into the Fire Worship Cult of the Indus Valley Civilization (IVC) as my subject, I knew it wouldn't be an easy undertaking. The complexity compounded when I aimed for a comparative analysis with the Vedic *Yajna*. Initially, I presumed that, having extensively studied the *Vedas*, I'd encounter fewer hurdles. However, in reality, familiarity with the *Samhita* portion of the Vedas didn't suffice for comprehending the intricacies of the *Yajnas*. Understanding the procedures necessitated delving into the *Brahmana* part and other sections of the *Vedas*. Fortunately, prior knowledge of the *Samhita* facilitated the study of the *Brahmana*.

Subsequently, organizing my research became a formidable task. The sheer volume of books I immersed myself in on a daily basis seemed boundless. Beyond that, a crucial challenge lay in simplifying the subject for others to comprehend, once I had grasped its depth. I endeavored to convey complex concepts in plain language, catering to the curiosity of the general readers.

Accessing reference books posed a significant challenge in the writing process. Despite possessing an extensive collection, the need for additional readings persisted. Countless individuals provided invaluable assistance in this regard. Without the unwavering support of institutions like Delhi University, JNU, IGNCA, Amity, and ASI, completing this book would have been an insurmountable task.

To delve into the subject thoroughly, I've encompassed discussions on *Vedas*, *Vedanta*, and pertinent Vedic literature within the book's limited scope. Likewise, a concise exploration of the IVC in a separate chapter aims to aid the reader's understanding. The Stone Age is significantly discussed, and for detailed reference, readers are directed to Appendix A, which outlines the terminology and chronology of that period. Appendix B serves to list the units of measurement used in Vedic Yajna, catering to interested readers.

Aligning with contemporary conventions, I've opted to use BCE (Before Common Era) in place of BC (Before Christ). The book discusses fire altars from various archaeological sites, drawing comparisons with Vedic fire altars. While this might result in repetitive explanations, it aims to ensure clarity for readers. This repetition, though, may seem unnecessary to some. However, it is intended to prevent readers who progress slowly from losing the context by not placing the facts in a chronologically coherent setting. I hope readers will excuse this slight deviation for the sake of contextual clarity.

This book would have brought immense joy to my father if he had the chance to see it before his passing in December 2020. He always encouraged me to write, and I regret not embarking on this project sooner! At various junctures, I found myself at an impasse, wishing my father were here to offer his guidance and wisdom. His collection of books has been an invaluable resource that aided me throughout this journey. Another individual of immense support is

Bahata Angshumali Mukhopadhyay—a friend whose counsel has been invaluable.

Rajesh Deb, an incredibly talented artist, made the cover and sketched the fire altars and furnaces with precision, barely needing descriptions. No work is complete without expressing gratitude to one's *Guru*. Padma Shri Dr. R S Bisht, a foremost expert on the IVC, generously shared guidance during our extensive interactions. I'm immensely grateful for his mentorship.

Then there are those who have consistently tolerated my idiosyncrasies—my wife, Godhuli, and my son, Rik. Their smiles have been a balm, alleviating my own sorrows. Lastly, Bibekananda Chatterjee, a beloved elder brother figure, facilitated the tremendous task of transliterating this book—a contribution deserving of heartfelt appreciation.

Dipan Bhattacharya

INDEX

Chapter 1

THE BEGINNING

What was the religion of the people of Indus Valley Civilization? Describing the religion of the Indus Valley Civilization is a challenging task as it conceals a profound mystery that goes far beyond the surface of this seemingly simple question. First, it is hardly possible to describe in brief, the religion and culture of such a civilization that existed in the vast areas between distant Balochistan to Western Uttar Pradesh, and from Jammu to Maharashtra for almost three thousand years!

Let us consider an example to explain the subject. Today, in our country, that is, in India there are people practising same religion at different areas, yet their religious customs are different in many ways. The practices of the same religion are never alike in Bengal and Kerala. Perhaps one would not be able to recognize the same deity at different corners of our nation. Besides, there are cult worship and sectarian faith, even in religions like Hinduism, Buddhism and Jainism. There are sects of *Shiva, Shakti, Vaishnava* or *Mahayana, Hinayana* and so on! There is another factor - evolution of religion. The Indus Valley Civilization existed for almost three and half thousand years. Religions too, undergo evolutionary changes with time and Gods are not immune to change. New ideas emerge and new influences are adopted. Sometimes, religion, faith and practices are influenced by old and apparently outdated ideas and thoughts that existed in a different spatial and temporal setting. Region-wise, these practices also assume diversities. In the same manner, it is hard to determine exactly how many such diverse religious practices are embedded in the Indus Valley Civilization.

In this regard, we must explore ancient worship. Presently, it would be safe to avoid the term "religion" with its conventional meaning, lest that lead our discussion to a different level. So, we shall keep our perception of analysis confined to the field of archaeology; which means, readers should consider this book only an earnest attempt to pursue research-based knowledge. As scholars, we diligently seek proof of innumerable concepts and theories of history from archaeology. We also consider a theory established, from antiquities; although, the major component of history is the evolution of mankind and the subjective perception of mankind is different for each human being. Similarly, the interpretation of shared history may also vary from person to person. On the other hand, the driving forces of the development human civilization that we now comprehend governed human beings of another time. Thus, we cannot generalize their ideas and thoughts in a restricted manner. Above all, we analyse history or other events from our perspectives which are shaped by our surroundings, social norms, and knowledge, but these are entirely relative. Much of those perceptions of the distant past remains inaccessible to us. Hence, alongside archaeological evidence, we must find out the remainders of those ancient beliefs that somehow survived the test of time in our customs, practices, mystical powers and rituals, etc. And we must attach these parameters with archaeology, so that, we will more or less, get closer to truth.

Mark Kenoyer has mentioned in his paper 'Cultures and Societies of The Indus Tradition': *"Furthermore the connection of pre-historic communities with later literary texts or historically known communities must proceed with great caution, and that all interpretations must be taken as suggestions and not as facts"*.

At present, as new archaeological sites and artifacts are being discovered, modern scientific techniques are being employed during archaeological investigations helping us uncover unknown facts or, at times, challenging our previous concepts, which is inevitable. We cannot assume any particular theory as gospel truth only because it is predominantly popular. Hence, we need to keep an open mind and let our analytical faculties remain alert all the time.

Many a time, we observe that similar types of culture, worship and symbolism had been prevalent in various civilizations. Avid readers often chance upon the distinct similarities between Vedic Gods and Goddesses of ancient Greek, Sumerian, or Egyptian mythology. This is true for any ancient idol-worship or pagan culture! In most cases these religious tenets developed independently, despite the civilizations being connected otherwise through trade, travel, and cultural flux. In this context, famous archaeologist Mark Kenoyer wrote in the same article (as quoted above) *"Another example is the use of symbols such as the swastika. This is a symbol that has been found distributed throughout the world beginning in the Palaeolithic period. It is found on pottery in Mesopotamia dating to around 4000 BC, at Harappa beginning around 3300 BC (Kenoyer and Meadow 2000) and widely used in the Indus cities from 2600- 1900 BCE" (Kenoyer 1998).The presence of the swastika in Mesopotamia and the Indus valley is not necessarily connected in any cultural or religious way but is evidence of independent invention of a symbol that probably had very different ideological meanings. Kenoyer Jonathan Mark, ibid"*

The history of worship is probably rooted in the genesis of thoughts and ideas of mankind. An idol of "Lion-man" around 35 to 40 thousand years old was found in a cave named "Hohlenstein-Stadel," in Germany. The "Löwenmensch figurine" also called the Lion-man of Hohlenstein-Stadel, was a prehistoric ivory sculpture found in 1939. The German name, Löwenmensch, meaning "lion-person" or "lion-human", was used most frequently after it was discovered and exhibited. Those stone-age people sculpted this Lion-human, one of the most ancient sculptures by carving mammoth ivory. The Lion-man had a head of lion and body of a human. This figure was kept in a specially constructed chamber in the cave alongside some beads, chert-tools and other paraphernalia. Clearly, it was a place of worship. This was an important discovery to establish the interlink in that distant past between human imagination and their trait for worship.

These primitive principles of worship are similar everywhere in the world. The human-beast synthesis evolving in *"Nrisingha* (Lion-man)" is widely worshipped in India. The Indus Valley Civilization was no exception. Men, at that time were hunters - gatherers. They were equally fearful of nature as they were of wild beasts. So, we cannot suggest that they would not worship nature since they feared and revered beasts. We found many human-beast figurines which belonged to that era. Human trepidation against natural calamity led to nature-worship. Among these natural forces, one was fire. Like other animals, humans experienced the infinite power of fire. It is clearly understood that in the beginning, primitive humans too, dreaded fire like other animals. Slowly, they learned to overcome their fear and use it to their advantage. When lightning struck ground to start wildfire, people took it as a gift from God! Humans first received fire from forest fire, caused by lightning. Then they learned to kindle and rekindle the fire and control it, during the Palaeolithic age. If anything was poured, sprinkled or dropped in the fire, it turned into smoke. Just like the flames that leapt towards the sky, the smoke also billowed in the same direction. Now, sky was where the Gods lived. Hence it was perceived that things or foods dedicated to the Gods reached them through the fire. In the legends and folklores of various countries, we find that "Fire" is a very personal possession of Gods. Man received fire from the heaven. So, like the worship of sun, moon, water and wind, "Fire worship" was also prevalent in the societies from Neolithic to Chalcolithic age.They all initiated this worship in their own ways and carried on; it underwent evolutionary changes with time. Later, these indigenous practices faded under the influence of other religions and worshipping methods; or survived in various forms as subsidiary rites. So, we should not tag any specified model with our quest of the methods of fire worship in Indus Vally Civilization. After the discovery of "Fire Altars", furnaces, kilns and hearths in Harappan archaeological sites, it was natural (for the archaeologists) to compare them with the Vedic fire Yajna altars. A comparative study of the two similar worshipping practices of ancient times in largely common geographical territory, was inevitable. Our present attempt is also to undertake a comparative analysis of the two worshipping practices, but that comparison would be essentially drawn on the basis of the constructions of the fire devices and artifacts found in the archaeological sites.

We do learn a great many things about Vedic customs from different available sources. Major among those, is the Vedas. The importance of Yajna in the Vedas is limitless. It is said in the Rigveda that: -

dadhann ṛtaṃ dhanayann asya dhītim ād id aryo didhiṣvo vibhṛtrāḥ | atṛṣyantīr apaso yanty acchā devāñ janma prayasā vardhayantīḥ ||

- Rigveda 1.71.3

"the great "Angira" sages possessed the fire in the form of Yajna as wealth. Later those Yajmans (Religious patrons) who were wealthy, yet owned up the Yajna and offered services for the fire, renouncing their personal materialistic pursuits, were able to bring about prosperity of the human race by sacrificial activities and then departed through the fire. (as translated by Ramesh Chandra Dutta in his Bengali edition)

Undoubtedly, the Yajnas stood at significantly high ground in Vedic worship. The rituals of Vedic fire worship or various Yajnas are extensive in nature, and they are linked with several contextual life situations. If we embark on discussing all Yajnas, it may distract us from our primary purpose. So, our investigations will progress along the facts related to the "Fire-altars". During the Indus Valley Civilization period, the altars or the *Kundas* found were of two major types. One type of Kundas was found inside residential houses and the others in open areas. It was established that one or more groups of people existed in Indus Valley civilization who regularly worshipped fire! There was another indication of collective fire worship with the discovery of large Kundas that were found at open areas or public places. In many of those Kundas, archaeologists found ash, charcoal, and remains of other sacrificial items. Historians concluded that there was substantial technological progress in IVC. As many industrial furnaces and kilns were constructed in the well planned Harappan settlements. We need to be careful and not mix-up those furnaces and kilns with worshipping Kundas. And this is not an easy task as the outward structures or the exteriors and the items found in those fire-sources were, in many cases, similar.

Here comes an important question; were those Harappan fire worshippers Vedic sages? We will attempt to find out the answer to this question. But, to establish a link or to challenge popular belief, we need to obtain adequate physical evidence. A series of Kundas were excavated at the archaeological site of Kalibangan with seating arrangements, facing east. Since the eastern direction was also suggested as sacred and most appropriate in the Vedas, one is often driven to label those Kundas as Vedic altars. We cannot afford that luxury, even if endorsed by some archaeologists. We need to examine the remaining Kundas and find out whether the same eastward seating formations were followed elsewhere. Only with such complete justifications, we could reach a conclusion. So, we will not select one or two Kundas and instead, scrutinize all of them in order to develop a clear idea on the subject. An unbiased and analytical mind-set is essential to make headway into this complex subject. With a comparative study in mind, we have a barrage of information regarding Vedic Yajnas and rites against nothing except some rugged remnants of the Indus Valley Civilization. Even the Harappan script is yet to be deciphered. So, we only have those excavated objects for our explorations. At the same time, we need to remember that we would not have the same advantage as studying the Vedic Yajnas supported by available sources in the commentaries and literature. The Harappan culture would have to be assessed with parameters which are based on archaeological facts, supported by physical presence of relevant excavated objects and artifacts for our comparative study. Again, this is not going to happen with the Vedic practices for which we have to rely on Vedic precepts alone with no physical evidence to support the assertions. Our arguments, however, would essentially be referenced within the confines of the Vedas as the essence of all the Yajnas are found in the great precepts. Also, our primary purpose will be to seek comparison with the most ancient forms of the Vedic Yajnas. We will desist from delving deep into other fire worship practices, like among the Iranians or in Steppe areas, as these would again divert us from our primary goal. We will try to elucidate the subject supported by original facts extracted from relevant archaeological reports verbatim, leaving space for the reader to shape his or her own opinions. During the Harappan period, some objects of fire worship were found in archaeological sites, especially in Kalibangan, Lothal, Kunal, Banawali, etc. We will also try to understand the characteristics of those artifacts vis-à-vis histories of those archaeological sites, in accordance to their archaeological significance.

At the outset, we will study the fundamentals of Vedic Yajnas and then try to compare these with the fire worship of the Harappans. Since our findings in the Indus archaeological sites include Kundas, potteries and other sacrificial items, our scrutiny will focus on extensive study of these artifacts in the light of Vedic Yajnas.

In the Rigveda (1.140.1) Fire or "Agni" is named as "Vedishade"

vediṣade priyadhāmāya sudyute dhāsim iva pra bharā yonim
agnaye | vastreṇeva vāsayā manmanā śuciṃ jyotīrathaṃ
śukravarṇaṃ tamohanam ||

Vedishade means that Agni is inherent in the Vedi (Altar). In the Vedic Yajnas, the significance of the fire-altar or Yajna Vedi is supreme. First, we will look at the measurement of the various Yajna altars as prescribed in the Vedas, that is their sizes, lengths, etc. The Vedic Yajna spots are popularly known as *Vedi* (Altars), except in a few cases, where they are referred as "Kundas". So, while studying the Vedic Yajnas, we will use the term "Altar". With this we will also note the sizes of the bricks which were used to construct those altars. The second task would be to identify the position of these Yajna altars signifying the seating position of the devotees, Yajmans, priests and other members. Then we will find out the details of the pots related to the Yajnas, their shapes, sizesand making process. Finally, we will consider the sacrificial offerings, the oblations through the invocation and kindling of the Agni. Merely describing these three or four aspects of Yajnas and its few corollaries will not suffice to convince the readers, nor they will understand the Vedic terminologies associated with it. So, we will append brief descriptions of each of these Yajnas, that may offer a concept to the readers for their own judgements.

Readers need to keep the above aspects in mind while we discuss the Vedic Yajnas so that later, while comparing these with their Harappan counterparts in terms of Kundas, altars/fire-pits, sacrificial offerings, directions of the worship and positions of the worshippers, the readers would find it easy to reconcile. After discussing the details of Vedic Yajnas we will step into the subject of Indus Valley Civilization that include a few of its unique features. The relevant chapter (Chapter 3) would help the reader. The Stone-age will also come into play for which readers may read Appendix - A, beforehand. The terminology and chronology are mentioned in it.

Chapter 2

THE VEDIC YAJNAS

Thousands of words are written about the definition, nature, and procedures of Yajna. More will be written in future. However, the significance of Yajna was reflected in the third chapter of *"Bhagavad Gita"*

saha-yajnah prajah srishtva purovacha prajapatih

anena prasavishyadhvam esha vo 'stvishta-kama-dhuk

devān bhāvayatānena te devā bhāvayantu vaḥ

parasparaṁ bhāvayantaḥ śhreyaḥ param avāpsyatha

iṣhṭān bhogān hi vo devā dāsyante yajña-bhāvitāḥ

tair dattān apradāyaibhyo yo bhuṅkte stena eva saḥ

- Bhagavad Gita 3.10-12

In the beginning of creation, Brahma created humankind along with duties, and said, "Prosper in the performance of these yajñas (sacrifices), for they shall bestow upon you all you wish to achieve."

By your sacrifices, the celestial Gods will be pleased, and by cooperation between humans and the celestial Gods, great prosperity will reign for all.

The celestial Gods, being satisfied by the performance of sacrifice, will grant you all the desired necessities of life. But those who enjoy what is given to them, without making offerings in return, are verily thieves. (Commentary by Swami MuKundananda)

In Rigveda, Yajna is defined as: -

pṛthak prāyan prathamā devahūtayo 'kṛṇvata śravasyāni duṣṭarā |

na ye śekur yajñiyāṃ nāvam āruham īrmaiva te ny aviśanta kepayaḥ ||

evaivāpāg apare santu dūḍhyo 'śvā yeṣāṃ duryuja āyuyujre |

itthā ye prāg upare santi dāvane purūṇi yatra vayunāni bhojanā ||

- Rigveda 10.44.6-7

"They go separately (to the worlds of the Gods); first those who offer oblations to the Gods haveattained reputation difficult to surpass; those who have not been able to ascend the ship of sacrifice, have gonedown (in the world), wretches, in debt."

As we developed our familiarity with the Vedic religious scriptures, it became clear that the great influence of the Yajnas comprehensively governedthe lives of its adherents in the Vedic era;both from religious point of view to social codes of conduct. This very truth was philosophically professed in the *"Upanishads"* (Late Vedic and post Vedic philosophical Sanskrit texts that documented the transition from the archaic ritualism of the Vedas into new religious ideas and institutions) as *the entire human life is a Yajna*.

We will therefore,study the major Vedic Yajnas. But, before that we need to understand the constitution of Vedas and the various scriptures, commentaries and disciplines associated with it which will be useful for our study as references in this book; and once understood, will not put the readers in confusion at the later stages of analysis, inferences and comparisons.

The Vedas were in four parts – The *"Rigveda"*, the *"Samaveda"*, the *"Yajurveda"* and the *"Atharvaveda"*. The Vedas had many branches. According to *"Kurmapurana" (chapter 52)*, Rigveda had 21 divisions, Yajurveda had 100, Samaveda had 1000 and Atharvaveda had 9 divisions.

The statistics of these branches or divisions appeared a little exaggerated! At present, the existence of three *"Shakhas"* (Schools of thought) of Rigveda are established. They are *"Sakala"*, *"Baskala"* and *"Sankhayana"*. Two other branches namely *"Asvalayana"* and *"Mandukayana"* are now extinct. The *"Sakala"* branch of the Rigveda was the most popular among those three disciplines. The *"Yajurveda"* had two parts *"Krishna (dark) Yajurveda"* and *"Shukla (white, pure) Yajurveda"*. The *"Krishna Yajurveda"* furtherbranched out to *"Atreya"*, *"Kathak"*, *"Apastamba"* and *"Haridrabiya"* while the *"Shukla Yajurveda"* included two *"Shakhas"*, *"Madhyandin"* and *"Kanwa"*. The *"Atharvaveda"*held two *"Shakhas"* – *"Paippalada"* and *"Shounakiya"*. The remaining seven *"Shakhas"*, *"Tauda"*, *"Mauda"*, *"Jalala"*, *"Jalada"*, *"Brahmavada"*, *"Devadarsa"* and *"Chaarana-Vaidya"* are now extinct. The *"Rigveda"* consisted of ten thousand five hundred fifty-two *"Mantras"* (hymns), *"Samaveda"* had one thousand eight hundred seventy-five, in *"Yajurveda"* there were one thousand nine hundred seventy-five hymns while *"Atharvaveda"* had five thousand nine hundred seventy-seven hymns. The total number of hymns in the four Vedas stood at twenty thousand three hundred seventy-nine. The central part of each of these four Vedas was the *"Samhita"*, that comprised the *"Mantras"*. All the Mantras of Rigveda are in verse-like rhythm and ought to be recited. In Samaveda, mostly the commentaries and the mantras of Rigveda were musically composed to create chantable melodies. Samaveda, however had a few of its own unique Mantras and sung with prescribed musical tunes. Many techniques were adopted while reciting the Vedas to ensure unwavering attention, like the *"Nirbhuj"* and *"Pratrina"*. *"Nirbhuj Path"* (recital) was meant for chanting the Mantras verbatim. But the *"Pratrina"* technique, had subsidiary methods of chanting, like the "*Padapath*", "*Jatapath*", "*Kramapath*", etc. All the Mantras of Yajurveda were written in prose. Further, the Mantras of Yajurveda were not dedicated to specific Gods as it is in the case of Rigveda Mantras. We mentioned earlier, of the Krishna Yajurveda and Shukla Yajurveda. Their actual names are "*Taittiriya*" Samhita and "*Vajasneyi*" Samhita.

The story of Taittiriya and Vajasneyi Samhita went like this - according to "*Vishnu Puran*", Rishi (Sage) Vaishampayana was cursed for his deliberate absence in the conglomeration of sages at "*Mahameru*". As a redemption, he held a "Vrat" (Practice of austerity, in terms of food and drinks) ceremony with his disciples. One of his disciples, Yajnavalkya, driven by pride, defied Vaishampayana and went on to perform the rituals on his own. Vaishampayana disowned his disciple for this contemptible act and asked him to return all his acquired knowledge. The otherwise devoted disciple Yajnavalkya vomited the entire Vedic knowledge he had learnt. Otherpupils of Vaishampayana took the form of *Tittiris* (birds, partridges) and swallowed the Vedas thus thrown up. Therefore, it came to be known as Taittiriya Samhita or the Krishna Yajurveda and those disciples were called as "*Charak Adhwaryus*". Later, Yajnavalkya appeased the Sun who restored his Vedic knowledge, which came to be known as Shukla Yajurveda or Vajasneyi Samhita. Most of the Vedic Yajnas' religious rites were included in Yajurveda alone. One of the major attributes of the Vedic Samhitas was the discipline, "*Brahmana*". The Brahmanawas more like a ready reckoner. Brahmana explained the meaning of the Mantras of Samhita and clarified the methods of Yajna and Vedic worship. Understandably, the scriptures ofBrahmana are a littledifficult to understand. Considering Brahmana as the first part and the Samhitas second of the four Vedas, the third part of Vedas was known as "*Aranyakaa*". Aranyakaa described and discussed rituals from various perspectives but primarily from a philosophical standpoint. The material Yajna transcendedinto Jnana-Yajna (Yajna of knowledge). The seeds of spirituality sowed in Aranyaka later blossomed philosophically in the "*Upanishads*". The Upanishads related to

Brahmanawere called "*Brahmanaopanishad*". Likewise, "*Kenopanishad*"was part of "*Jaiminiya Brahmana*", which in turn was a section of Samaveda. Some parts of Upanishads were related to Aranyaka and thus, called "*Aronyakoponishad*". "*Oitoreyopanishad*"was a part of "*Oitareya Aranyaka*". The categorization of the Vedic Mantras was elaborately dealt in "*Mantropanishad*" which was unique and was also known as "*Ishoponishad*". They were part of Shukla Yajurveda's Mantras.

Every Veda entailed separate Brahmana, Aranyaka and Upanishad. The major categories are given in the table (2.1) below. To understand the physical aspects of the Yajnas, the most useful part is the "*Satapatha", which* is the Brahmana part of Shukla Yajurveda.

Parts of Veda (table 2.1)

Veda	Brahmana	Aranyaka	Upanishad
Rigveda	Oitareya, Kaushitaki or Shankhyana	Oitareya, Kaushitaki or Shankhyana	Oitareya, Kaushitaki or Shankhyana
Samveda	Tandya, Sharabingsha, Chandogya, Jaiminiya, Sambidhan, Arsheya, Bansha, Devata Adhyaya	Chandogya	Chandogya, Ken
Krishna Yajurveda	Taittiriya	Taittiriya	Katha, Shwetashwar, Mha Narayana,Taittiriya
Shukla Yajurveda	Satapatha	Vrihadaranyaka	Vrihadaranyaka, Isha
Atharvaveda	Gopatha	---	Prashna, Mundaka, Mandukya

There were six *Vedangas*. Vedanga could be literally translated as "the limbs of the Vedas," referring to the six auxiliary disciplines associated with studying the ancient Indian spiritual texts, the Vedas. These texts laid the foundation for both yoga and Hinduism.

Those six "limbs" could together support the study, preservation and interpretation of the Vedas. In ancient India, where they developed, they were designed to provide students of the Vedas with a holistic and integrated understanding of the scriptures. The six Vedangas were *"Shiksha"*, *"Kalpa"*, *"Nirukta"*, *"Vyakarana"*, *"Chhanda"* and *"Jyotisha"*. Shiksha dealt with the phonetics and pronunciation of the Vedic texts. It provided rules for correct enunciation and recitation of the Vedic verses. Nirukta, created by "Yaska", a narrator involved etymology and interpretation of difficult or archaic Vedic words. It aided in explaining the meanings of obscure terms in the Vedas. Vedic commentator Yaska, in his writings also described the Vedic Gods. Vyakarana is the study of grammar and linguistic analysis. It helped in understanding the grammatical structure and rules of the Vedic language. Jyotisha was the study of astronomy and astrology in relation to the Vedas. It involved calculating auspicious timings for performing Vedic rituals and understanding celestial phenomena. Lastly, the Kalpa, the most relevant aspect of our study.   Kalpa was instrumental in conceiving and aiding the Yajnas. It dealt with Vedic rituals, ceremonies, and rules for proper conduct. The Brahmana part of Vedas comprised descriptions of the Yajnas while the guidelines, rules and regulations were stipulated in *"Kalpasutra"*. Kalpasutra was divided in three parts *"Shrautasutra"*, *"Grihyasutra"* and *"Dharmasutra"*. The four original social or public Yajnas, *"Hom"*, *"Isti"*, *"Pashu"* and *"Soma"* along with many other auxiliary Yajnas culminated in *Srhautayajna* for which Shrautasutra was its application. All codes of conduct for the domestic individual, from childbirth to last riteswere prescribed in the Grihyasutra.The Pancha(five) *"Mahayajnas"*: - *"Brahmayajna"*, *"Nriyajna"* or service to guests, *"Devayajna"*, *"Pitriyajna"* or paternal funeral ceremony and "Bhutayajna"were also dealt by Grihyasutras. The Dharmasutra provided guidelines for ethical conduct, religious practices, and social duties based on the principles found in the Vedas. Dharmasutra also outlined various aspects of human life, including rituals, responsibilities, and moral conduct, drawing inspiration from the Vedas and framing them in the context of dharma or righteous living. They helped individuals understand how to lead a moral and harmonious life in accordance with the teachings of the Vedas. The Shrautasutra and Grihyasutra are both relevant to our present study. They do not contain any Vedic scripture related to Vyakarana, Chanda or the Jyotisha. Besides, we need to seek credence from *"Shulvasutras"* that was considered as the manual of construction of the Yajna altars. It contained the measurements and many other geometric aspects of Vedic Yajnas.

Sutras of vedas (table 2.2)

Veda	Shrautasutra	Grihyasutra	Dharmasutra
Rigveda	Asvalayana, Shankhyana	Asvalayana, Shankhyana	Vashishtha
Samveda	Latyayana, Drahyayana, Jaiminiya	Drahyayana, Jaiminiya, Gobhil, Khadir	Gautama
Krishna Yajurveda	Baudhayana, Apastambha, Manaba, Hiranyakeshi, Vaikhanasa	Baudhayana, Apastambha, Manaba, Hiranyakeshi, Bhardwaj, Baraha, Kathak, Lougakshi, Vaikhanasa, Badhul	Baudhayana, Apastambha, Manaba, Hiranyakeshi, Vaikhanasa
Shukla Yajurveda	Katyayana	Paraskara or Vajasaneyi	Shankhalikhita
Atharvaveda	Vaitana	Kaushika	Pathinasi

Prior to our journey into the Vedic Yajnas in their entirety, it is essential to expect completely unfamiliar descriptions of some Yajnas. Some of the Yajnas related to birth, death and marriage are still performed with much less embellishment. But their deeper implications are likely to be unfathomble for the layperson and decipherable only by experts. At the same time, rudimentary dictates concerning the proceedings may also dissuade the reader from appreciating the true essence of the fire worship culture and customs. So, we seek access to various interpretations andunderlying messages from the Mantras and also the myths attached to those Yajnas to understand the subject.

It would not be an exaggeration to consider Agni as the primary driving force of the Vedic Yajnas. Rigveda begins with the term "Agni": -

agnim īḷe purohitaṃ yajñasya devam ṛtvijam |

hotāraṃ ratnadhātamam ||

"I glorify Agni, the high priest of the sacrifice, the divine, the ministrant, who presents the oblation (to the Gods), and is the possessor of great wealth."

The number of Mantras in adulation of Agni was the second largest after the laudatory hymns about Indra, the king of Gods. Again, the first Mantra of Samaveda about Agni reads: −

"O Agni, we invoke your presence for joy and purity of our thoughts. Assume the form of worshipper and come to carry the offerings to the divine Gods of the heavens. O convener of the Gods, please sit before the Yajna!"

Rishi Aurobindo said on Agni − *"Sublime mediator between earth and heaven"*. A bridge between the heaven and the earth, Agni is the face of the creator, he is the *"Habyabaha"* meaning carrier of the sacrificial offerings to the Gods. Thus, Agni should be protected with care.

Many hierarchical entities were involved in the Vedic Yajnas. Major among them were the *"Yajmans"*, religious patrons for whose welfare the Yajna was conducted and the *"Ritwik"* (priest) who performed the Yajna. That the Yajnas In Vedic era were held in accordance with prescribed period of time and in appropriate seasons is clearly understood by the Mantra given below. In fact, the term Ritwik evolved from Ritu (season). According to Krishna Yajurveda (1.7.3), the Ritwik was an emissary of God. The duty of a Ritwik was to perform the Yajna perfectly as mentioned in -

34

"O Suryadeva (Sun-God), epitome of knowledge! Thou art the all-containing, absolute radiance! O giver of light (enlightenment) bestow wisdom upon me. Let me follow your all-revealing sphere and embark on good deeds." (Shukla Yajurveda 2.26)

During the Vedic Yajnas, Rigveda was recited while Samaveda was chanted melodiously. He who chanted the Rigveda Mantras and invited the Gods was the *"Hota"* (religious convener). One who submitted the offerings in Agni was the *"Adhwaryu"* (Vedic priest). Adhwaryu chanted the Mantras of Yajurveda, sacrificed the offerings was also responsible for preparing the holy offerings. Adhwaryu was the most important person as he invigorated the Yajna. The Samaveda hymns were sung by *"Udgata"*. These three individuals were led by *"Brahma"* who also had three aides but those assistants were not summoned for every Yajnas. The priests or Ritwiks and their three aides were thus: -

Adhwaryu – "Pratiprasthata", "Neshta", "Unneta"

Brahma – "Brahmanacchanshi", "Agnidhra", "Pota"

Hota – "Moitravaruna", "Acchabak", "Grabastut"

Udgata – "Prostota", "Pratihorta", "Subrahmanya"

Besides these sixteen priests, there was one more general assistant called *"Sadasya"*. So, the maximum number of Ritwiks who performed the rituals was seventeen.

Vedic Yajnas consisted of three elements, the *"Dravya"* (general offerings), *"Deva"* (the Gods) and the *"Tyaga"* (sacrifice). There were mention of various offerings like *"Ghee"* (clarified butter), milk, curd, honey, *"Somaras"* (An organic herbal beverage), a type of cake called *"Purodash"*, animal flesh, porridge, etc. The offerings were dedicated to the Gods, like Indra, Soma, Agni, Surya (Sun), Mitra, etc. Agni, as mentioned earlier is the deliverer of these offerings to the *"deva loka"* (heaven) and also the abode of the ancestors. According to the Vedas, there were two types of Agni for worship, the *"Grihya-Agni"* and the *"Shrauta Agni"*. Every Yajna had its unique feature called *"Prakriti Yaj"* or *"Pradhan (main) Yaj"*. They also hadotherauxiliary disciplines called *"Vikriti Yaj"*. Two Vedic rites need to be mentioned here

"Hom" and "Isti Yaj". For our study we will relate "Hom" to "Pak Yajna" that follows the "Grihya Sutra" and "Isti Yaj" to "Habiryajna" that follows "Shrauta Sutra". "*Hom*" (holy fire) was characterized by two rituals "Pratarhome" and "Sayanhome" depending on dawn or dusk, and "Isti Yaj" was performed with "*Darshapurnamasa*" rites. The essence of "PashuYaj" was "*Daikhsha*" or "*Prajapatyapashu*". The characteristics of "SomaYaj" is "*Agnistoma*". The Yajna which concludes in one day was called "*EkahaYaj*". Yajnas that were completed in less than twelve days were called "*Aheen*". Those crossed the limit of twelve days were "*Satras*". From the sacrificial point of view there were three types of Yajnas - "*Pakyajna*", "*Habiryajna*" and "*Somayajna*". Only Pakyajna is performed with Grihya-Agni, "*Abasakhya-Agni*" or "*Smartya-Agni*". This Yajna included conducting Hom daily, in the morning and evening and rituals as "*Sthalipak*", "*Navayajna*" and "*Pitriyajna*", etc.

Habiryajna included "Dasapranamasa", "*Agnihotra*", "*Agnadheya*", "*Agrayan*", "Chaturmasya", "Pasubandha", etc, while Somayajna entailed "*Agnistoma*", "*Shorashi*", "*Agnicayan*", "Bajapeya", etc. It is almost impossible to describe all the Yajnas. We will select the major Yajnas with brief descriptions of the positions, sizes and shapes of the Vedis and the types of paraphernalia involved in those Yajnas.

Let us first understand the Pakyajna. It was mentioned earlier that Pakyajna was performed with Grihya-Agni, "Abasakhya-agni" or "Smartya-Agni". The rituals under this household obligations were known as "Shrauta Karama". Agni was invoked on a domestic altar. Only a married man could kindle this Agni at home. The house of an unmarried person was not considered as home as he was not a family-man. Most of the Vedic religious activities were essentially performed by a patron or Yajman alongside his wife to ensure the presence of the Gods. Sacrifices for the Gods were made in the form of supplication. Edible items of the Yajnas were "*Habyas*". The woods and sticks used to produce the fire in Yajnas were called "*Samidh*". There were also household or domestic Vedis to kindle the Agni. The process of kindling Agni at home was called "*Agnidhyan*". The descriptions of the indoor Vedis are importantto understand the subtleties of Vedic Yajna fire altars or the Vedis. These descriptions would also separate Grihya-Agni from Shrauta-Agni. In Vedic households, an entire room (*Agnishala*) was dedicated to accommodate the Agni. On an auspicious day, the homeowner along with his wife rekindled fresh fire with the help of Ritwik (priest). A north- south partition walldivided the room into two smaller chambers. The east-side chamber held the "*Ahavaniya*" (invitational) Agni while the west side chamber made space for "*Garhapatya*" (domestic) Agni(Apastamba Grihyasutra 5.4.3, 6.2.11). These two Agnis were placed on the same axis. Garhapatya Agni was mortal as it helped the family while Ahavaniya Agni represents the divine world. Offerings and sacrifices were madethrough this fire. According to Vedic concept the Sun rose from the divine world, paradise, and set in earth! So, the Ahavaniya Agni was placed on an eastwardly direction and Garhapatya Agni on the west. The two worlds, that of the God's and the humans were governed by the movement of the Sun. In between the Ahavaniya Agni and the partition wall, there was a Vedi (sacrificial altar) which was called "Oistik Vedi". Now, at the south of the space that was left between the Oistik Vedi and Garhapatya Agni, "Dakshinagni" was placed (It was not precisely to the south). According to "Apastamba Srautasutra" (5.4.5), Dakshinagni was positioned southeast of Garhapatya Agni, at a distance of one-third of the distance between Ahavaniya and Garhapatya Agni. The south direction denoted the kingdom of "*Yama*" (Lord of Death, hence this direction was selected to make sacrifices and offer "Pinda" (funeral cakes) to the deceased ancestors. D.M.Knipe correctly assessed that these three fires or Agnis actually represented the three worlds. Each of the three Agnis were of same area, that of a square with sides measuring one "*Aratni* (measure of the elbow to small finger of the Yajman or religious host)" in length and one Aratni in breadth, regardless of their actual shapes.

The shape of the Garhapatya Agni was circular and was considered to be representing the house owner and welfare of the family. Ahavaniya Agni (also known as Vaitanik Agni) was square-shaped and belonged to the Gods, while Dakshinagni's shape was semi-circular. This particular shape presumably halfway between circular and square, led many to believing that Dakshinagni denoted the journey from the mortal world to the heaven. Garhapatya Agni and Dakshinagni were situated in the Garhapatya chamber (westside) with its main exit-door in the west. Inside the Ahavaniya Griha(chamber), the Ahavaniya Agni and the Vedi were situated and its exit door was in the east side. But in Shrauta Yajna, the three Agnis being used simultaneously, a door between the two chambers was necessary. However, many Yajna spots were found with only one chamber accommodating all three Agnis and one Vedi. To sum up, Ahavaniya Agni, Grihya Agni and the Dakshinagni, all were Shrauta Agni. The chronicles of Vedic culture were significantly influenced by these three Agnis. There is a story about those three Agnis in the Chhandagya Upanishad 94th Prapathaka, 1-13th Khanda)

Upakosala Kamalayana lived with Satyakama Jabala as a student of Brahamavidya (sacred knowledge). For twelve years, he tended the Agnis. But his teacher did not allow him to return home nor taught the Brahmavidya. Thereupon, Upakosala was filled with grief and began to fast. Then, the three Agnis, in turn, taught him the Brahmavidya and revealed their true nature to him.

"The three Agnis addressed him conjointly 'O, Upakosala, dear boy, thus has been expounded to thee our philosophy, the Agnividyā, Philosophy of the Fires, as also the Philosophy of the Self."

"Breath is Brahmana, Ka (bliss) is Brahmana, Kha (sky) is Brahmana.' The Teacher will expound to thee, the process, —for the acquiring of the final reward of knowledge."

Garhapatya Agni said to Upakosala – "The earth, the fire, the food and the sun are my nature. The cosmic being pervading in the solar system is me. I am "He". Dakshinagni told Upakosala – "The water, the (ten) directions, the stars and the moon are my nature." The cosmic being, permeating the lunar sphere is me. I am "He". Finally, the Ahavaniya Agni said to Upakosala – "Breath, sky, heaven and the thunder are my nature. The cosmic being who reveals himself in the thunder is me. I am "He".

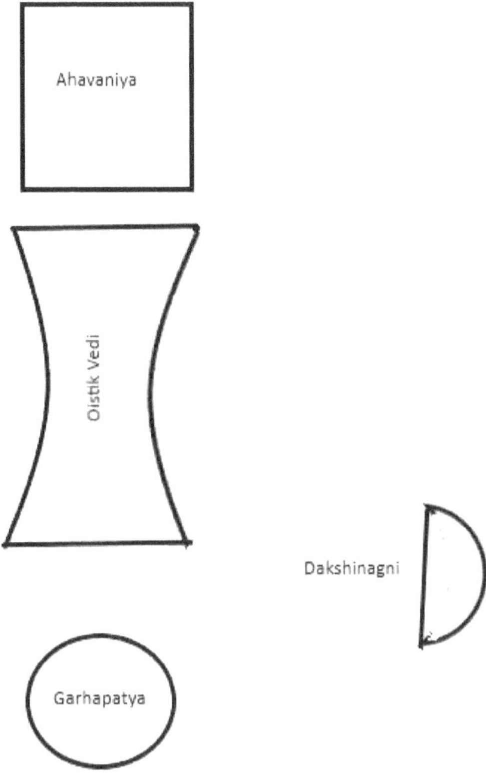

Fig. 2.1 Location of three Agnis and Vedi in an Agnishala

We discussed the Shrauta Agni and studied their shapes, areas and their positions. Now we will discuss "Grihya Agni" also known as "Garhasthya" Agni. Besides the religious fires inside the houses, we find mention of Garhasthya Agni in "KhadIda Grihyasutra". Here, another structure, called *"Sthandil"* was introduced. This was a smaller Vedi, made of earth and sand and placed at the eastern section of the houses. It was regularly plastered with cow dung. Sthandil was circular in shape and situated in a "one arrow's length" square space. *(Ashvalayan Grihyasutra 1.3.1)* The length of the arrow was approximately 74 centimetre, little more than two feet. The entire third paragraph of the first chapter of "Ashvalayan Grihyasutra"explained the process of preparing of this Agni. The

Ritwik(priest) sat south of this Agni with the holy water vessel*(Shankhayan Grihyasutra 1.8.6-8)*. This is of importance us because it was that Grihya Agni which was kindled inside the houses. Similar description of Sthandil is found in *Hiranyakeshi Grihyasutra (1.1.1.9)* where the ideal position of the Ritwik was suggested as North or North-east corner of the house."Paraskar Grihyasutra" alsointroduced a process of constructing the Vedi (Altar). However, in the last two references the term "Sthandil" was missing. This was the Grihya Agni that a Vedic family head was supposed to keep aflamein his home round the clock. When an unmarried individual studied in the Gurukul (religious learning centre) or under an *Acharya* (religious teacher) he was assigned to perform Hom every morning and evening, invoking the Agni with Samidh (wood, sticks). After convocation, he returned to his home, married and instituted the Grihya Agni, also called "Abasakhya Agni" or Smartya Agni in his own home. He was obligated to perform the Yajnas that were prescribed in the Grihyasutra with this Agni. The *"Grihi"* (family man) needed to sustain this Agni lifelong.

Another Vedi, situated between the circular Garhapatya Agni and the square-shaped Ahavaniya Agni was the Oistik Vedi.This Vedi was constructed along an east-west axis, with its middle part having the lowest breadth, like that of a concave lens. The eastern corners of the Vedi were called *"Angsa"* meaning "shoulders" while the western corners were known as *"Shroni"*, which meant "waist". According to the Vedic precepts, the shape of this Vedi was *"Krishamadhya"*, similar to a *"Damaru* (a percussion instrument of concave shape, often appeared in the hand of lord Shiva). One could not help but envision this Vedi as the torso of a woman. The terms "Angsa" and "Shroni" supported this view and it emerged that the Oistik Vedi was the depiction of a woman's body whose (imaginary) arms embraced the Ahavaniya Agni *(Satapatha Brahmana 1.2.5.15)* and *"Katyan Shrautasutra" (2.6.1)*, as if a Goddess was engaged in copulation with the Ahavaniya Agni that represented the Gods. Many historians drew inferences from the positions of Vedi and Agni with "Fertility Cult". In *Vrihad Aranyaka Upanishad (6.2.13)*, the Vedi was compared with the body of a woman. The union of the Vedi and Ahavaniya Agni was assumed as a divine ritual to espouse the radiance of the Agni.According to *Satapatha Brahmana (7.1.1.36)*, construction of this Vedi required 21 bricks, denoting the total of 12 months, 5 seasons, 3 worlds and 1 fire. There was a Vedic reference of a corpus of texts known as *"Shulvasutra"* that described the methods of the construction of the smaller Vedis. For more elaborate Yajnas, larger Vedis were erected, called *"Mahavedi"*. In "Agnicayan" yajna, five layers in the Vedis were constructed with one thousand bricks. The strategically important bricks were separately named in the related Vedic scriptures. Those names are not important for our purpose, but they would definitely address the curiosity of the interested reader.

Let us return to the Vedis. According to Prof Staal: -*"The Iranian fire ritual is in many respects similar to the Vedic. Fires were installed on three altars. The domestic altar is circular, the sacrificial, square."*

The Indo-Iranians were confirmedly a sect of the Vedic Sages (Rishi) hence worshippers of fire. The presence of an Indo-Iranian Vedic sect in India was an established fact, and they were fire worshippers. Archaeological findings suggested that people in the transition from the Sintashta-Petrovka to the Andronovo culture around 1500 BC practiced fire worship and cremation rituals and fire worship was a common practice in the ancient realms of religions of the Vedic and Iranian civilizations.We found the existence of Iranian *"Ahuras"* or the "Asuras" (evil spirit) in Indian Vedic fire rituals.

It is clear to us now, that primarily there were three Agnis for Vedic fire worship. The invocation of Grihya Agniand performing the Pak Yajna rituals were parts of the Vedic daily life andtraditionally the basic steps of worship described in the various Grihyasutra. The Grihyasutra also prescribed about the source of Grihya Agni that included fire from "Thunder-struck, top branches of Banyan tree"to inflammable materials kept on heated pan. The *Apastamba Grihyasutra (5.14.1-2)* and the *Kathak Samhita (8.12)*suggested that Agni may be brought from any prosperous household, provided its owner was powerful as the Asura, regardless of his caste, implying that even the Asuras were entitled to worshipping Agni and left its mark in the Vedas. This is quite an important aspect. As this entitled the "Anaryas" (non-Aryans) to performing Yajnas and other Vedic practices. But we willnot explorefurther details of this *"Agnyadhyan"* process. We have already collected useful material for our study. After the kindling of the Agni and prior to commencement of the Yajna, the Vedis were consecrated by "IstiYaj".

The positions of the Yajna Vedis are clear now – theOistik Vedi with four corners alongside a square-shaped (Ahavaniya) Agni to its east, a circular (Garhapatya) Agni to its west and another (Dakshinagni) Agni tothe south (Pic – 2.1). The exact spot of the three Agnis were demarcated with bricks and earth. The Garhapatya Agni was eternal, never to be extinguished and constantly resisted the evil. Ahavaniya and Dakshinagni were not always invoked. They were rekindled from the fire of the Garhapatya Agni. The Adhwaryu(main priest) poured Ghee in the Agni with a wooden ladle called *"Juhu"*, while the Yajman sat behind, holding him. This was*"PurnAhuti"*. In *SatapathaBrahmana*, there was a story on Vedic oblation about Manu, who appeared in the sacred literature of Vedasas the performer of the first sacrifice.After the great deluge,Manuperformed the Purn*Ahuti* Yajna. As he offered ghee, milk and curd, Goddess Ida appeared from it. This was the first Pak yajna in the form of*"Adiyajna"* (original Yajna)and this Goddess Ida was the Goddess of livestock, imagined and worshipped in much earlier ages when the human race learned cultivation and domestication of animals. This proverbial Yajna was Adiyajna and its components were also quite simple. Its offerings only includedmilk products and cereals. During IstiYaj, one type of pie or cake (known as "Purodash") was prepared and offered to the Gods. The residual part was distributed among the priests and the patrons to complete the ceremony. A part of the Purodash was laced with Ghee (clarified butter) and was named after Ida. Before consuming this part, Goddess Ida was invoked, a practice known as *"Idopahbhan"*. So, Adiyajna was all about offering milk products to the Gods through Agni andThe practice of Adiyajna originated during the time when humans began domesticating animals and it continued to be observed throughout the Vedic era.The Vedic Agni was perceived as, and compared with many entities, one being the sun. Sun was the God of the daily morning rituals of Agnihotra. The Mantras of its oblations considered Sun as the recipient, thus: –

Sooryaya Swaha

Sooryaya Idam Na Mama

Prajapataye Swaha

Prajapataye Idam Na Mama

Vedic Rishis considered Sun as the Agni of the heavens. Agni and the Sunrepresented two "*Jyotis*" (divine lights). The Agni, in the form of "fire" belonged to the earth. It took the form of "thunder" in the Antarikhsa (space) and that of the "Sun" in the heavenly realms of the Gods. The Agni, thunder and the sun were manifestation of the same spirit. Agni was life! Agni was also represented in the Vedas, as "fertility". Thus, the process of producing fire by the friction of two pieces of wood (*Arani*) was called "*Manthan*" (Churning). Rigveda (3.29.1-3) commented that Agni dwelled in those wood as in *mother's womb!*

We have understood the positions, shapes, measurements, directions and other aspects of Garhastya Agni. A few significant Pak Yajnas were performed by Grihya Agni. According to *Ashvalayan Sutra* there were only three Pak Yajnas - "*Huta*", "*Ahuta*" and "*Prahuta*". The "Paraskar" Grihyasutra mentioned about another Pak Yajna, "*Prasita*". The list added a few more, considering, other Vedic commentaries on the subject. They were "*Shravanakarma*", "*Sthalipak*", "*Astakahom*", "*Astaka*", "*Pratyavarohan*", "*Shulgab*", "*Baliharan*", "*Sarpabali*", "*Ashwayuji*", etc. The Agni-based daily ritual of a "*Grihi*" (family-man) was "*Aupasana* Hom" that included "*Pratarhom*" (morning rituals) and "*Sayanghom*" (evening rituals), and was compulsory for every household. Either the Grihi himself or his representative could perform the Hom. Before sprinkling water on the fire, permissions were sought from three Goddesses – "*Aditi*". "*Anumati*" and "*Saraswati*". After the "*Pratarhom*", it was necessary to recitetheVedas. This was also a part of daily rituals. Besides, there was "Brahma Yajna" and"Astaka Yajna" that were performed at night."Astaka Yajna" was performed on"Ashtami" or the eighth day after the full moon in the month of "Agrahayana"for which offerings of *"Charu"* (oblation of rice, milk and sugar boiled together) and *Apoopa* (pie or pudding cake) were prepared. On the same day i.e "Ashtami" after the full moon, in the month of Pausha *"Mangsashtaka"* (meat) was offered. During this event the *"Hom Agni"*was initiated with *"Bopa"*, or fat from navel area of sacrificed bovine or other livestock. On Ashtami in the month of *Magha,"Sakashtaka"* (herbs) offering was made.

Now, we will study the *"Habiryajna"*, that came under Shrauta Karma. It implied that, after the rites of "Agnyadhyan", this Yajna was required for kindling the Ahavaniya Agni and Dakshinagni. Here, our three Agnis and one Vedi were involved. The most important Yajna in this category was "Agnihotra". The "Agnihotri" (One who had undertaken the duty of Agnihotra) invoked the Ahavaniya Agni two times (morning and evening) every day dedicating the rituals to Sun (in the morning) and Agni (in the evening), the dual manifestations of the divine light.

This was what Agnihotra was all about except that, it had an element of controversy about its timings. There was no doubt about the period of *"Sandhyakal"* (evening) which was *"after the sunset and before it got dark"* (implying twilight or dusk). But whether morning meant dawn, before sunrise or after, that was obscure! An interesting answer to this question was found in a lesser known *"Shankhayan"* or *"KaushitakiBrahmana" (2.9)*. It declared *"If Hom is performed after sunrise, then (he) concludes his "Atithya" (host-duties) for a departing great Deva (Sun) but if (he) performs Hom before sunrise then he properly offers hospitality to an arriving Sun God."* So, it was appropriate to perform Hom before sunrise. Milk was indispensable for those rituals. Every morning and evening, milk was contained in an earthen pot and warmed by the Garhapatya Agni. Two wooden ladles were required for the oblation process. The smaller one was called *"Shruba"* and the larger, *"Agnihotrahavani"*. Before the Habiryajna, the Yajman and his wife entered the Agnishala and rekindled the Ahavaniya and Dakshinagni from the Garhapatya Agni.

The most popular of the Shrauta Yajnas was"Isti Yaj". Isti Yaj wasmostly similar to PashuYaj and SomaYaj. The Agnihotri *"Grihi"* (houseowner) performed Isti Yaj on every full-moon and new-moon.The Yajman (Religious Host), during the ritual was required to sit with his wife in the presence of more than one Ritwik (priest). These details would be useful later in order to assess the space required for these Vedic Shrauta Yajnas as opposed to those Kundas found at the Indus Valley Civilization archaeological sites.

Besides the Yajmans there were at least four Ritwiks required. A Rigveda Mantra was chanted before the "Yaj" (worship) which was called *"Puronuvakya"*. And the Mantras related to the Yaj were known as *"Yajja"*. Yajja began with the supplication – *"Ye Yajamahe"* and ended with *"Vaushat"* The beginning and end were termed as *"Agu"* and *"Vashatkar"*. We have already discussed the names, shapes and measurements of the Agnis and the Vedis wherein the "Oistik Vedi" was also mentioned which was situated between Garhapatya and Ahavaniya Agnis. Let us see its functions. *"Kusha* grass"was laid on the surface of the Vedi, called *"Prastar"* on which the components for the Yajna, including a water-pot were placed. We will study the process of the Yajna, in order to get an idea of the space between the fire pits and later compare with the Indus "Kundas". At the start of the Yajna, Adhwaryu moved from north of the Vedi to its south, with two ladles, "Juhu" and *"Upabhrith"* and stood in front of the Ahavaniya Agni. This movement was called *"Atyakraman"*. Hota, who was positioned to north of the Vedi chanted the *"Anuvakyamantra"*, "Agu", "Jajjyamantra" and "Vaushat", after which Adhwaryu kindled the Ahavaniya Agni. Thereafter, the Yajman chanted the *"Tyagmantra"* and then Adhwaryu returned back to his original position to the north of the Vedi, his retreat known as *"Pratyakraman"*. From those positions, movements, and the mantras, we get an idea of the distance between the Vedis. Now, let us consider the items meant to be bequeathed to the Agni and other associated rites. Material oblation (*"Ahuti"*) was an important part of the Yajna and also important for us in order to compare those offerings with articles found in the Harappan archaeological sites. The first offerings went to the Agni and the second was servedboth to Agni and *"Soma"*.Purodash was also offered as *Ahuti*. Purodash was a type of pie made with rice or barley powder and baking it on a square-shaped dice. Itspreparation also required a special wooden ladle, Agnihotravani to carry the rice or barley and crushed by a pestle known as "*Udukhal*". Then a winnowing fan (called "*Surpa*") separated the chaffs from the grains before being mashed on a grinding stone to prepare the paste. A dice was used to give shape to the Purodash. Two more things were required, a wooden block called "*Shamya*" and skin of a black buck (*Ajin*) that was laid for the preparation. The pestle Udukhal and the grinding stone were the required stone implements here. The entire process from preparation of "Purodash" to its offering was undertaken by "Adhwaryu". Besides "Purodash", Ghee (clarified butter) was also offered. We have known that this Ghee was known as "*Ajjya*" and the earthen pot that contained the Ajjya was called "*Ajyasthali*". Therefore, the "Ajyasthali" was always to be found in close proximity of the Yajna Agni. Mention of four types of wooden ladles used for oblation was found in the Brahmanas. They were the "Shruba", "Juhu", "Agnihotravani" and "Upabhrith". Besides, another type of ladle was found, known as "*Dhruva*". Those are, however not much relevant to our study since it was never possible to find perishable, wooden ladles from the Harappan era. The rituals of "Shrauta Yajnas" did not include "*Samagaana*", the melodious chanting of the Sama Veda, so there was no "Udgata" present. On the first day, The Yajman (with his wife) prepared the Agnishala kindling the three Agnis. Then they took some religious vows known as "*Vratagrahan*" and spent the night in the Agnishala. This meant there used to be enough space in the Agnishala to accommodate the worshippers. Next day, in the morning the rites of "Isti Yaj" commenced after the daily ritual of "Agnihotra". Some more items of this Yajna were the three pieces of wood, placed along the perimeter of the circular space surrounding the "Ahavaniya Agni" called "*Paridhi*". A part of the rites of Ishti Yag was "*Praneeta Pranayan*". Praneeta was the water kept to the east of the Vedi, beside the Ahavaniya Agni. We will keep in mind the specific location of the water, situated to the east of the Vedi, for future reference. It was crucial that the water pot resting on the "Prastar" remained undisturbed until the Yajna was completed, as it was believed to safeguard the Yajnas from any interference by "Rakshasas" (demons) and "Asuras" (evil spirits). After all these preparations in place, the Habiryajna commenced. Agni, envisioned as the emissary of the Gods, was represented by a sage titled "*Prabar Agni*," who belonged to the same religious denomination or "Gotra of the Yajman.

A series of five "Yaj" or worship rituals took place after this – "Prayaj", "Ayabhag", "Upangshu", "Swishtakrit" and "Anuyaj". Those Yajs required a wooden sword called "Sfya".Major offering during those rites was "Purodash". Other "Isti Yaj" rites followed more or less the same procedures.

Our next subject of study is "Pashu Yaj",a Vedic worship aided by animal sacrifice.In many excavated "Agni Kundas" at Harappan archaeological sites, bones of animals were found. In fact, a carved image of animal sacrifice ritual was also found in one of those sites. So, for comparison purpose, we need to understand the nature and functions of those Vedic sacrificial rites.

One more Vedi was added to the traditional "Oistik Vedi" for "Pashu Yaj", and this new Vedi was positioned to the east of the "Ahavaniya Agni". The additional Vedi was actually an assortment of two separate Vedis, one smaller Vedi, called "Uttar Vedi" placed atop a larger one, called "*Pashuk*". Agni was rekindled at the centre of the "*Uttar Vedi*" (known as "*Navi*" or umbra) from the fire of "Ahavaniya" Agni. The process was called "*Agnipranayankarma*". During the rituals, this Agni placed at "Navi" played the role of "Ahavaniya" Agni. Like the "Oistik" Vedi that held the offerings and elements of that particular ritual, the "Pashuk" Vedi was also used to place various organs of animals, among other items, needed for "Pashu Yaj". A thick log, called "*Yupakashtha*" was planted to tie the sacrificial animal. This log, known as "*Astashree*" was shaped as an octagon and was five arm's length long. It was buried four arm's length under the ground with one arm's length protruding over the ground. A crown-like topping known as "*Chashal*" completed its shape. The pit for this "Yupakashtha" was dug at the east side of the "*Pashuk*" Vedi. So, the "Pashuk" Vedi was to the east side of the "Ahavaniya" Agni and the "Yupakashtha" to the east side of this new "Pashuk" Vedi. Understandably, the "Yupakashtha" stood quite far from the Vedi. The rope, that was used to tie the animal was called "*Rashna*". A piece of wood was also attached with the rope, known as "*Chakkhal*". The rope was not fastened to the animal by its neck but by its horns, a process called "*Pashu*

Niyojan". It is worth noting that there were fundamental differences between conventional *"Bali"* (animal sacrifice) traditions of present times and that of Vedic era. Vedic custom did not permit beheading of animals with sharp weapon. They were strangled with ropes! The process of asphyxiation was called *"Sanjyapan" (Aitareya Brahmana 2.6.3)*. The sacrificial altars found in the later periods were non-existent in Vedic times and in no way resembled the "Yupakashtha" that only acted as a fastening post. The actual sacrifice took place at a different place, afar from the pole. The Yajna area was off-limits for animal sacrifices or other acts of violence. A separate place, called *"Shamitra desh"*, north of the "Pashuk" Vedi was reserved for the purpose. Fresh fire was made to cook the animals on that spot. The person who killed the animals was known as *"Shamita"* or *"Adhrigu"*. Another interesting aspect of the proceedings was that the Yajman and the Ritwiks did not witness the "Bali" (killing) of the sacrificial animal and sat in front of the "Uttarvedi" turning their back against the killing zone or "Shamitra desh". After the killing, the wife of Yajman washed the body of the animal with water and the "Adhwaryu" sliced its belly with a sharp knife to extract the fat (Bopa) from its navel area to be offered to the Agni. A different version of "Purodash" was made adding flesh of the sacrificial animal. We have studied the process of "Purodash" in "Isti Yaj". In the present case, animal flesh was the major ingredient. Eleven body parts of the animals were considered appropriate for performing the "Pashu Yaj", they were – Heart, tongue, chest, liver, the kidneys, the left foreleg, the rib-cages, right buttock, the anus, Bopa and Basa (Fat from Chest area). The blood, not being of any use was disposed of and believed to be consumed by demons who in turn would desist from sabotaging the Yajna. Those duties were performed by the "Shamita" or "Adhrigu". Thereafter, "Adhwaryu" collected all the above organs in an earthen vessel and boiled it before adding *"Prasadajya"* (Curd and ghee) to prepare the offering for oblation to the Gods. So, those earthen vessels were closely associated with the "Pashu Yaj".

From "Pashu Yaj" let us move on to "Soma Yaj", the most enigmatic of all the Vedic Yajnas! The prescribed period to perform this Yaj was in the month of Chaitra – Vaisakh. This was because the Soma plants grew during those period (Krishna Yajurveda, 3.2.8).

During the excavations of Indus Valley Civilization sites, archaeologists found open or outdoor Agni Kundas, presumably used for collective social rituals, rather than domestic purposes. Accordingly, we need to examine the larger outdoor Yajna rituals of Vedic era and study the proceedings. "*Soma*" is a type of plant with divine attributes. One school of Vedic thoughts considered it as the "King", another –God! The generally accepted fact was that the "Soma plant" acted as the intermediary between God and the King. The beverage extracted from the plant was of divine nature. "*Soma ras*" was the primary offering in the "Soma Yaj".

In the Vedas, the term "Soma" was used to refer to the beverage, the plant, and also its divine form. Consumption of Soma was believed to grant immortality *(Amrita, Rigveda 8.48.3)*. Both Indra and Agni were depicted as consuming copious quantities of Soma. Within Vedic belief, Indra was portrayed as consuming large quantities of Soma while battling the serpent demon *Vritra*. The act of humans imbibing Soma was well-documented in Vedic commentaries. "*Soma Mandala*"part of the Rigveda (9th Manadala) wasdedicated to Soma "Pavamana" and concentrated on a specific moment in the ritual: the pressing, straining, blending with water & milk, and pouring into vessels of the Soma. These actions symbolized various concepts, including a king expanding his territory, the Sun's voyage across the universe, or a bull's pursuit of mating with cows (symbolized by the milk). One of the most significant myths concerning Soma revolved around its theft. According to this narrative, Soma was initially imprisoned in a celestial fortress by the archer Krishanu (Agni, personified). A falcon managed to steal Soma, eluding Krishanu, and delivered it to Manu for sacrificial purpose. Additionally, in the later Rigveda and Middle Vedic period, Soma became linked with the moon. Surya the Sun's daughter, is also periodically identified as Soma's spouse.

Coming back to Soma Yajna, the central sacrament of the Yajna was "*Jyotistom*" which was divided into four phases, containing three, fifteen, seventeen and twenty-one Mantras from Rigveda. Those mantras were chanted by "Hota" before invoking the Agni, hence the name, "Jyotistom" (lighting of the fire). "Jyotistom", in general terms can be understood as an oblation process to various Vedic Gods. According to *"Kaushitaki Brahmana"*, there were seven types of *"Jyotistom"*- *"Agnistoma"*, *"Atyagnistoma"*, *"Ukatha"*, *"Sodashi"*, *"Bajpaya"*, *"Atiratra"* and *"Antoryam"*. Among these, the particular types of oblations were appropriated through a process called *"Samastha"*. In the realm of Vedic rituals, particularly within the framework of the Soma Yajna, "Samastha" held significance as a type of offering. The Soma Yajna was an intricate Vedic ceremonial practice involving the preparation and presentation of "Soma ras" to various Vedic Gods. This ritual was extensively mentioned in ancient Vedic scriptures like the *"Krishna Yajurveda"*. During the Soma Yajna, diverse offerings were presented to a consecrated fire as acts of devotion to distinct Gods. These offerings contained elements such as grains, clarified butter (Ghee), milk, and the Soma ras. The term "Samastha" often conveyed the notion ofblending those substances for collective offering.

In the context of the "Soma Yajna", oblations termed "Samastha" were typically dedicated to Agni, the fire God, along with other celestial beings perceived in the rites. Those offerings formed an integral facet of the ritualistic practices within Vedic traditions, believed to invoke divine blessings, foster cosmic order, and uphold equilibrium in the cosmos.

The basic form of "Somayaj" or "Somayajna" is the *"Agnistoma-Somayaj"* (*Krishna Yajurveda 7.1.1*). Yajurveda describes a war between the Gods and the "Asuras" (Evil spirits)" where the former began a Yajna to ensure victory. Learning this, the "Asuras" also started their own Yajna. Then the Gods decided to perform the great "Somayaj", unbeknownst to the "Asuras". The "Somayaj" was performed behind the façade of "Agnihotra". This deceived the "Asuras" who were ignorant about the power that the Gods derived from "Somayajna" and subsequently lost the war against the Gods. *(Krishna Yajurveda 3.2.2)*.

The various stages of "Soma Yaj" required complex procedures and different time-periods to complete. They could take from one day to one year. "Agnistoma" is the simplest. We will study its components and later compare them with the HarappanKunda-related arrangements.

Since a large space was required for "Agnistoma Yajna" it was not possible to perform this Yajna indoor, inside a residence. An area was demarcated outside the house, called "*Devayajan Bhumi*". The most important aspect of this Yajna, was the positions and number of Vedis involved. "Isti Yaj" was performed before and after "Agnistoma", so, a separate "Oistic Vedi" was erected on the spot. The three Agnis – "Garhapatya", "Ahavaniya" and "Dakshinagni" accompanied the "Oistik Vedi". This outdoor format was known as "*Prachinavamsasala*", and occupied an area of a square having sides of twelve "Aratni" (one Aratni wasthe measure from the elbow to small finger of the Yajman or religious host). To the east of the "Oistik Vedi" a large Vedi was constructed, known as the "Mahavedi" or "Soumik Vedi". The "Mahavedi" (fig. 2.2) was a paved floor with the shape of a trapezium. Its eastern side being shorter than its western side although they were parallel to each other. The northern and southern sides were equal but obviously not parallel. Manyscholars visualized thisas the torso of a male human figure! One part of the Vedi is called "Angsa" and the other – "Shroni (shoulder and waist)". The measurements of the four sides were determined on the basis of the body-measures of the "Yajman". We calculate this by the unit of "*Prakram*" or the length of a step, which is approximately two and half feet, or thirty inches.

Accordingly, Vedic measurements of the sides of the trapezoid can be noted as: -

West side	75 feet
Ease side	60 feet
North and South sides	90 feet

Those standard measures were often altered depending on "Yajman's" physical dimensions.

A few "Mandapas" (religious canopies) were erected on the Vedi with the help of poles. The one at the centre was called "Habirdhan Mandap". There were separate names for the other "Mandapas".

We will, however, only study the Mandapas where Agnis were instituted. On top of the "Mahavedi", an "Uttara Vedi" (mentioned in "Pashu Yaj") was constructedto the east side which measured "*Dashapada*" (or 2.5 metres), it literally meant ten times measure of the foot. Human foot is approximately twenty-five centimetres. Like the Oistik Vedi, this Vedi also had an inward narrow curvature at its middle part where Agni was instituted exactly at its navel or central spot. The Vedi which was erected at the western side on the "Mahavedi" was called "*Sadahsala*" or "*Sadogriha*", which was 18 arms in length and 9 arms in breadth. 'One arm' is the distance from elbow to tip of the middle finger of the Yajman, approximately 1.5 feet. So, the "Sadahsala" measured 27 feet in length and 13.5 feet in breadth. Besides, there were six fire altars or "*Dhishnyas*" from north to south on top of the "Mahavedi". Separately, they were "*Acchabak*", "*Neshta*", "*Pota*", "*Brahmanaacchangshi*", "*Hota*" and "*Maitravarun*". These names may sound familiar to those who remembered the names of the Ritwiks mentioned earlier who performed the Yajnas. The fire altars were thus named after their religious custodians. There were also two "Dhishnyas" at the north and south sides of the "Mahavedi", they were called "*Agnidhriya*"(north) and "*Marjaniya*" (south). The measurements of these "Dhishnyas" were significant, as we would requireto refer those while comparing the physical characteristics of the Vedic fire altars with their Indus counterparts excavated at the Harappan archaeological sites. The "Dhishnyas" were mostly square-shaped with its' sides measuring "one (Yajman's) arm" or "18 fingers'" length. However, within this exact area they were sometimes circular in shape. (*Apastamba Srauta Sutra 16.15.1*). It is now obvious that all the measurements of the Yajna Vedis were connected to the body measures of the "Yajman" who performed that particular Yajna. One finger was identified as a length of approximately 2 centimetres. So, 18 fingers called for 36 centimetres or 1.25 feet. Going by the arm, which was sum of 24 fingers gave an average length of approximately 1.5 feet. From this, we can infer that the areas of "Dhishnyas" were between 36 – 48 centimetres or 1.25 to 1.5 feet. For a circular shape with the same area the diameter would be more or less, the same. Now, we get a total of nine "Agnis" on the "Mahavedi" (six in a series, two across, and one on the navel of "Uttara Vedi"). The Agni that was invoked on the navel of "Uttarvedi" acted as "Ahavaniya" Agni while the original "Ahavaniya" Agni was renamed *Shaladyarya* and its fire was used to initiate the "Dhishnyas". Two pits "Chatwalak" and "Utkar" were found dug, three and two feet (literal meaning) away from the "Mahavedi" implying that the "Chatyalak" was dug to obtain earth for construction of the "Mahavedi", while *"Utkar"* was a waste disposal pit.

"Soma Yaj" was performed by the Yajman along with his wife. Both invited the Ritwiks through proper religious rites and received "Diksha" (preparation or consecration for a religious ceremony). Then, they took their seats in front of the Vedi (*Krishna Yajurveda 3.5.6*). Soma was bought from a seller outside the Yajna venue and brought to the Yajna by bullock cart. The Soma was attributed royal status so the cart was parked right in front of the "Habirdhan Mandap", at the centre. The religious reception of "Soma" included offering of "Gharma", a mixture of warm milk and ghee, through a ritual known as *"Prabargya"*. During this ceremony all the Ritwiks and Yajman (his wife too) touched the offering and took oath to perform the Yajna with devotion and righteousness. After this, four-days long rituals for "Ishti Yaj", "Pashuyaj" and other related rites ensued. "Soma Yaj" started from the fifth day. A ritualistic tradition of fetching water from nearby water sources at dawn still prevails in Bengal. Similar tradition was found during this Yajna wherein the Ritwiks and the Yajman's wife brought water separately in vessels. This water was used to prepare "Somaras", adding it to crushed Soma plant.

The extract of Soma was thus produced while chanting Mantras, referred as *"Abhishava"* in the *Krishna Yajurveda (3.1.8)– "Osadhi is the subject of Soma and Lord Indra is his God"*. There were three stages in the preparation of Soma – *"Pratahsaban"*, *"Mandhyandin-saban"* and *"Tritiya-saban"*. During the first two stages the "Somalata" (Soma leaf, branch or plant) was grinded while at the "Tritiya-saban" stage, the water brought at dawn was mixed with the paste and distilled. *(Krishna Yajurveda 3.2.2)*. The "Somaras" was then dedicated to Lords Prajapati, Indra and other Gods, and the offering of "Somaras" through sacred Agni commenced thereafter. "Hom" (or "Havan", a Vedic fire ritual) was instituted with chants of the Mantra- "Svaha" (The final word, at the end of specific Mantras, before sacrificing the offering to the

Vedic Gods). "Pashuyaj" and "Ishtiyaj" were repeated at the end of "Somayaj".

We have, so far inspected the "Somayaj" and the Vedis, shape of the fire altars, directions and measurements. Before concluding "Somayaj", it is noteworthy that the definition and sublime identities of "Soma" encompasses different Vedic interpretations, whether it was the plant or the intoxicating extract, or, for that matter carried its literal meaning which is moon (note the sense of lunacy)! In the scriptures of the Vedas, all those attributes are supported and mostly mentioned in the commentaries in Rigveda as God. The entire "ninth Mandala" of Rigveda (also called Soma Mandala) is dedicated to "Soma". Although personified in many Vedic myths, the "Soma" of Yajna was purely the religious potion extracted from the "Soma" plant. The Vedic scriptures administer every detail about its procurement, preparation and rites of offering.Although, Rigveda has about 144 hymns on "Somas", two are quite significant and specific about its nature.

pavasva soma madhumāṁ ṛtāvāpo vasāno adhi sāno avye |

ava droṇāni ghṛtavānti sīda madintamo matsara indrapānaḥ ||

Rig Veda 9.96.13

O Soma, who have exhilarating Juice, who are connected with the sacrifice, clothed with water flown upon the elevated fleece; alight upon the water-holding pitchers, you who are most exhilarating, intoxicating amongst the special beverage of Indra.

pavasvendo pavamāno mahobhiḥ kanikradat pari vārāṇy arṣa |

krīḻañ camvor ā viśa pūyamāna indraṃ te raso madiro mamattu ||

Rig Veda 9.96.21

"Flow Indu, purified by the venerable (priests), seep through the filter of fleece, enter the pitcher playfully from the (stone) plaques. Let your exhilarating juice be distilled and thence inebriate Indra."

The connection of these Mantras with the preparation process of "Somaras" is evident. The grinding of the "Somalata" on two stone-slabs (analogically, plaques), the filter made of lamb fur (called "Pavamana"), the final stage of the beverage finding its way into the pitcher containing ghee -all are described, albeit with poetic cadence.

That the "Somaras" was intoxicating, was an established fact. Both Mantras describe it as exhilarating!

Before we conclude, two Yajnas – "Rajasuya" and *"Asvamedha"* call for mention. These two Yajnas, made famous by the Hindu epic Mahabharata, were forms of "Soma Yaj" in the "Shrauta" tradition. Let us not misconstrue "Asva (horse)medh" as a "Pashu Yaj". It was indeed a "Soma Yaj" where the horse symbolized the royal sacrificial offering. Both the Yajnas were conducted by kings or the Kshatriyas (warrior aristocracy) to establish, popularize and strengthen their sovereignty over a vast dominion. Performing "Rajasuya Yajna" was also an exclusive right of the Kshatriyas. The "Rajasuya Yajna" commenced on the first day of the bright lunar fortnight (Shukla Pratipada) in the eleventh month of the traditional Indian calendar. It began with Ishti Yaj, followed by year-long rituals of various Yajnas. It commenced with *"Chaturmasya Yajna"*, followed by *"Pavitra Yaj"* that included *"Dikshaniya Ishti"* and *"Upashad Ishti"* for its completion. The next stage was performing the *"Hom"* "Ishti Yaj",*"Pashuchaturmasya"*,*"Indraturiya"*, *"Apamarg"*, *"Devikahabih"*, and *"Devasubahih"*. After this, the enthronement ceremony of the king took place. The king also engaged in a mock war against an imaginary adversary on a chariot driven by three horses and invariably won. He performed *"Rathbimochaniya Hom"* after alighting from his chariot. It drew an end with the *"Pasha"* (a royal board game with dice) followed by Ishti Yaj.

In the *"Asvamedha* Yajna" a consecrated and specially chosen horse was allowed to roam at its will for a specific period in various designated territories while an elaborate set of rituals, prayers, and offerings were performed at home by King's priests during this period. If any other king dared to capture the horse, the consequence was war. If it returned unharmed, the horse was ritually sacrificed, followed by a royal feast. Interestingly, the rituals included the queen acting out a sexual union with the horse, which was later related with "Fertility theory" by many. This was followed by a ceremonious enthronement of the king with much fanfare. In fact, "*Asvamedha* Yajna" turned out to be a festive occasion for people in Vedic era. Bullock carts were loaded with "Somalata". People engaged in mock fights over possession of Soma lata. Animal sacrifices were rampant.

In the early stages of Vedic era, the "*Asvamedha* Yajna" was much simpler as described in the *Rigveda (1.162 – 163)*. Subsequently, the "*Asvamedha* Yajna" held a complex and symbolic significance within later-Vedic traditions, representing not only the king's supremacy but also spiritual and cosmic aspects as mentioned in ancient Vedic texts, most notably in the "*Yajurveda*" and the "*Mahabharata*".

We will now study the last of the important Yajnas – "Agnicayana", one of the most significant Yajna rites among the Shrauta Karmas. "Agnicayana" literally means "piling up of fire". Earlier, we discussed about "Shulvasutra" as another set of precepts found in Vedic literature, that contained precise measurements concerning construction of Vedi or fire altars. In fact, the Shulvasutra commentaries were part of the larger corpus of texts called the "Shrauta Sutras" and comprised a collection of ancient mathematical texts that emphasized geometry and measurement. Their main focus was on constructing fire altars used in Vedic rituals. Those texts, referred to as the "Shulvasutras," were among the earliest examples of Indian mathematical genius, believed to have been written between 800 BCE and 500 BCE. The term "Shulva" translatedinto "cord" or "rope," while "sutra" denoted concise rules or aphorisms. The primary goal of the Shulvasutras was to provide precise instructions for crafting various types of altars essential for performing Vedic rituals. These altars had specific geometric shapes and dimensions, necessitating accurate measurements for the rituals' success. The "Shulvasutras" delved into concepts such as the Pythagorean theorem (pre-dating Pythagoras by centuries), properties of right-angled triangles, and techniques for constructing squares and rectangles with predetermined areas.

One prominent text among the Shulvasutras was the "*Baudhayana Shulbasutra*," connected to the ancient Indian mathematician Baudhayana. This text outlined rules for creating different altar types, including the Agni-Kunda or fire altar, the pivotal element in Vedic rituals. While primarily concerned with practical applications, the "Shulvasutras" also introduced advanced mathematical ideas that were remarkably progressive for Vedic times.

"Agnicayana" yajna wasincluded in Soma sacrifices. The primary requirement for construction of its "Yajna Vedi" was bricks. The height of these Vedis was generally "Knee-length" of the Yajman or patron-sacrificer. Most popular Vedis had five layers of bricks but sometimes extended to ten to fifteen layers. Among other Vedic Yajnas, "Agnicayana" or "Syena (hawk) Yajna" held special significance. According to famous Indologist Naoshiro Suji – *"Agnicayana, as the pinnacle of Vedic ritual, occupies a special position among the Shrauta sacrifices owing not only to its elaborateness but also to the fact that it contains many remarkable rites and ritual elements."*

In 1975, an "Agnicayana Yajna" was performed in Kerala, India. Renowned researcher of Vedic rituals Prof. Frits Staal recorded an in-depth description of the proceedings in his book. He observed an Agni Shala accessible to commoners and a *"Mahavedi"* constructed beside it, as in "Soma Yaj". Similarly, to the west of the "Mahavedi", the religious hearths of "Garhapatya", "Ahavaniya", "Dakshinagni" and the "Oistik Vedi" were constructed to create the "Prachinavamsasala". On the top of the "Mahavedi, "Habirdhan Mandap" were erected on the middle section and "Sadahsala" over its western edge. Readers may remember the "Uttara Vedi" that was constructed for "Soma Yaj" to the east-side, on top of the "Mahavedi" and the secondary "Ahavaniya Agni" thatwas initiated at its centre or "Navi (navel)". But in "Agnicayana" another larger Vedi was constructed and "Ahavaniya Agni" was established at its centre. Various shapes of altars were prescribed (in different disciplines of the Vedas),but the broad categories were *"Khsudracayana"* and *"Mahacayana"*. A compiled phenomena of these Yajna Vedis from the precepts of *"Taittiriya Aranyakaa"*, *"Taittiriya Brahmana"*, *"Apastamba Shrauta Sutras"* and *"Baudhayan Shrauta Sutras"* depict the following variations: -

1. Sabitracayana   Sun-shaped Yajna Vedi

2. Nachiketayana   Resembled the sage Nachiketa

3. Chaturhotracayana   Indicated positions of the four "Hotras"

4. Vaischaryacayana   Depiction of original form of creation

5. Arunaketucayana   Resembled the sage Arunaketu

6. Syenacayana   Hawk-shaped Yajna Vedi

7. Kurmacayana   Tortoise-shaped Yajna Vedi

It is difficult for us to perceive the shape of the "Syenacayana"Yajna Vedi as either depicting four Hotras (similar meaning as Hota) or the original form of creation. It requires further exploration.

"Mahacayana" was divided into three parts which differed, not in shape but in height. For "Khsudracayana", a pit was dug and the Vedi was erected by filling the pit with stone-chips andpebbles. But in case of "Mahacayana" the Vedi was made of bricks. Its height varied according to specific purposes. It could be five times knee-length (of the Yajman) or ten times the height of the individual's navel or in certain cases, fifteen times the height of individual's face from ground. Among so many types of altars, the "Syenacayana" version was most popular. Indian Sage and Grammarian Panini, in his *Ashtadhyayi Sutras (3.2.92)*" metaphorically compared the "Agnicayana" or "Agniciti" with a hawk that flew to heaven and delivered the oblations to the Gods. The oldest evidence of this Vedic "Syenacayana"Yajna Vedi was found during the excavation of Kaushambi. A description of the Vedi is given in Appendix C for interested readers. Regardless of the shape of the Vedi,its area had to be eight and half square *Purusha*" (one "Purusha was the measure of height of the Yajman with raised hands). But when the same Yajman performed the Yajna periodically, with specific *"Kamya"* (desire) in mind, the area of the Vedi was increased each time by one square "Purusha" within a limit of 101 square "Purusha". The "Mahavedi" of "Agnicayana" was constructed from bottom to top by laying bricks in layers.Some bricks layers were special and named accordingly. The first layer consisted of *"Apasya"* bricks meant for *"Apa(water)"*. The bricks were also part of worshipping items and Mantras were chanted while bricklaying. This religious process was called *"Upadhan"* and was performed by *"Adhwaryu"*. Each layer contained a minimum of 200 bricks that formed the structure with five layers with 1000 bricks. Thus a *"Mahavedi"* with 10 layers had 2000 bricks, and with 15 layers, 3000 bricks. For the layers, there were religious practices of animal sacrifices and gold offerings. Some of the *"Mahavedis"* did not form the exact shape of the hawk, instead symbolically represented by one square-shaped altar with two rectangular blocks by its sides to portray wings and another rectangular block behind as its tail. We will later find the significance of this arrangements.

Let us, now consider the "Dhishnyas" which were the eight subordinate or side-altars. We recollect that six "Dhishnyas" were in series placed side-by-side and two across the middle part. These six "Dhishnyas" often appeared in our study. In the "Agnicayana", these "Dhishnyas" are also constructed and religiously initiated. Constructions of the *"Agnidhriya"*(northsideDhishnyas) and *"Marjaniya"* (south) required six and eight bricks respectively. *"Acchabak"*, *"Neshta"*, *"Pota"*, and *"Maitravarun"* required eight bricks each, while *"Brahmanaacchangshi Dhishnya"* needed eleven and for *"Hota"*, twelve bricks were required to fullfil the "Agnicayana" prerequisites.

The Yajna Vedis were symmetrical, lengthwise, by both sides across an imaginary line called *"Prishtha"* or *"Prachi"*. It divided the Vedis like a backbone of an animal into two equal sections. Due to this feature the Yajna Vedis were known to be *"Pashudharmi"* or animalistic in shape. Earlier, we have seen that the "Mahavedi" of "Soma Yaj" could be an isosceles trapezium, concaved at its middle section, like the shape of "Oistik Vedi". These altars were Yajna-specific and slightly varied in measurements. *"Pakyajniki"* altar was for "Pak Yajna", *"Darshapournamasiki"* altar was for a specific *"Darshapounamasa"* Yajna, "Pashuk Vedi" was reserved for "Pashu Yaj", etc.

Besides the shapes of the altar, another important aspect of*"Agnicayana"*were the bricks. In fact, there were quite a few restrictions about those Vedic bricks. In the *"Satapatha Brahmana (8th Kanda, 8.7.2.16-19)"* it was suggested that the bricks should be of pristine red colour and without any black core. Broken, over-burnt or decayed bricks were also scrapped. The slightest impurities like bloating, efflorescence, etc, meant outright rejection. The unit of "Purusha" (defined earlier),was used in the manufacturing of bricks. There were two types of bricks – The common *"Lokamprina"* and the special, *"Yajusmati"* bricks. The latter were used to fill-in designated parts, containing specific designs like the head, wings or tails of a figure that shaped the altar. Obviously, the shapes of "Yajusmati" bricks came in various shapes and sizes in accordance with the designs, but never exceeded 395 *"Satapatha Brahmana (10.4.3.14-20)"*. These commentaries precisely dictated the numbers, names and the laying process.

The first layer contained 98 bricks, out of which 15 were "Apasya", 5- "Chhandasya", and 50 – "Pranbhrit" bricks, rest were without names. In the second layer there were 41 bricks in total. The named ones were: 5 – "Ashwini", 5- "Vaishyadevi", 5- "Pranbhrit", 5- "Apasya" and 19- "Vayasya" bricks. The third layer had 71 bricks among them named ones were 1 "Vishwajyoti", 10 "Pranbhrit", 36 'Chhandasya" and 14 "Balakhilya". The fourth layer was made of 47 bricks, all without names. The fifth and last layer contained 135 bricks that included 5 "Asapatna", 40 "Viraja", 29 "Stombhaga", 5 "Naksada", 5 "Pancachuda", 31 "Chhandasya", 8 of "Garrhapatya", 8 of "Punashiti", 1 Vishwajyoti" and 1 "Vikarni" brick.

These layers held 395 special "Yajusmati" bricks, the rest were "Lokamprina" or common bricks with no names. The number 395 has a mystery attached to it too. No of days in a particular year (considered 360 days in Vedic era) added to the period of new moon to full moon which is 24 days and 12 representing 12 months, adds up to the number 396. The surplus of one day accounted for one extra "Yajusmati" brick that was used as filler in the fifth layer. Now, the small gaps and crevices were filled with small "Lokamprina" bricks. These bricks were called "*Muhurta*" a unit of Vedic time period wherein there were 10800 "*Muhurta*" in a year. Accordingly, a maximum number of 10800 small "Lokamprina" bricks were permissible. To sum up, a total number of 11195 bricks including big and small ones were used to construct the altar of "Agnicayana" that completed the shape of the of hawk or other symbolic figures.

Besides those bricks, there were some other bricks of specific shapes and sizes required for the construction of Yajna altars. There were those square-shaped bricks whose sides equalled one-fifth of the height of the Yajman, hence named "Panchami" bricks. Some other Vedic preceptssuggested this to be one-fourth of the height of the Yajman. Some bricks were made on the basis of the size of Yajman's foot, known as "*Ekpad*". Another brick named "*Sapada*" was rectangular in shape, with a length of one-fourth of "Panchami" bricks. The breadth of these bricks were prescribed as one-fifth of the distance from Yajman's knee to his foot. In this context, the largest brick equalled the thighbone (femur) of the Yajman, in length. Now we know that the bricks required for the construction of the Vedis were never uniform and had different measurements. It was strictly observed that the joining of two bricks of a particular layer did not align with the joints of bricks either of the upper layer or beneath it. The brickwork was done in symmetry with every alternate layer, viz, first, third and fifth; second, fourth, sixth and so on. Different bricks were additionally used to build circular or curved parts.

Stones were also required for the construction of Yajna Vedis and essentially placed around the three "Shrauta Agnis" – "Garhapatya", "Ahavaniya" and "Dakshinagni". Those holy stone slabs or blocks were known as "*Parisrita*". For the "Garhapatya" Agni" 21 "Parisrita" stones were required, for "Ahavaniya Agni", 261, and for "Dhishnyas" 78 "Parisritas" were prescribed totalling 360 stones *Satapath Brahmana (10.4.3.13)*, In the commentaries, the stones were compared with night.

Vedic pottery too, played an important role in the Vedic Yajnas. In the descriptions of the Yajnas, we have seen that the Yajna pots were unique in their features. Some of the vessels were made of wood, hence not relevantto our study. We cannot expect to find the remnants of perishable wooden pots in Harappan sites. We will scrutinize the major potsand vessels of theVedic period and compare them with the artifacts, found around the fire worshipping Kundas of Harappan times. Like the chanting of Mantras or the religious rites, the preparation of the pots were of equal religious importance. The common name for these pots was "Ukha". It was not easy to produce those pots and they demanded a complex procedure to obtain the finished products. Besides "Ukha", there were two more special types of pots, "*Mahavira*" and "*Pravargya*". We will closely follow the Vedic religious procedures for the manufacturing of pots and understand the shapes, sizes and functions of the pots. The prescribed methods of the process was not generic in nature nor flexible, but strictly guided by Vedic principles and work ethics described in "*Ukhasamvarana*" which was a part (Kanda) of *"Satapatha Brhamana"*. The process was indeed complex. Grinded potsherd, charcoal ash, threshed husk or chaff, gravel, and deer-hair were added to the clay to make it suitable for pottery. Ingredients for "Pravargya"includedant-hill mixed with earth, dug-up by wild boars and the root-soil of a particular type of grass named "Adra". It was then added to goat milk to prepare the perfect pottery-clay. These details are of academic interest and not quite relevant to our study. We will, however have to touch upon the fundamentals and, to an extent the physical properties in order to avoid supplementary information about these religious objects. The kilns for the heating and firing of the wares were made of earth and constructed traditionally at the east side of the "Agnishala", consisting the Vedic Agnis. This fact will help us to find out possible links between Vedic Yajna and the Indus fire worship. According to" Ukhasamvarana", manufacturing of pots was entrusted with a skilled potter and was accomplished by hand without the use of potter's wheel or scrapers. No woman or unskilled person was allowed to undertake the job or even witness the proceedings. Later, in the "Shrautasutra", there was a dictate for the Yajman's wife or the "Adhwaryu:" of the Yajna to make the pots, thus replacing the potter in the Yajnas. In any case, without his wheels and scrapers, the absence of the potter did not make much difference! From this, archaeologists concluded that the Vedic potteries were mostly handmade.

Now, we will study the method of manufacturing Vedic earthenware. Three lumps of the processed clay were taken to shape the top, middle and bottom parts of the pot. Pitchers or pots for keeping Ghee, the earthen covers, milk-pot and various other containers were shaped and dried under sunlight. Later, when they became a little hard (as leather) a coating of 'slip' was applied. In the context of Vedic pottery, a 'slip' was a mixture of clay and water that was spread on the surface of a pottery object prior to the firing process. This technique served multiple purposes, including enhancing the visual appeal, providing a smoother texture, and even introducing colours to the pottery. However, this practice was not unique to the Vedic period and also found in traditional pottery in other contemporary civilizations. The earthenware then, were purified by smoke from dry horse dung, a process called "*Dhupayati*" followed by firing of the objects (called "Pakati") in an open kiln which was, as mentioned earlier, located at the east side of the Agnishala. The pots were placed upside down on the kiln. After lighting the fire, the wares continued to be fired throughout the day. Those pots cracked by heating were rejected. Here, a little insight would not be out of place. The ingredients or "grogs" that the Vedic people added to the clay like grinded potsherd, charcoal ash, threshed husk or chaff, gravel, and deer-hair made the substance almost impossible to be shaped by a potter's wheel. On the contrary, the lumps of the same clay were quite easy to handle manually and obtain the desired shapes.The grogs improved the workability, strength, and thermal shock resistance of the clay bodies. Furthermore, grog contributed to the aesthetic qualities of Vedic pottery by imparting texture and creating a slightly roughened surface.Itwas earlier mentioned that, before heating, the wares were exposed to dry horse dung smoke. Besides purification, it was also intended to blacken the surface of the pots. The black particulate matters of the smoke, filled the pores on the surface of the pots leaving them with a black exterior. Since ancient times, potters had followed this method to create black potteries. During the later periods, the "Northern Black Polished Ware (NBPW) displayed excellent black shades inside and out of the pots. The Vedic methods of colouring the innermost parts of the potteries are now almost extinct. It may be construed that the NBPW artisans used the same methods.

For shapes and sizes, the important vessels like "Mahavira", "Ukha", and *"Prashitraharan"* types may be discussed. "Mahavira" was one *"Vighat* (tip of the stretched thumb to tip of the stretched ring finger) in length. It had a flat top and bottom with its middle area being comparatively narrow. In another context, "Mahavira" was described as a cup. Some pots also had "spouts" to pour liquid into other vessels. The egg-shaped *"Ukha"* pots too, were one *"Vighat"* in length with breadth, exceeding their length. An embossed band on the pot's surface held a motif depicting woman's breast and nipple as the spout. The milk pitchers had elephant-lip-shaped spout or, in some cases shell shaped spouts. *"Prashitraharan"* category pots resembled "Chamas (cow's ears)". These pots held "Ida". We discussed earlier about "Ida (name of Goddess and also of the oblatory clarified butter or Ghee) being linked with farm animal establishing the fact that the nascent form of Yajna was contemporary with rearing of animal.

We have studied the important Yajna pots, method of their manufacturing, their colour and unique shapes. Now we will discuss the *"Ahuti"* that referred to offering or oblation made during a Yajna. *"Ahuti"* wasspecifically a ritualistic sacrifice and involved the symbolic act of offering various things into a consecrated fire while chanting related Vedic mantras. Besides food of the Gods, the Yajman usually sacrificed articles he held dear. Complete surrender of 'self' by Yajman was considered to be the ultimate sacrifice. The offerings were believed to reach the Gods through Agni. The preferences of each deity for specific sacrificial animal were also revealed in the Vedic scriptures. We discussed about edibles and articles of oblations earlier. However, a deeper look will help us to understand the evolutionary aspect of the *"Ahuti"* through the Vedic period. During the budding stage, things that were easily available were offered as *"Ahuti"* such as milk, curd, ghee, etc. With the expansion of the Yajnas and associated rituals, *"Ahuti"* also assumed greater importance and included much more than dairy products. As kings, warriors and elites adopted the religious implications of Yajnas, *"Ahuti"* became something of a royal affair with "Somaras", animal sacrifice, "Purodash" (pie made of wheat), etc, being added to traditional offerings. The *"Satapatha" Brahmana (1.2.3.6-7)"* and *"Oitareya"*

Brahmana*(2nd Panchika, 8th Kanda)*offer an interesting narrative on the subject:

"Initially, the Gods desired "Human" to be the primary sacrificial object or "*AhutiDravya*". Out of fear the human essence of Yajna ejected from the human body and took refuge in 'horse'. When horse was chosen for sacrifice, the essence entered the body of oxen. Likewise, it travelled through horses, oxen, lambs, goats and finally fledbeneath the earth. The essence existed in the harvest (wheat and rice). Hence, offering edibles like the "Purodash", made of staple cereals was believed to bestow same benefits as any other item of sacrifice.

This Vedic narration held and still holds significance. One theory exists, that many believe to be Vedic advisory meant to prevent people from unabated killing of animals discourage religious fervour. It is also believed that there was a natural "focus shift" from animal sacrifice. Sacrifices, involving animals like horses, cows, and goats, were a part of Vedic rituals, but even these sacrifices gradually declinedas Hinduism evolved over time. Ramendra Sundar Trivedi wrote in his book "Yajnakatha": - "*It is safe to conclude that Vedic people turned repulsive against animal sacrifice....*". It may not be completely true, though. Yajnas like "*Asvamedha*" in which the horse was ultimately sacrificed, continued unabashedly. The most acceptable interpretation of the Vedic narrative would be a fair judgement about the patron of the Yajna.Oblation and offeringswere to be befitting within the means and affordability of the sacrificer. If the Yajman could afford to sacrifice a horse or a goat there was no reservation. Otherwise, there was no dearth of sacred virtue in offering pie ("Purodash"), made of barley to the Gods that indirectly amounted to sacrificing animals. "*Oitareya Brahmana (2nd Panchika 9th Kanda)*" explained it thus: "*Ahuti*" of "Purodash" equals animal sacrifice in terms of "*Karma*" because, the hay attached to the cereals represented animal hair, the husks were skin, the rice – meat of animal, the hard parts were animal bones and the disposed broken bits of grains and other impurities were blood of animal. This was the metaphoric transformation of "Panchmukhi (five-point)" animal sacrifice. In the *Rigveda (1.162-163)* commentary, the stages from animal sacrifice to their cooking process are described in detail. We find mention of "Astaka" yajna.On the 8th day or

"Ashtami" after the full moon in the month of Pausha, it is named as "*Mangsashtaka*"during which meat and fat from the navel area of cow or other livestock known as "*Bopa*" were offered. On "Ashtami" (after the full moon) in the month of Magha "*Sakashtaka*" *Ahuti* was performed that included various creeps and herbs, uncooked rice-grains, etc. There were two other Yajnas "Navayajna" and "Agrayan" performed during "new harvest" period. "Charu" (Porridge) made from fresh cereals was offered during those Yajnas. The tradition remains to this day as "Navanna","Pongal" or "Lohri" festivals in different parts of India. During "*Devayajna*" or "*Vaishyayajna*", cooked rice and curries were offered through the "Grihya" Agni. "Charu" was also offered in the "Sthalipak" and "Shravanakarma" yajnas. Some dairy products were considered spoilt, as those needed curdling. One of these products in Vedic term was "Amiksha (type of cheese)" which was generally prohibited, except for "*Varunapraghash yajna*" during which nine items were offered including "*Amiksha*", specifically for Gods "*Maruta*" and "*Varuna*" ("*Kaushitaki*" *Brahmana* 5.3) by "Adhwaryu" and his assisting subsidiaries. Hence cheese-like milk products were not always taboo, but offered in some Vedic Yajnas.

So, we have a variety of offerings as oblations, Ghee, milk, curd, charu (porridge), staple-cereals and grains, purodash (pie), animal flesh, bopa (fat), Somaras, etc. The sacrificial animal was "Nishkraya" (bred and owned by Yajman) and considered as the Yajman himself in animal form. This again raised some debates. Since it was a religious practice to spare a portion of the "*Ahuti*" after the oblation, called "Habih" which was consumed by the Yajman and the Ritwiks, did it mean that the Yajman was actually consuming his own flesh? Or that the Ritwiks were actually consuming human flesh? The answer came from *"Oiteriya Brahmana (2.6.3)"* where the episode of "Vritrya" was referred. Vritrya, a devil spirit or "Asura" was vanquished and killed by "Indra" with assistance from Agni and Soma. A grateful Indra conferred a divine grant to Agni and Soma and decreed that all animals sacrificed in the Yajnas should be dedicated to them, thus turning the residual oblation into "Prasada", holy leftovers of the Gods. The Vedic dictate, in one stroke, upheld the spirit of the

Yajna and also endorsed legality in consuming the remains of sacrificed animals as "Prasada".

The subject of human sacrifice inevitably barges in here. Was there a religious practice of human sacrifice in ancient Vedic era? Answer to this question again ends in debate. A Yajna named *"Purushamedha"*, part of the Soma Yaj tradition was found in the scriptures of Vedas - *Taittiriya Brahmana (3.4)* and also in *"Satapatha Brahmana (8.6.1-2)*. In *Rigveda (10.90.7)* it was commented that *"The foremost Purusha who took birth before all was sacrificed as offering in the (Yajna) Agni performed by Gods and the abled rishis"*.The 30th chapter of *Shukla Yajurveda* also mentioned this "Purushamedha" Yajna describing the sacrifice of one or more "Purushas". Most experts labelled this as a symbolic event. D.M.Knipe wrote *"(there) is no inscriptional or other record that a purusua-medha was ever performed, leading some scholars to suggest it was simply invented to round out sacrificial possibilities"*. However, the Yajna may have existed before the Vedas were written. In this context, Satapatha Brahmana (13.6.2.19), commented: -*"If the Brahmana performs the (Purushamedha) Yajna, he will be granted everything"*. In Apastamba Shrautasutra (20.24.2) it was, thus: *"Any Brahmana or Kshatriya can perform the Yajna"*. The *"Purushamedha"* Yajna was referred in *"Sankhyan Shrautasutra (16.10-14)"* and in the only Shrautasutra of Atharva Veda, *"Vaitansutra"*, *"Purushamedha Yajna"* found mention with its rituals resembling the *"Asvamedha"* Yajna. In *"Sankhayan Shrautasutra(16.10.4)"* it was observed that the Yajna resembled all rites of *"Asvamedha"*. The *"Vaitansutra(37.10)"* also described the *"Purushamedha"* Yajna" as similar to *"Asvamedha Yajna"*. The sacrificial human must be Brahmana or *Khsatriya* whose value would be equivalent to 1000 cows and 100 horses. He would, like the horse of *"Asvamedha"* wander around for one year escorted by 400 skilled soldiers. On return, he would be sacrificed in the same way as *"Asvamedha"*. In *"Agnichayan" Yajna"*, while arranging the "Citi" on the altar, five animals were recommended by "Satapatha Brahmana". They were "Purusha (human)", horse, ox, lamb and male goat. According to *"Satapatha Brahmana (6.2.2.15)"* the sacrifice was dedicated first to "Prajapati", then to other Gods. But, traditionally, "Vayu" was the only other deity besides "Prajapati", considered suitable to receive human sacrifice. In this context, archaeologist Asko Parpola observed that a transgender who was also a musician, was chosen for sacrifice. He wrote: *"Based on textual evidence,I propose that the human victim in Vedic sacrifices was a harp-plying bard"* – Roots of Hinduism.

The most powerful evidence in support of human sacrifice in Vedic era came from the excavations in Kaushambi. Among the remnants of "Agnicayan Yajna" found in the archaeological site, there were several human skulls. A sculpted Vedic brick was also found in the site with picture of a sacrificial human, tied up with pole. (Ref.Appendix C)

There is a popular legend in "Oitareya Brahmana" about Raja (king) Harishchandra, known to be the epitome of generosity, devotion and truth. The king had 100 queens but none could bear him a son. "Narada" (Vedic demiGod) advised King Harischandra to worship God "Varuna". Following his advice, King Harishchandra worshipped God "Varuna" who subsequently granted him a son, but on one condition; that the boy would be bequeathed to "Varuna". The king agreed and after the childbirth named him "Rohitasva". But "Varuna" asserted his rights over the new-born while the king delayed to fulfil the obligation under various frivolous pretexts. An angry "Varuna" entered the stomach of the king which swelled up, endangering his life. Here, "Devraj Indra" (Lord of the Gods)intervened to sort out the matter amicably. Initially Rohitasva agreed to be sacrificed for "Varuna" but "Indra" advised him to flee! Rohitasva went on the run and wandered into the forests where he met a Brahmana named "Ajigarta". This Brahmana had three sons – "Sunahpuccha", "Sunahsef" and "Sunahlangul". The Brahmana was deprived and hard-pressed. Rohitasva planned to buy one of his sons, pass him on as "Niskraya (not purchased) and get him sacrificed to "Varuna". The Brahmana refused to sell his eldest son while his wife would not part with the youngest. Finally, Rohitasva bought the middle one, Sunahsef for 100 cows. He returned to his father Harishchandra, with Sunahsef. Together, they also convinced "Varuna" to accept Sunahsef as a compensation for the prince.The king prepared for a "Rajasuya Yajna" and set the day of enthronement as appropriate day for the sacrifice of Sunahsef. The stalwarts among the Rishis attended the Yajna as Ritwiks. Widely venerated Rishi Vishwamitra acted as "Hota". Rishi Jamadagni was "Adhwaryu". Rishi Ayashya was"Udgata" and Rishi Vashistha was "Brahma" in the "Rajasuya Yajna". But after Sunahsef was brought into the Yajna site, no Ritwik agreed to attach him with the "Yupakastha" (tying pole). Brahmana Ajigarta, father of Sunahsef was again persuaded to do the dirty job for an additional 100 cows. But even after tying the victim no "Shamita" or "Adhrigu" came forward to behead him. Ajigarta, now became willing to kill his son himself for another 100 cows. At this "Sunahsef" started chanting the Mantras of Rigveda. Hearing the hymns, "Varuna" had a change of heart and freed the boy. When Ajigarta wanted his son back, Rishi Vishwamitra intervened and adopted Sunahsef as his son. Despite all the ingredients "Rajasuya Yajna", "Niskraya" and sacrificial human being present in the legend, the bottom line was that no execution took place, and the Ritwiks were unanimously against the (human) sacrificialritual.

Yet, it cannot be denied that the stigma of human sacrifice was attached to the "Rajasuya Yajnas". In the epic, Ramayana the same episode is described with different names. King Ambarish replaced King Harishchandra there and coincidentally both belonged to the "Ikshaku" ancestry. Earlier, we have seen the sacrificial element of Yajna ejecting from the body of human and taking refuge in other animals to escape the vehement desires of the Gods hungry for sacrifice. The element finally entered the earth and manifested in harvest. It is also evident from the religious anecdote that human beings were considered supreme among all other living things. *"Satapatha Brahmana (6.2.2.15)"* explains that a horse has mane, a sign of superiority, it does not have horns, but it has hoof. Other animals have both horns and hooves. But humans have beard for mane but no horns or hooves thus being the most superior.

Another distinctive feature of the so called "Purushamedha Yajna" was the "Dakshina" or the religious offerings to the Ritwiks after the Yajna was accomplished. The Yajman renounced all his worldly possessions and went in exile into the forest. After the completion of Yajna, the "Hota" received everything to the east side of the sitting Yajman, the "Brahma" staked claim on everything to his south. The possessions to the west of the Yajman belonged to the "Adhwaryu" and "Udgata" and other Ritwiks received everything located to the north side of the Yajman's position.

The various purposes of Yajnas also included a few humorous ones. Such a Yajna was "Sautramani Yaj". The Yajna was performed to seek salvation for those who indulged in excessive drinking of Somaras. The methods of "Sautramani Yaj" was in the possession of "Asuras" as they needed it most. Later the Vedic Gods reclaimed it with the help of Agni *(Satapatha Brahmana 12.9.3.7)*. An overthrown king or any person who lost his livestock was eligible for this Yajna. Once Indra consumed such a large quantity of Somaras that the substance flowed through all his bodily organs. Then Ashwini brothers, twin Vedic Gods of healing, cured Indra by performing "Sautramani Yaj". In Vedic terms "Sutrata" means restoring from afflictions. Thus, the name "Sautramani yaj" was acquired.

The diagram below depicts the positions of the Vedis and the seats of the Yajman and Ritwiks.

PLAN OF SACRIFICIAL GROUND.

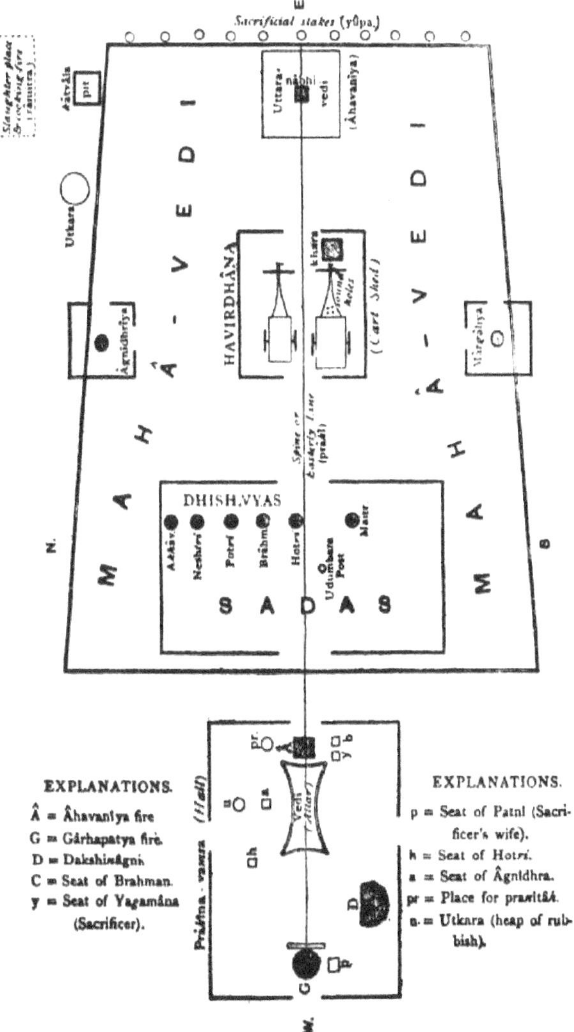

Fig. 2.2 Plan of a Somayaj ground

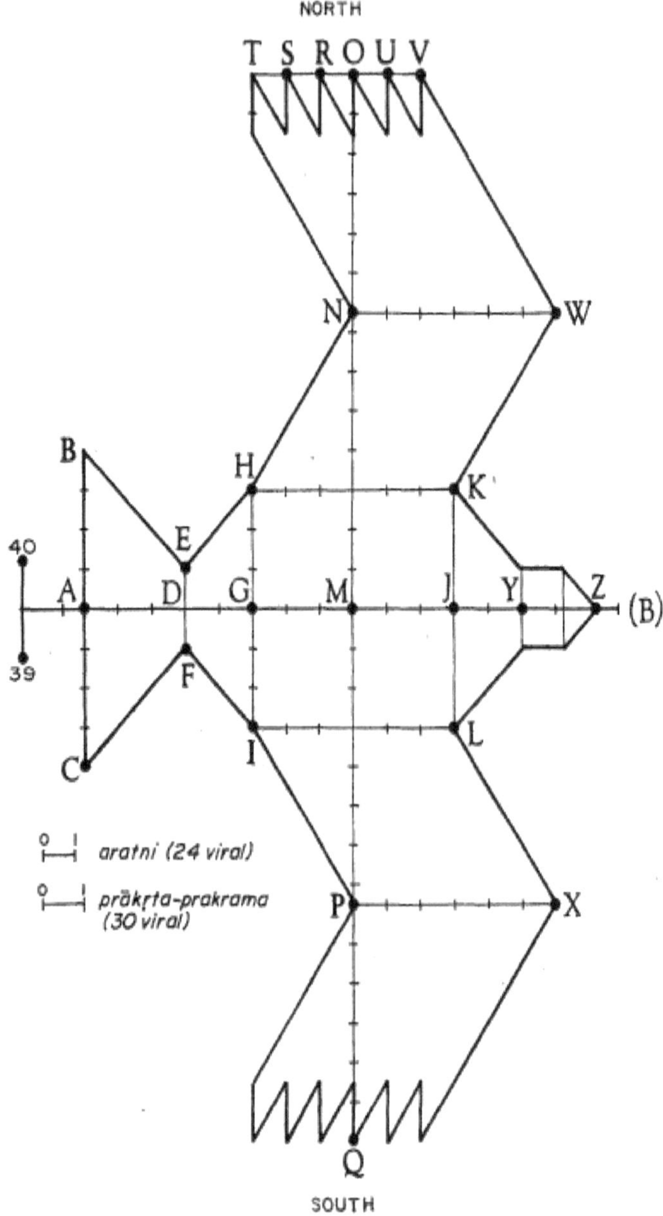

Fig.2.3 Shyenaciti as made during Agnicayana yajna ritual in 1975

Chapter 3

THE CONTOURS OF IVC

Having accomplished a journeythrough the Vedic Yajnas, the rites and the rituals, we are ready to delve into the distinctive features of fire worship in the IVC also known as the Harappan civilization. Our explorations will be based on the excavation reports that provided factual information, devoid of hypothetical opinions or, even worse, archaeological bias.There were a few sites that lacked detailed excavation reports, and in such cases, we will rely on the "preliminary finding reports" as well as published theses, articles, and treatises.

Before we embark on this journey of exploring fire worship in the IVC, it would be fitting to establish a brief understanding of the civilization itself. This will help set the stage with a well-defined archaeological timeline.

Chronology of IVC (Table 3.1)

Period	Approximate timescale
Hunter gatherer phase Mesolithic and Microlithic	10000 – 2000 BCE
Advent of agriculture and Pre Harappa Phase	7000 – 5500 BCE
Early Harappa Phase	5500-2600 BCE
Mature Harappa Phase	2600-1900 BCE
Later Harappa Phase	1900-1300 BCE

The Indus Valley Civilization, also known as the Harappan Civilization, was one of the world's oldest and most enigmatic civilizations that flourished in the vast landmass of Indian subcontinent. It was a testament to the remarkable achievements of an ancient society that thrived in the fertile river plains what is now situated in modern-day Pakistan, Afghanistan and India. Despite its antiquity, the Indus Valley Civilizationleft behind a legacy of sophistication and innovation that continues to captivate scholars and enthusiasts alike. However, compared to two other contemporary civilizations, the Egyptian and Sumerian,much of this enigmatic civilization remained obscure and shrouded in mysteries due to its undecipheredscript. Although thousands of inscriptions were found on seals, tablets, and pottery, scholars have yet to decipher their meaning. This script remained undeciphered, and as a result, our understanding of their language and the historical implications they might contain is limited and continues to challenge linguists and historians, leaving much of the civilization's story untold.

Like the Egyptian and Sumerian civilizations, Indus Valley Civilization too, corresponds to copper-bronze age. The term "Copper Age" was sometimes used interchangeably with the early phase of the Bronze Age, as it represented a period when people were primarily using copper for tools and implements. In the context of the Indus Valley Civilization, it is more accurate to say that it belonged to the late stages of the Copper Age, transitioning into the Bronze Age.The inevitable transition was a result of bronze being an alloy composed of copper and tin or other metals, that provided several advantages over pure copper, including increased hardness and durability. The people of the Indus Valley were skilled coppersmiths who eventually developed the technology and knowledge to produce bronze by alloying copper with tin that marked the transition from the Copper Age to the Bronze Age throughout their dominion. This transition allowed for the creation of more advanced tools, weapons, and artifacts, contributing to the civilization's technological advancements and material culture during the Bronze Age. They also knew the use of gold but did not have any knowledge of iron.

The first discovery of IVC or the Harappan civilization happened in 1920-21. The first excavation of the ancient city of Harappa, a key site of the Indus Valley Civilization, was conducted in 1920-21 by anIndian archaeologist Dayaram Sahni. In accordance with an archaeological convention of naming a civilization after its first excavation site revealing distinctive features, the name, Harappan civilization became synonymous with Indus Valley Civilization. Both the terms identify the same civilization. Immediately after Harappa, another major Indus Valley site Mohenjo-Daro was excavated by renowned archaeologist Rakhaldas Bandopadhyay, playing a pivotal role in identifying the existence of a series of invaluable archaeological sites and this ancient civilization to the attention of the world. His findings provided crucial insights into the urban planning, culture, and technological advancements of the Indus Valley Civilization. Besides cities like the Harappa and Mohenjo-Daro, many small villages were also discovered. The expanse of the civilization was calculated as vast as both Egyptian and Sumerian civilizations put together. The population peaked at fifty million. The geographical expanse covered a diverse range of habitats from Shortughai, an ancient settlement that was found in present Afghanistan, to Alamgir Pur in Western Uttar Pradesh and again from Manda of Jammu to Daimabad of Maharashtra.

More excavated sites are being added to the list. In Mehergarh of Baluchistan, existence of population that transitioned through Neolithic age to Bronze-age was recorded. Many believe that IVC had its root in Mehergarh. Although there were other settlements at different places adopting Neolithic and bronze-age culture and traditions, eventually they merged into the IVC fold. The term "culture" interprets into a relatively smaller domain with limited social implications compared to a civilization like the Harappan civilization that embraced the regional human settlements with its entire tenet of governance, technology, script, religious beliefs, arts, potteries, etc.

The chalcolithic age began in 7000BCE. This was pre-Harappan era marked by people learning agriculture, making sun baked clay-pots and bricks. Subsequently, pre Harappan phase moved towards Early Harappan phase. New crops and animals were introduced into agriculture and domestication process. Commerce too, gained momentum and Harappan script garnered popularity. This early Harappan period continued for three thousand years from 5500 to 2600 BCE.Thereafter commenced a period of "Mature Harappan Phase" that lasted for 700 years, till 1900 BCE. During this period, Harappan civilization reached its zenith.Numerous Indus settlements flourished and expanded annexing even more territories as the civilization progressed, giving rise to meticulously planned cities with grid-patterned streets, advanced drainage & sewage systems, public wells, water storage, indicating a high level of civic and organizational planning. Harappan houses were equipped with bathrooms, wells, stable for the cattle, cooking arrangements, garbage disposal units and other household amenities. The sophistication of Harappan script, measurement system, city planning, and hydro-engineering were indicative of a developedpopulace and continued to fascinate archaeologists and scholars through the ages. The Harappans were remarkably proficient in domestic as well as long-distance tradesinhigh-quality beads, pottery, ivory, and a wealth of commodities. Seals with Indus script bore witness to a well-organized, well-coordinated and well-balanced commerce and business ethics within its confines. Agriculture played a central role in the economy of the Indus Valley Civilization. The fertile alluvial plains of the Indus River and its tributaries provided an ideal environment for cultivation. People grew a variety of crops, primarily wheat and barley during winter. In the eastern part, cultivation of linseed, peas, lentils, horse gram and rice, and various pulses were evident, while sesame and cotton were found in the west. Archaeological evidence also suggested the development of an advanced irrigation systems to maximize agricultural productivity. Alongside agriculture, the domestication of animals, such as cattle, Zebu cows, buffalos, sheep, pigs, dogs, goats and donkeys was an integral part of Harappan economy. These animals not only provided food but also labor for plowing fields and transportation. A mysterious image often appeared in the seals of the Harappan's – that of a Unicorn; although the impression did not represent a horse but was akin to an Ox or bison/Neelgai. Miniature figurines of domestic and wild animals were also found in the sites.

It was not difficult to imagine that, in order to control and maintain law & order over such an extensive civilization, a formidable governing mechanism was evolved. But we have no idea regarding the political system of that civilization. There was "Acropolis" like demarcated segment in the larger cities presumably the citadel of power that be. But the political structure of the Harappan Civilization, remained one of its enduring mysteries. Despite extensive archaeological excavations and research, there was limited direct evidence to definitively describe the political organization or political structure of this ancient civilization. However, over the years, scholars proposed several theories and made educated guesses, based on available evidences. One major aspect of the political structure of the Harappan Civilization was the absence of monuments or conventional palaces;unlike some other ancient civilizations, such as Egypt or Mesopotamia, the Harappan Civilization lacked monumental structures like royal palaces, temples, or grand tombs that would suggest the presence of a centralized monarchy or rulers. The political structure may have been less hierarchical.The presence of standardized weights and measures, as well as seals with inscriptions, indicated an organized system for trade and economic regulations. These seals, often depicting animals, possibly represented clans or guild symbols, hinting at a decentralized or clan-based political system. The political structure of the Harappan Civilization might have been decentralized, with various city-states or chiefdoms operating semi-autonomously. These regional states were governed by local elites, trade guilds, or clan-based chiefs.Another theory suggests that religious leaders or clergy classes could have held political power or influence in Harappan society. Some of the artifacts and symbols found at the sites, such as the "Unicorn" figure, are interpreted as having religious significance. It was possible that the

Harappan Civilization had a system of cooperative governance, where decisions were made collectively by representatives from different communities or social groups. For any political structure, conflict is a necessary evil that results in confrontations, war, overthrow and change. Surprisingly, this vital aspect did not reflect in the governing dynamics of Harappan civilization, let alone remnants of war. There was no evidence of soldiers' barracks or armaments. According to many historians, the surrounding walls of the cities were constructed mostly to resist flood water and not intruding army. Although, Harappan societies were not completely free from violence. Some skeletal evidences found in the sites pointed to domestic violence.

In essence, due to the lack of written records and definitive archaeological evidence, the exact political structure of the Harappan Civilization remained a subject of ongoing research and debate. It was likely that the civilization had a complex and multifaceted political organization, with different regions and urban centers potentially having variations in governance. The absence of a deciphered script and historical records makes it challenging to provide a comprehensive understanding of the civilization's political system.The social structure of the Indus Valley Civilization was relatively egalitarian. There was no marked social hierarchy, and cities were characterized by uniform housing and city planning. Religion likely played an integral role in the common Harappan   lives, as evidenced by the presence of religious buildings, including the famous "Great Bath" at Mohenjo-Daro. Statues and figurines of some mysterious figures and animals have also been discovered, suggesting a polytheistic belief system.Despite its decline and the mysteries that shrouded it, this ancient civilization left an indelible mark on the history of human civilization. It reminded us of the enduring human spirit to create, innovate, and build thriving societies, even in the most ancient of times. The dockyard of Lothal, public bath at Mohenjo-Daro, water reservoir, stadium and signboard of Dholavira., the cultivated fields of Kalibangan continued to unravel its secrets and marvels to this day.

Major transport of Indus Valley civilization were bullock carts and boats. It the cities of Mohenjo-Daro, Harappa and Kalibangan the existence of depression or deep rutmade by bullock carts was found. Evidence of the existence of these marks came from the excavated roads, lanes and by-lanes of these Harappan cities. Surprisingly,the same distance between the two wheels of a bullock cart is prevalent to this day. These cities had well-planned grid-like street patterns with carefully constructed drainage systems. Bullock carts were in common use for transportation and trade within the cities. Compared to bullock carts boats were much faster means of transportation inter-linking the cities. In some Harappan seals, and potteries, images of sailing boats with awning shade were found. Indus merchants set sail up to Oman, Bahrin and Iraq by those boats.

Knowledge of religious traditions and beliefs of the Harappans was mostly based on the artifacts and worship related objects found in the archeological sites. In needed an array of hypotheses and inferences to arrive at a few stunning revelations that have been discussed in subsequent chapters.

Fig 3.1 territory of Indus Valley Civilization
(Courtesy: Kenoyer & Possehl)

A rapid decline of this great civilization started in 1700 BCE with the cities becoming decayed, disorganized, and finally abandoned. It was like a great tree with a rotting root. The major cities of the Harappan civilization experienced a deterioration in their infrastructure, including the public buildings and streets. This

80

may have been a sign of urban decay or lack of centralized authority. At the end, the popular Harappan script, its famous seal, and the superbly planned cities were scarcely noticeable. Regional cultures and traditions took precedence over the homogeneous religio-cultural identity of the vast Indus dominion. But these isolated settlements too, melted away by 1300 BCE.

There is no consensus on a single cause for the decline of the Harappan civilization, and it's likely that a combination offactors contributed to its downfall. Additionally, the lack of a deciphered script from the Harappan civilization made it challenging to access detailed historical records, leaving much about its decline open to interpretation and ongoing research. Prevalent theories included: -

Environmental Factors:

a. Climate Change: Changes in the monsoon patterns and shifts in the courses of rivers may have resulted in altered precipitation and disrupted the agricultural system upon which the civilization heavily relied. Prolonged droughts or flooding events could have severely impacted food production and water availability.

b. Deforestation: Extensive deforestation to clear land for agriculture and for building materials may have led to soil erosion and reduced the capacity of the ecosystem to support the population.

c. River Shifts: The gradual shifting of the Indus River and its tributaries could have disrupted the reliable water supply for irrigation, which was essential for the agricultural surplus that sustained the civilization.

Social Factors:

a. Urban Decay: Some evidence suggested that the major cities of the Harappan civilization experienced a decline in their infrastructure, including the deterioration of public buildings and streets. This may have been a sign of urban decay or a lack of centralized authority.

Economic Factors:

a. Trade Disruption: The Harappans were known for their extensive trade networks, but disruptions in trade routes or a decline in the quality of goods may have had economic repercussions.

b. Resource Depletion: Overexploitation of resources, such as agricultural land and water, might have led to a decline in agricultural productivity and eventually the collapse of the civilization's economic base.

Migration and Abandonment:

a. Population Migration: Some theories suggested that people from the Harappan civilization may have migrated to other regions in response to environmental or social pressures, leading to the abandonment of urban centers.

We will refocus on the areas of our interest and get familiar with a few technological necessities of the Harappan people for which they constructed furnaces and kilns. Often, common fire altars or the Yajna Vedis are confused with the furnaces used for masonry or other manufacturing processes. In the later chapters we will discuss and compare the Harappan fire altars and various furnaces used for industrial purposes. As such an overview of the these typical Harappan industries becomes necessary.

One of the distinctive features of Harappan craftsmanship was pottery. Besides utensils, skilled Harappans also produced earthen jewelry, measure-weights, small figurines, statuettes, toys, etc. The process not only involved roasting or firing but also applying decorative coatings, painting and etching. Those Indus craftsmen were adept at all the stages of the manufacturing process. For pottery, they requireda potter's kiln thatplayed central role in the production of fired clay objects. A separate chapter is dedicated to the descriptions of the Harappans' kilnsand furnaces.

Lapidary or making of beads

Much significance is attributed to this specialized field of bead products.Besides metals, fired-clay, faience, bones, ivory and conch-shells, the Harappans also crafted beads from a wide variety of stones. Stone beads were an important aspect of the material culture of the Indus Valley civilization. These beads were significant artifacts that provided insights into the craftsmanship, trade networks, and cultural practices of the Harappan people. Some of the commonly used semi-precious stones included carnelian, agate, jasper, lapis lazuli, steatite and (soapstone). Those stones came in various colors, allowing for diverse and colorful bead creations. Those stones were heated prior to cutting and etching. Subsequently, they used various techniques to shape and polish the stones into beads. These techniques included drilling, grinding, and polishing. The presence of various types of stone beads made from materials not locally available in the Indus Valley region suggested long-distance trade networks. Beads crafted by the Harappans from red carnelian stone were much admired in Sumer. These beads were sometimes coated with alkaline organic sap from plants and heated in kilns, to created etched designs. Another type of beads was produced from steatite after carving and heating. Numerous stone beads were found at Harappan sites, including well-known locations like Mohenjo-Daro and Harappa. These beads were also found in burial sites, indicating their use as personal adornments and possibly as burial offerings.

Metalworks

Metalwork was another branch where furnace was used. The Harappans worked with several metals, including copper, bronze, gold, and silver. Copper was the most commonly used metal for various tools and ornaments which was procured from various mineral-rich areas including places which are now in Rajasthan. It also came from as far as Bahrin. The use of furnace was not limited to the extraction of copper from its ore.Copper was alloyed with tin to produce bronze. Copper and bronze were used to make various metal objects, ornaments, and implements for which the furnace played an important role. Harappan artisans used the lost-wax casting technique for creating metal objects. This method involved creating a wax model, encasing it in clay, heating it to melt the wax, and then pouring molten metal into the cavity left by the wax. This technique is still used by "Dokra" artists for creating their figurines. The famous bronze sculpture of the "Dancing girl" found in Mohenjo-Daro was created by this method.

The Seals

The intricate and beautifully crafted seal engravings of Harappan era are another of its characteristic features. They are small, square or rectangular pieces of stone, typically made of steatite (a type of soapstone) and sometimes other materials like terracotta. They were invariably heated in a controlled manner for hardness and durability. The famous engraving of the "Priest-king" of Mohenjo-Daro on a seal is an example of steatite etching.

Faience craft

Many consider faience artifacts as the most amazing find from the Indus valley archaeological sites. The Harappans made this glass-like material by crushed stone mixed with Potash (Potassium carbonate) and oxide of copper. It resembled ceramics although no clay was used.Due to the presence of copper, it displayed a hue of cyan, azure or a shade of blue copper vitriol. Faience artifacts were also found in contemporary civilizations like the Egyptian, Crete and other places. A mixture of crushed quartz, potash and a few other ingredients were melted in the furnace. The molten product was then passed through specially designed dices to obtain various desired molds and shapes. Bangles, beads, small figurines, etc., were found as Harappan faience artifacts. The faience process required the use of furnace from the start and throughout its execution.

Textile

The Harappans knew the use of cotton and weaving threads to produce cloth. A variety of earthen spindle whorls were found which were used for spinning threads. In the present Sindh region, there is a traditional method of dyeing and printing designs on cloth called "Azrakh" which may have evolved from the ancient methods of the Harappans to dye textiles. Their dyeing process required various natural ingredients like clay, plant-sap, stone dust and animal excreta, etc., and the preparation of the dye needed firing/heating by furnaces.

Apart from the above craftworks, many other disciplines of the Harappan life required the use of oven, hearth or furnace. From daily cooking to manufacturing bricks, the uses of those fire-sources were indispensable. The most important areas of craftmanship with specific skill-based produces and crafts will figure in our subsequent studies.

Another very important article worth mentioning was the terracotta cakes used for controlling the heat inside the kilns, furnace or hearth. Every civilization has its own 'signature artifact' that becomes its identifying symbol. These identifying artifacts are of great significance to the archaeologist. The terracotta cake is one such intriguing artifact which are found in plenty in almost all the archaeological sites of the Harappan era. These cakes were of four categories. The first one was of triangular shape resembling Indian "Parathas", the second one was also comparable with another south Indian staple diet, the "Idly". They were saucer-shaped, circular-bi-convex cakes made of clay. These two types were most popular. The exact function of these cakes was not understood clearly. They were found even in ordinary household-kitchens, especially beside the oven or hearth. This led to the hypothesis that the Harappan terracotta cakes were extensively used to control the heat of the fire-source. Lighting a fire was not as easy as it is now. An 'all-night' fire was kindled from which torches were lighted at night, if required. The terracotta cakes may have played vital role in controlling the fire. When kept on the oven, the cakes helped subduing the flames and kept the sparks from scattering and causing accidents. Some believe that heated terracotta cakes were used to keep their food warm. Many of these cakes especially those found inside the kilns of potters and masons bore marks of being repeatedly fired and burned after they were made, a result of being exposed to intense heat of the kilns, furnaces or hearths. They were used also to seal the breaches of Muffle (closed) kilns after the firing chamber were sealed with clay-coverings and they couldcontrol temperature and oxygen levels more effectively than open kilns. Another use of the triangular-shaped terracotta cakes were as tiles in household flooring and as road construction material.

One of the two other types of terracotta cakes were the wheel-shaped cakes, rarely found in the IVC archaeological sites. Those cakes were known as "Mushtika" and were lumps shaped by hand and dried by firing. *(The author has, in his collection, some "Mushtika" which bore the fingerprints of its makers).*Those "Mushtikas" were found inside ancient Harappan furnaces, kilns and hearths in copious quantity and used for controlling temperature of the heat sources while they were functional. Also, mixed with charcoal, the "Mustiks" were used for indoor flooring in the Harappan houses found at Kalibangan. It was seen that this particular type of flooring prevented dampness and repelled termites. The "Mustiks" were found in all the IVC archaeological sites. At the Harappan site of Mithathal, Haryana, a particular type of terracotta cake was found *(by the author)* that was unique in shape (see picture). It was circular-bi-convex with wavy edge. This type of terracotta cakes was not found in any other Harappan sites. The cakes (in the picture) bore marks of firing and burning.

Fig. 3.2. Various types of terracotta cakes

Triangular terracotta cake at the lower right corner. Idli shaped (wavy edged), Mushtika and round shaped are shown clockwise from triangular one. On the Mushtika, one may notice the fingerprints of the Indus craftsman. Collection and photo: Author

Figure 3.3 Terracotta cakes found in a kiln at Binjor 4MSR site (Courtesy: ASI).

Chapter 4

The kilns of Indus

Now we are familiar with the fire altars of Vedic Yajnas and have been acquainted with a brief history of the IVC. The last chapter also dealt with Harappan fire-based crafts and industries. And there we found the importance of furnaces in IVC. In our study of Harappan installations regarding use of fire, the mention of various furnaces could be expected repeatedly. As such we need to grasp the idea of these furnaces. Instances of identifying fire-pits without substantial evidence of actual fire being instilled in those spots are commonplace. A major component of every civilization is its industrial furnaces. The 'fire' as an indispensable commodity had its applied aspects beyond the religious practices. Thus, different kinds of furnaces were invented by the Harappans to suit their needs. There were the ovens and hearths, the furnaces and the kilns. These again evolved into newer versions according to their specific purposes. The Harappan furnaces were built to produce heat by burning fuel and was used for multiple purposes, from heating water to extraction of metals. The fire needed oxygen to burn hence provision for adequate oxygen along with the fuel inside the furnaces had to be ensured. We have known that the furnaces were used in their maximum capacity. In simplified terms, the Harappans were aware of the importance of maximum utilization of the total heat generated by those furnaces minimizing unnecessary wastage of fuel and

89

substandard quality of their finished products. So, the Harappans took every care to seal the cracks and crevices of the heat chambers preventing heat from getting out. Their craftsmen used broken pieces of pottery (potsherds), clay or terracotta cakes to perform this task. In some IVC site, some conical shaped earthen objects were found that were likely to have acted as 'kiln settler'. The furnaces were closed from all sides except the area where the containers were placed for heating, leaving only a vent for oxygen flow and inlet for the supply of fuel. The religious Vedic altars had no such conditions. The Harappan furnaces essentially had inlets for oxygen and re-fueling since the combustion and heat generation was of primary concern while the Vedic altars were all about the sacrificial fire and rekindling it; even heating something for ritualistic purposes were done easily from outside. The sole purpose of the Vedic Yajna fire was 'sacrificial offering'. This Yajna fire was considered sacred and represented the divine presence of Agni. It was carefully maintained throughout the ritual, protected from all sides.

The second difference between the Vedic fire altars and the Harappan furnaces was that the latter were generally placed behind walls or at the corners to avoid smoke while the Yajna fire was kindled on the altars or *"Vedi"* leaving space to accommodate maximum number of participants. These basic principles are being followed to this day and based on it, the infrastructure of the Harappan "Kundas" would be studied in the later chapters.

In the context of craft making, the IVC presented a unique technological invention, The "Double chamber updraft kiln" (DCUK). A pillar-shaped elevated platform was constructed inside the combustion chamber that held a heating pan on which pottery, beads or figurines were placed. The most important feature of this heat treatment process was that the materials never came in direct contact with the fire. We will see the pictures and descriptions of these kilns the later chapters. Double chamber updraft kilnswere found in the archaeological sites at Harappa, Amri, Balakot, Kot Diji, Cholistan etc. The kiln of Balakot was found in almost intact condition and some earthen figurines ready for firingwere found inside. Six DCUKs were excavated at Lal Shah, near Mehergarh which were pear-shaped and constructed blending the characteristics of two types of furnaces.

At 'Mound-E' in Harappa, two DCUKs were found. The one (kiln-100) at the northwest side attracted considerable archaeological interest. These three meters by two meters sized gigantic pear-shaped furnaces had its inside walls completely vitrified by continued exposure to extreme heat. Anthropologist-historian Rita P. Wright remarked on the potsherds found inside the kilns that those resembled the earthen pots exported by the Harappans to Oman implying that the DCUKs were used to produce high-quality pottery. British Archaeologist Ernest J.H. Mackay also found this type of Harappan kilns during his excavation of DK-G area at Mohenjo-Daro. Many 'pointed base goblets' were discovered at the site, which were produced for the elite class. Another aspect of those kilns were the walls. In some cases, leaning walls were erected to accommodate the fire chambers. Those industrial kilns were always positioned adjacent to walls to get enough frontal working space and avail the lighting arrangements set up in the alcoves of the walls. However, in both the domestic ovens and industrial combustion chambers, the presence of terracotta cakes was ubiquitous.The terracotta cakes were found alongside all kind of firing kilns of the Harappan era. Their domestic utility was to regulate the heat and keep their food warm. In the industrial kilns those clay-cakes were used to regulate the air flow. Inside the fire chambers, those terracotta cakes were probably used to maintain uniform temperature for a long time even after the fire was extinguished.

Now we will take a glimpse at different kinds of Harappan ovens and kilns. The two broad categories were the domestic ovens and the industrial kilns. There were various types of household ovens including tandoors (for baking and grilling), big stoves for boiling animal feed and the ones used for cooking in large scale on occasions.

The industrial kilns were used by craftsmen, potters and metalworkers. Apart from pottery, fire was essential for bead-making, metal-extraction and metal works. So, kilns of various shapes and sizes were constructed by the Harappans. We will thoroughly study these kilns, one at a time. Interestingly, there has not been much change in their characteristics even after thousands of years.

Domestic ovens were found in every Harappan household. Besides the cooking ovens inside their kitchens, many built large hearths and fireplaces in their courtyards. The open fireplaces for boiling animal feed and cook for extra heads on special events are found even now at places in Rajasthan and Haryana states of India. Ovens constructed by digging a pit and the others, erected above ground were both conventional. The former below the surface also had a passage dug for supply of wood. Maintaining its circular shape, the front portion of the oven looked like a bridge over the dug passage. The interior as well as the exterior of the oven was plastered with mud. The erected ovens too were made of clay or bricks and mud plastered. These were elevated round-shaped ovens and had space beneath for inserting fuel-wood. The most popular domestic ovens were of "Horse-Shoe"shape: The defining feature of these ovens was their distinctive horse-shoe shape. They were often constructed in the form of a semi-circular or U-shaped structure with a frontalopening for stoking. These industrial ovens were found at the archaeological sites of Dholavira. At one place (Trench No. 25X2) small figurines were found to have heated in such U-shaped ovens. In another settlement, Hulas, at Harappa domestic U-shaped ovens were found that were possibly used for boiling harvest. Two subsidiary round-shaped ovens and a dug-out pit for storing the crops were found adjacent to those ovens. One distinctive feature of the IVC was their division between residential and industrial zones. In an area of about 200 square-meter at Hulas, 32 houses were clustered to form a craftsmen community that was divided by a thick wall. One part consisted of a series of mud-houses used as workshops while the other half had round-shaped hutments that housed the artisans. The significance of having a wall beside the kilns to avoid the smoke and sound was typical of this civilization. Such large walls acting as a screen to smoke and sound, were found to have alcoves possibly for keeping lamps for their work. Apart from the round-shaped ovens at Hulas, a large rectangular-shaped (2.28 X 0.48 meters) kiln was also found with a few faience beads and copper rings, implying that the place was quite developed in producing high quality ornaments. At another spot in Hulas (STR 42), three adjacent walls formed a triangular space that held a rectangular fire chamber (1.55 X 0.07 meters). The concerned excavation report clearly identified the fireplace as a craftsman's kiln. It recorded that *"A survey of the objects in situ suggested that this very house could be a workshop of a craftsman"*, as some copper objects and ingots were retrieved from the site. A fireplace inside of a similar structure was found at Banawali but that was identified as a worshipping altar.

Another type of oven, a cylindrical-shaped drum or "Tandoor" was popular during the pre-Harappan period. The same type that are used in today's world for baking bread by placing it on the inner wall of the fire chamber. It is surprising that these popular ovens of pre-Harappan era were lost during the mature Harappan period. It resurfaced during the beginning of "Historic era". Archaeologist Dr. B.B. Pal, in his excavation report of Kalibangan wrote about this mystery – *"The innovation of this advanced technology of baking wherein thick roti is baked in almost closed tandoor (a barrel shaped furnace with an open mouth) of which evidence has come to light from Early Harappan levels and suddenly disappeared in Mature Harappan levels and reappears in the early historical period. It is an enigma as why this superior technology of baking roti was not continued and discarded during the Harappan times innovated and used the terracotta chaklas for preparing phulka roti"*. The terracotta roller-pin and hotplate to shape and bake roti (bread) were widely used in the Harappan civilization. In many archaeological sites those earthen plates were found. Some of them had engravings on them, possibly displaying their owners' names.

Some large round-shaped clay-furnaces were found in Lothal for extraction of copper. Their clay plastered interiors turned into glassy walls due to extensive heat. A channel was found behind the furnace. The metal workers preferred those channels as they required plenty of water for copper smelting from their ores and hardening the molten extracts. At level 5 in Lothal, five small rectangular furnaces were found which were used for copper smelting. Each furnace was three feet in length and two feet in breadth. A channel was also found alongside. Some terracotta crucibles were required for the smelting process and few necessary tools confirmed those furnaces to be used for extraction of copper. *"In spite of the destruction of the town in phases III and IV because of the flood, the coppersmiths re-established their workshop near the nullah in phase V. Five small rectangular sink-like brick-pavements skirted by bricks-on-edge and interconnected with runnels (pi. LIV B) are laid bare in the workshop wherein several coppersmiths must have been working under a single roof Near each sink a pot-furnace containing ash and bits of muffles are noticed. The sinks are too small (3 x 2-6 ft.) to be used as bathing pavements. Among important finds mention may be made of two terracotta crucibles, small lumps of copper and a crescentic sleeved axe used for shaping copper and bronze objects. It bears hammer marks".* (Lothal excavation report).

Bead making was an important craft in the Harappan civilization.As a part of adornment, those beautiful beads were crafted from terracotta, ivory, animal bones, shells, semi-precious stones like carnelian, agate, and jasper, as well as metals like copper and gold. Besides, steatite was a very popular ingredient for bead making in IVC. Steatite is a soft and easily workable stone when freshly quarried, which makes it suitable for bead-making. Artisans made beads with steatite paste and made it ready to use after heating and hardening using simple tools, such as stone or metal implements. We have seen in an earlier chapter that the beads crafted by the Harappans from red carnelian stonewere much admired as an export-item inMesopotamia, Afghanistan, and Central Asia. These beads were sometimes coated with alkaline organic sap from plants or soda and heated in kilns, for etching designs. Generally oval-shaped (or pear-shaped) kilns were used by the artisans for heating the beads. Some round-shaped hearths were also excavated that were used for the process. In one of the archaeological sites at Harappa, a cylindrical kiln for bead-making was found inside a lapidary workshop. This kiln had four holes on the top as an outlet for smoke, and at the bottom, there was an opening beside the fuel inlet possibly for an over ground blower to be attached.

The crafted beads were slowly heated inside those kilns by covering them with sawdust. The kiln temperature gradually reached approximately 1200 degrees when the firing process was complete.

Various ovens, kilns and furnaces wereexcavated in the Harappan sites. In the courtyard of an excavated Harappan house at mound ET, five earthen structures were found with pillar-like raised platforms inside. Unmistakably, those were furnaces! Another interesting construction was found in the same area in 1995 that had a fire-pit inside a room with intersected walls like a "+" sign. A similar feature was found in Banawali which we will study later. In another courtyard of 8 meters X 6.5 meters area, three makeshift fireplaces were seen near the center adjacent to diagonally intersecting walls with a chamber located in the southeast side which had a few circular and semi-circular silos were dug for storing objects. One more chamber behind it had similar storage pits and a wall with an alcove that extended from east to west. A massive amount of industrial waste heaped to a height of two meters was noticed around the spot that contained charcoal and metal nodules. According to historians, a big industrial workshop was situated there with those strange pits being used as storage for food grains for the workers. A further study of the waste indicated the presence of various crafts around the area. Besides the remnants of raw-materials, drill-bits used for beads, broken faience objects and semi-precious stones were also found in the site. We developed an insight into the industrious efforts of those Harappans who instituted workshops in every household and furnaces of specific shapes while maintaining a peaceful dwelling side by side. More than two dozen of industrial kilns and furnaces were found in this site alone at Trench-9. Most of those furnaces had raised inner platforms. Some of them bore marks of repeated repairs and reconstructions as a result of extensive use. Many Harappan seals were also found amidst the waste, connecting them with trade of those crafts. Perhaps the traders stamped their seals on the finished products. This was believed to be an important aspect of the Harappan seals. Besides the furnaces of metallurgy, stonework, and beads-making, some clay-brick kilns were also excavated around Trench-9.

Mehergarh was an important Harappan site from an archaeological point of view. Many artifacts from the early stages of IVC were found here. In Mehergarh and Nausharo, potter's kilns and implements from different periods of IVC were found. In Mehergarh, archaeologists found 'open air' potter's kilns where the pots were placed at an open space and then covered with clay before firing them. Here, another six-meter-long oval-shaped potter's kiln was found intact, with 140 earthen vessels. Those kilns spoke volumes about the basic stages of Harappan pottery and their firing methods. The potter of this oval-shaped kiln cleverly used part of a wall and adjacent space to construct the hearth. The vessels were kept in rows over a maximum of four stacks.Potsherds were placed between the vessels to keep the vessels tightly organized inside the kiln. The top of the kiln was covered by mud mixed with shards, hay, ash and limestone pebbles. These types of kilns were also found in Nausharo. Agricultural waste was the major fuel. Usually, the kilns were located behind a wall that had an outlet on its upper part to allow for the billowing smoke. Those were 'Single Chamber Firing Structure' which were also found at Mohenjo Daro. Many 'Double Chamber Firing Structures' were found in Mehergarh and adjacent Lal Shah site.

Many small kilns for bead-making were found at Dholavira that were used for firing semi-precious stones and also terracotta beads. Finely dusted clay was used to produce those beads. Sometimes, the beads were coated with colors to add luster. Closed kilns were used to fire these beads. Small-size kilns were found in many archaeological sites including Rangpur, Binjor and Lothal. In Harappa's mound-F, two rectangular-shaped furnaces of unequal size were excavated. One measured 3.25 ft X 1.5 ft and the other 2.5 ft X 1.5 ft. Concerned excavation report reads *"consisting of three rooms and a courtyard (PI. XIX). Rooms Nos. 1 and 2 to the north and No. 3 is to the east of the courtyard No. 4, in which there is a pair of rectangular hearths of unequal size constructed side by side. The walls of these hearths are only half a brick thick, the east wall of the smaller hearth being composed of two rows of brick-on-edge making up the same thickness. The larger hearth measures 3 ft. 3 in. by 1 ft. 6 in., and the smaller one 2 ft. 6 in. by 1 ft. 6 in. Both of them contained ashes and charcoal, and also some fragments of terra- cotta cakes, nodules, and one or two bones from the surrounding debris. Here, attention may also be drawn to two pilasters abutting on to each other and projecting from the curtain walls behind the hearths. Evidently, they were constructed as supports, since all the walls of this house are only half a brick in thickness. In this section there may also be mentioned a 15 ft. long wall in square M 12/14, which is 2 ft. 8 in. thick. To its west is a small brick edging on both sides of which were recovered some bovine bones including two hoofed lower legs"(Harappa Excavation Report).* From this report it was inferred that the craftsmen took meals during their work and had no reservation against preparing or heating their food in the hearth fire. So many objects related to various crafts were retrieved from those Harappan houses and around the furnaces that no historian has ever remarked that the furnaces were Yajna altars. Animal bone fragments were also found at Kalibangan. Trench XB-8 of KLB -2 a hearth of almost rectangular (95 cm X 83 cm) shape was found having bones and terracotta cakes inside, reaffirming our opinion that the craftsmen took meals at their workplace. *("This hearth is nearly square in shape. Firing marks are seen around. A few terracotta cakes in situ were seen. Bone pieces are collected"-Kalibangangan Excavation Report).*

Like any other Indus archaeological sites, household ovens made of bricks and clay were found in all the excavated houses at Rakhigarhi. Most of those ovens or hearths were fashioned with a slope going deeper from the fuel inlet towards the opposite wall. This inclined or sloped domestic hearths ensured complete consumption of the fuel inside. In Rakhigarhi, rectangular, square and circular hearths were found. One was found to have conch-shell shape. A similar hearth in Rakhigarhi was once identified and recorded in the excavation report as a 'vagina-shaped worshipping altar'. Our study will reveal that it was actually a pear-shaped hearth with a duct or "fire tunnel" for supplying fuel. The average Harappan furnaces typically had those channels constructed that continued to be a feature till present-day, in the domestic hearths found in rural areas. The designs of those domestic hearths are further illustrated at the end of this chapter.

In Rakhigarhi (site RGR-1), a big Tandoor (cylindrical drum-shaped grilling fire chamber) was found. Also, inside a room in the settlement, three hearths were found. One triangular, one square-shaped and another T-shaped kiln were found constructed side by side (details in later chapter). A sizable bead workshop was found in Rakhigarhi. Two more U-shaped kilns were found in the courtyard of a Harappan house, with terracotta cakes and Mustika inside their combustion chambers. One of them was a 24-meters long kiln that was used for heating Agate and Carnelian stones for bead-making. In abead workshop at Lothal, a circular kiln could be seen. In the RGR -6 mound site at Rakhigarhi, a Harappan hutment dating back to pre-Harappan era was excavated. There, in a seven-room cluster, two had ovens that were round and triangular-shaped.

There were many pear-shaped Kundas in Harappa. Due to their resemblance with tear-drops, they were also called "Tear-drop Kilns". During the excavation in 1940 at mound-F areaat Harappa, sixteen tear-drop hearths were excavated from a trench (Trench-IV alone. Whether those kilns were 'Single chamber firing structures' or 'Double chamber updraft kilns' could not be ascertained. Three of those furnaces had raised platforms inside. The objects inside those kilns were subjected to heat treatment without letting them coming in direct contact with the fire. They were placed on a suspended plane or dish placed on the raised platform. In Mohenjo Daro, two pear-shaped kilns were found with such raised platforms, one of which contained the suspended dish, quite intact. Those kilns were often addressed as 'vagina-shaped' or 'conch shell-shaped' and misleadingly connected with religious practices. Pear-shaped kilns were found In Tarkhanwala archaeological site also.

But the perfect example of the "Double chamber updraft kiln" was found at Kanmer archaeological site in Gujrat (Fig. 4.21) with its inner pillar intact. Many faience objects were found in and around this kiln. Evidently the faience objects too were produced by the "Double chamber updraft kiln" *(Indian Archaeology 2007-08, A review, Page-47).*

We shall, now review the kilns and hearths categorically: -

Circular/Oval-shaped hearths/kilns

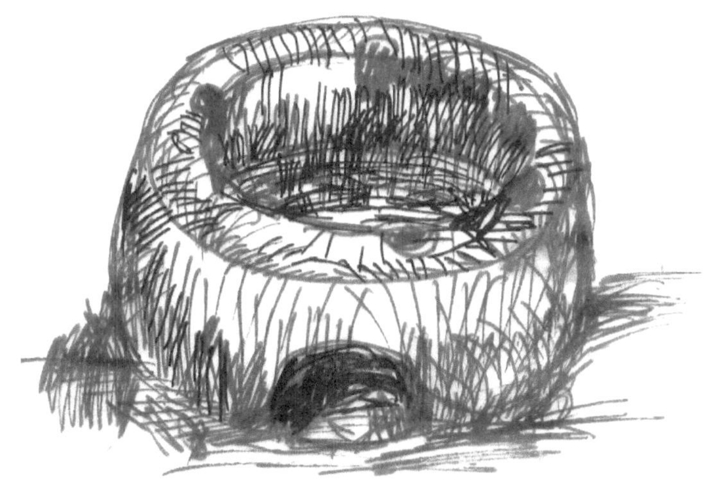

Fig. 4.1 Circular oven

Fig. 4.2 Tandoor from Kalibangan

The circular hearth or oven is still in use since pre-historic period. Made of clay, it had a channel by its side or at the bottom for supply of fuel or wood.Some came with multiple openings. Besides one inlet for supplying fuel, a dome like structure overhead allowed for two or more separate heating compartments for cooking vessels. This technique prevails to this day. In the rural areas of Bengal, date-juice is heated on such multi-openings clay-ovens to prepare molasses. These ovens can accommodate up to eight separate vessels saving both fuel and time in the process. The oval-shaped oven was a slightly modified form of the round-shaped oven.

Fig. 4.3 Circular and oval shaped ovens at Binjor 4 MSR site

Horseshoe-shaped or U-shaped kilns

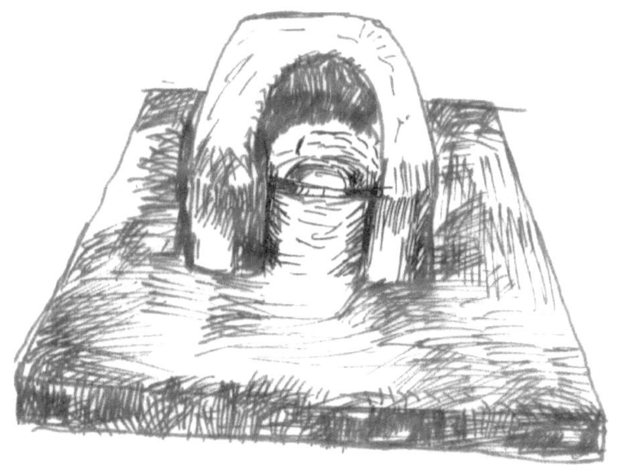

Fig. 4.4. U shaped oven

Fig. 4.5 Horseshoe or U shaped hearth/furnace excavated at Hulas (Courtesy: ASI)

This was also a widely used kiln/oven, generally constructed above ground level. These kilns were typically constructed with clay or mud bricks in a U-shaped fashion, leaving an open space for the hearth, with the open end of the "U" facing outward. The U-shape provided a channel for the stoking of fuel and also placing cooking vessels. During bead-making, the beads and stone pebbles were heated with sawdust on such furnaces. Harappan craftsmen controlled the temperature and provided a uniform heat-treatment to the objects by this method. In order to raise the temperature within the kiln, the Harappans replaced sawdust with sand. In Rakhigarhi, some terracotta cakes were found inside the U-shaped kilns indicating that the terracotta cakes also played a significant role in controlling the temperature within those kilns for this delicate craftwork. It can be mentioned here that the 'potter's kiln' also came under this category but those were generally of rectangular shape, surrounded by three side-walls with one side open.

Fig. 4.6. Vaulted-roof furnace of metalsmith

Fig. 4.7. Vaulted-roof furnace in situ in Harappa (Courtesy: ASI)

Fig. 4.8. Triangular hearths/kilns

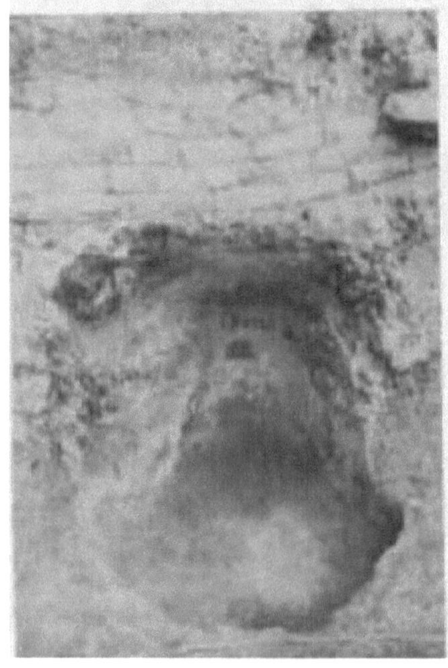

Fig. 4.9. Triangular kiln in Harappa (Courtesy: ASI)

These furnaces appeared in our study several times. In the rural areas in Bengal, these hearths are still in use. The three protruded edges resembled vertices while its combustion chamber was made of mud and closer to ground level. During the "IsMEO Surface Survey" In Mohenjo Daro (South of DK – B, C), a triangular, single-chamber hearth was excavated. But the archaeologist of the mission, Stefano Prachhia identified it as a pear-shaped kiln with some structural distortions.

Quadrangular hearths/kilns

Fig. 4.10. Quadrangular hearths/kilns

Figure 4.11 Quadrangular furnace found at Mohenjo Daro

(Courtesy: ASI)

105

The quadrangular hearths or kilns were also among the most popular Harappan heating sources. It was easily built above ground level and could be both rectangular and square, in shape. The lower part had space reserved for supply of fuel (logs, wood, etc.) and the open top held the vessels or objects for heating. Often, the top of the kiln was closed with multiple openings to hold as many vessels at a time enabling uniform heating of these vessels, minimizing fuel consumption.

Pit-kilns

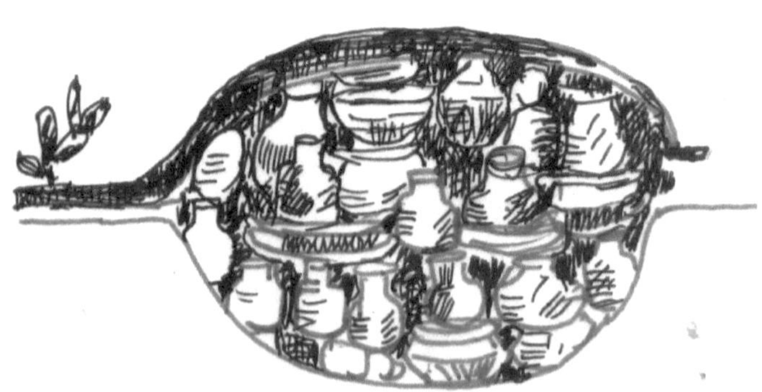

Fig. 4.12 Pit Kiln

Pl. VII. Tarkhanewala-Dera : Structure 4 (potter's kiln) See p. 24

Fig. 4.13 Portion of a Pit Kiln at Tarkhanwala Dera (Courtesy: ASI)

Those kilns were primarily used by the Harappan potters to fire their clay-pots. Earlier, we have seen the outdoor potter's kilns in Mehergarh, where the pots and vessels were placed at an open space and then covered with clay before firing them. Likewise, the "Pit kilns" were essentially dug outdoor. This advanced to a method where the potters dug a shallow pit and placed the pottery or clay objects in orderly fashion. Potsherds, pebbles, and one type of terracotta 'kiln settler' were stacked inside to keep the pottery firmly positioned within the kiln. Then, after laying hay and agricultural waste on the pottery, they were completely covered with clay, pot-shards, stone-pebbles and ash. There was a firing arrangement beneath the pottery and also sufficient opening for oxygen. The heat treatment lasted for 24 hours firing the objects evenly, and another one week for cooling. (These facts were derived from the size of the kilns and comparing them with the methods adopted by present-day potters).

Figure 4.14 Single Chamber Firing Structure

Figure 4.15. A Single Chamber Firing kiln found at Daimabad
archaeological site with remains of pots still inside (Courtesy: ASI)

A pit-kiln, constructed behind a wall with a smoke outlet on its upper part for disposal of the smoke, generated during the heating process was identified as a "Single Chamber Firing Structure".

Double Chamber UpdraftKiln

Figure 4.16 Double Chamber Updraft Kiln

Fig. 4.17 Double chamber pear-shaped Updraft Kiln found at Harappa, note the inner pillar (Courtesy: ASI)

The Double Chamber Updraft Kiln was one of the most popular and widely used Harappan kilns.By definition the kiln consisted of two chambers stacked on top of each other. The lower chamber was where the fire wasignited, and the upper chamber held the pottery or ceramics for firing.

However, the actual Harappan double chamber kilns were found to have employed more of the characteristics of the updraft system, than the structural settings which meant that the objects for firing never came in direct contact with the fire while heat and gases generated in the lower part of the round or pear-shaped kiln rose upward and evenly heated the pottery or objects that were placed on a pillar-like structureholding a dish apparently suspended from above. Sometimes the dish was perforated to ensure even distribution of heat and airflow. In most cases, archaeologists found the suspended floor of the kilns destroyed except in a few cases, where the broken parts of the suspended floor were strewn around. These Harappan kilns were extensively used for producing high quality ceramicsthat included a wide range of objects like pots, jars, figurines, and other utilitarian and decorative items as beads, bangles, faience objects and stone carvings. At archaeological site DK-G of Mohenjo Daro, the suspended floor of the kiln was found with a hole at its center. The upper part of the pillar (also known as stele) inside the kiln properly fitted into the hole, stabilizing the platform nicely for holding pottery and other objects. This also made way for replacing the one-piece suspended floor as and when required and continuing the heat treatment without much interruptions. It is also likely that the Harappan craftsmen dismantled the dish from the central stele after work. Archeologists also encountered conical stele in Banawali that was perfectly shaped to fit into the hole of the holding dish even if it had to slide down a little. This was an example of the ingenuity of the Harappan craftsmen.

Pear-shaped or Tear-drop kilns

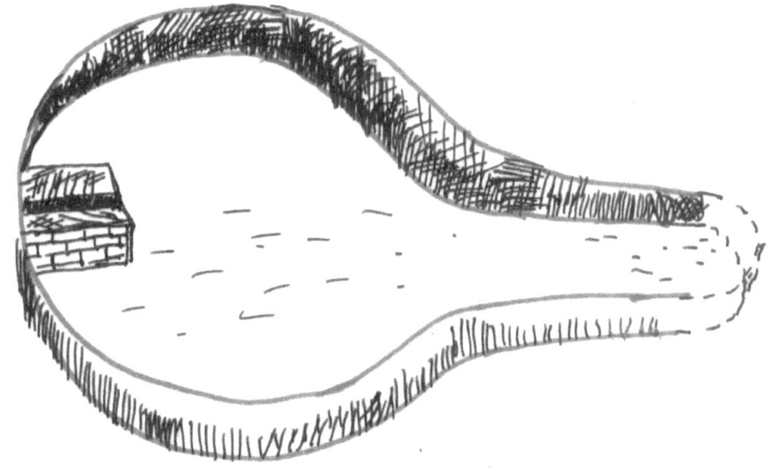

Figure 4.18 Pear shaped or tear drop furnace

Fig. 4.19 Pear-shaped furnace with brick platform at the centre at Rakhigarh (Courtesy: ASI)

Fig. 4.20 Typical pear-shaped furnace of Harappa (Courtesy: ASI)

Fig. 4.21 Double chambered pear-shaped furnace from Kanmer
(Courtesy: ASI)

These kilns had two parts, the round-shaped chamber where the combustion took place and the fire channel or tunnel, through which fuel (biomass) was supplied. The fuel partially burnt through the tunnel itself.

During the excavation of Trench-4, near mound-F in 1944 at Harappa, sixteen such pear-shaped kilns were discovered. Thirteen of them were found in identifiable shape with eight having brick lining while the other five were crude arrangements on dug pits. We learnt a few facts from those kilns. The kilns were made of either clay or bricks. The interior surfaces of the brick-walled kilns were plastered with a mixture of clay and sand. Since the interior of the firing chamber was exposed to extremely high temperatures during firing, its surrounding walls turned into a vitrified surface. Parts of these over-heated walls were often re-plastered to overhaul the kilns. The Harappan pear-shaped kilns were mostly used for beads-making. In some cases, the presence of an inner pillar was noticed, implying that the Harappan craftsmen, especially faience artisans and stone-masons employed the double chamber method in those kilns. Two different structural features were adopted. One was the conventional dish attached to the pillar and worked like the suspended floor holding firing objects. The other kilns had no central stele but only a slightly raised brick platform on which the vessels, beads and ceramic objects were placed inside a larger container for heating. Archaeologist M. S. Vats, in his excavation report recorded: - *"At Khairpur Mirs in Sindh a furnace for making glazed pottery with an astonishingly similar plan is still in use. (Excavations of Harappa by M. S. Vats: page 473).* He also drew a diagram of the kiln that clearly depicted the presence of the raised inner platform. The bricks of those platforms were laid with space between them to let the heat pass through the gaps and evenly heat the objects. The so-called conch-shell-shaped furnace of Rakhigarhi was actually a double chamber pear-shaped updraft kiln with a raised brick surface within. The spaces between the bricks were also visible. Another T-shaped furnace at Rakhigarhi bore similar characteristics. Two more arms branched out from this kiln probably for additional combustion openings, portraying the impression of "Anthropomorphic" furnace in the related excavation report.

Cylindrical kiln

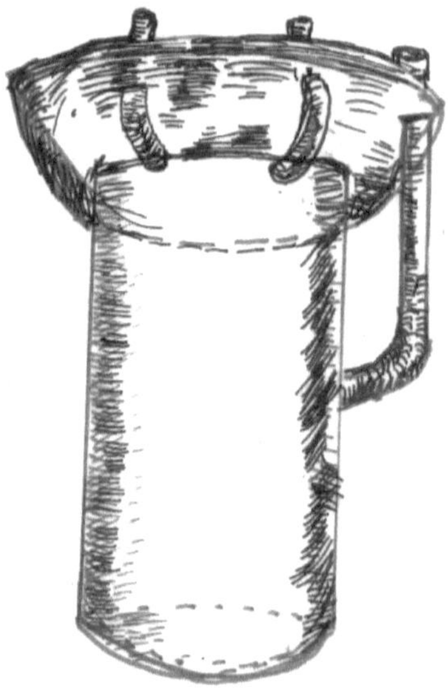

Fig. 4.22 Cylindrical furnace

Fig. 4.23 Site of the cylindrical furnaces found at Harappa

(Courtesy: ASI)

This is our last category of Harappan kilns. So far, there existed only one of its kind, excavated from Mound-F at Harappa. The particular kiln might have been experimentally devised but could not meet the expectations of Harappan craftsmen. This cylindricalkiln had one meter diameter and it was embedded underground at a depth of 1.6 meters. However, it bore the marks of combustion up to 1.1 meters only. Made with sun-dried clay-bricks, the surface of the kiln was plastered with clay and sand. Archaeologists believed that a good part of the kiln was above ground level. It was covered with a dome-like arched roof that was found in fragmented form alongside the kiln. The top part had four vents or flues probably as outlets for smoke. On the lower surface, another hole was noticed that entered the combustion chamber at an obtuse angle probably providing oxygen with an over ground blower. One part of the kiln being completely destroyed, the method of supplying fuel inside the kiln could not be ascertained. But according to archaeologist M. S. Vats there was a channel from ground level to the lower part of the kiln for this purpose that the craftsmen sealed during the combustion process.

The Harappan site namely Binjor 4MSR deserves special mention. During the excavation of this early and matured Harappan settlement site along the riverbed of Ghaggar, a plethora of artifacts including ovens, hearths, furnaces and kilns were discovered. Clearly, the Binjor site was an important Harappan industrial belt. In the excavated workshops various types of kilns and furnaces were found implying that often the Harappan artisans used different fire sources for the same craftwork. A picture (4.24) of such a workshop established the presence of round-shaped, oval-shaped and pear-shaped kilns at the same spot.

Fig. 4.24 Round, oval and pear-shaped furnaces from Binjor 4MSR site (Courtesy: ASI)

At Binjor, 4MSR, an ancient furnace used for extracting metals was recovered in intact condition (Picture 4.25). The place (A) where the blower was attached and the seat of the craftsmen (B) were designed in a planned manner. Besides gaining insight into the intricacies of Harappan kilns, archaeologists were able to form valuable opinions about the workshops of those craftsmen.

Fig. 4.25 Metal smelting furnace from Binjor 4MSR (Courtesy: ASI)

Having studied the furnaces, ovens, hearths and kilns of the IVC it emerged that these archaic fire sources are now seen in a generic

116

sense. The Harappans not only used different firing devices, but also engaged in continuous experimentations on their shapes, sizes and intrinsic structures. Another important aspect was the conformities of those designers. In the vast expanse of IVC, archeologists found astounding measurement and structural similarities in terms of the furnaces and kilns. Striking resemblance of the furnaces and kilns excavated in Mehergarh or Nausharo with those at distant Rakhigarhi are glaring examples. Not only the furnaces, the measurements of clay bricks, the weights, the script, seals, ornaments and many other items of daily use were all governed by an invisible conventional dictate which continues to amaze us.

A few remaining aspects of the Harappan kilns, furnaces and ovens are their evolutionary process. Over time, the ordinary pear-shaped kilns advanced to become pear-shaped double-chamber updraft kilns. But the old versions of these kilns were not entirely discarded and used in tandem with the advanced industrial furnaces. Even at present time, some of our ovens and especially our kilns retained their ancient characteristics. We would perhaps, never know the criteria or the selection parameters considered by the Harappan craftsmen in choosing their furnaces. We have seen different types of Harappan kilns being in use at different parts of their territory albeit for the same craft. The primary consideration was understandably the material being used. It was natural to use different combustion methods for pottery and bead-making. But when archaeologists found different kilns for firing their pottery or the presence of different furnaces in a bead-making workshop, it was concluded that they must have different heat-treatment methods for the raw-materials. The size of the objects or their intention to minimize fuel consumption with maximum utility could have mattered too. Investment (in any form, resources, manpower, etc.) might also have been a factor. For example, the double chamber updraft kilns required a demarcated place and skilled manpower. It also required a comparatively more expensive fuel - wood, instead of biomass or agricultural waste. On the other hand, those double chamber updraft kilns were much more efficient as the temperature within the heat chamber could be regulated easily and its extremely high heat-generating capacity. Some other kilns too produced desired temperature, but the provision for indirect heating in the double chambered kilns without the objects coming in contact with the fire, contributed to the quality of the products. Further, unlike the open-air kilns, the double chambered kilns were immune to rain or wind. Finally, the quality of the finished products was much superior to their counterparts from other kilns and without any discolorations or smoke staining. The double chambered kilns allowed the Harappan artisans to create high-quality, durable, and well-fired ceramics,including pottery, figurines, decorative and ornamental objects that served various purposes in Harappan society.

The kilns were also used in Harappan metallurgy. Blue ash was found in various sites which, going by the Harappan timeline could only come from copper derivatives. Copper was extracted and its compounds were processed in furnaces. We have seen that the Harappans invented a beautiful glass-like substance, called faience. The faience objects were often colored in blue with copper derivatives.

Chapter 5

FIRE WORSHIP OF KALIBANGAN

The primary obstaclesinstudying the fire worship of the Harappans, and their rituals and rites are the unavailability of any written scriptures or commentaries on the subject like the Vedas; and our inability to decipher their script resulting in a greater void in terms of the social, cultural and religious life of the Indus people. Even if the Harappan script were deciphered, it is unlikely that the daily life in this great civilization would unfold before us; reason being the apparently limited scope of the Indus script. The scripts were only found on seals and tablets; that too at an average of five characters on each artifact. Archaeologists believed that the Harappans mostly wrote on parchments, barks or other perishable medium that did not survive the long march of time.

We have studied the industries and crafts of the Harappans. We also scrutinized their furnaces and kilns. The task ahead will be exploring the religious aspects of the Indus society, especially their fire worshipping assemblage. Now, the ovens, kilns and furnaces were all fire sources and part and parcel of the average Harappan settlements. Categorically, we will, consider the ovens as one of domestic necessities for cooking purpose and kilns and furnaces as industrial requirements. As discussed earlier, their shape varied from being round or rectangular, oval or pear-shaped, or resembling a horse-shoe. Interestingly, the present-day ovens and furnaces retained their ancient characteristics to a large extent, especially in the villages and suburban areas where once the great IVC thrived.

Figure 5.1 Five fire pits found in the KLB 1 area of Kalibangan
(Courtesy: ASI)

The archaeological site at Kalibangan in Rajasthan spread along the dry riverbed of Ghaggar or, as many believe -the ancient river Saraswati, were excavated during the 1960s and 1970s. The three mounds explored were known as KLB-1, KLB-2 and KLB-3. KLB-1 presented the remnants of pre-Harappan era. Archaeological finds at KLB-2 indicated a blend of Pre-Harappan and Mature-Harappan culture. KLB-3 was specifically identified as a place connected with religious rites and rituals. Indus settlements existed at KLB-1 from 3000 BCE to 2700 BCE before a devastating earthquake forced the Harappans to abandon the area. Kalibangan was one of the major ancient settlements that were abandoned due to earthquakes. Like in many other Harappan cities, a fortified area that archaeologist named "citadel" was found during the excavation of KLB-1. The small fort-like establishment was surrounded by a thick boundary wall with rectangular towers at its entrance and four corners. The entire citadel complex area was divided by another wall, extended from east to west. This dividing wall too, had bastions. The northern part had a few raised platforms. Once, there may have been palaces or halls on those foundations, vandalized by brick robbers or decayed over time. The related excavation report mentioned two of those raised platforms bearing signs of ritualistic or religious practices. Five fire altars were found together at one courtyard (Pic -5.1). Earlier there were seven such fire altars. Two of them were demolished by the Harappans to make way for a drainage channel. Those are more like modified or structured "Agni-Kundas (fire-pits)" than conventional fire altars, rectangular in shape with rounded corners and placed along north-south direction. They were one meter in length, fifty centimeters wide and approximately twenty-five centimeter deep. The interiors of the altars were plastered with mud. They were guarded by a short wall to the west that also extended from north to south. Such was the structural design of those Kundas, one had to face east while seating in front the altars. Inside all those fire altars, small, round pillars or stone-slabs of 30–40-centimeter height and with a diameter of 15 centimeter were found. Archaeologists called it "Stele".

The measurement of clay-bricks used for those Kundas was similar to the bricks laid to construct the courtyards. They were 10 cm thick, 20 cm wide and 40 cm long. The Harappans tried to maintain this ratio 1:2:4, for their bricks. Ash, charcoal and terracotta cakes were found inside those altars. According to historians, a vessel (referred as a jar in the excavation report) containing ash and burnt charcoal that was found south of the series of the five altars connected the site with religious practices. The vessel was half entrenched below ground level, and most probably made by potter's wheel. A deep well with surrounding pavement were also found alongside the altars giving the site an impression of it being a public place. According to the excavation report, the well was used as a public bath before worship. A drainage channel was dug from the courtyard that passed through the so-called Agni-Kundas. The entrance to this area was from the south side.

Fig. 5.2 A separate fire-pit from KLB 1 (south) area of Kalibangan
(Courtesy: ASI)

Another separate fire-pit was found, south of those altars (pic 5.2) that was 1.3 meters in length, 0.9 meter wide and 0.60 meter deep. The bricks of that fire-pit were of unique feature, having a wedge-shaped or trapezoidal design. While one side of the bricks measured 40 cm, the other side was limited to 35.40 cm only! These bricks were easily recognizable due to their broader side tapering to a narrower end. One more significance of the pit was the traces of two types of faunal remains, bovine bones and antlers. The bones bore tell-tale marks of slaying of animals. Two square-shaped platforms of 0.45-meter length were found at north and south side of the fire-pit where (according to historians) the priests and participants assembled. A rectangular brick-paved courtyard of 12 meters length and 10 meters width was located at the south of

122

this fire-pit. Besides, a closed drain was found adjacent to the fire-pit that went towards the southwest side of the complex, probably for disposing animal blood and waste water.

So, the spot for killing the animals was situated at the southwest side of the fire-pit. A relevant fact for archeologists was the discovery of a triangular-shaped terracotta cake that had etchings. On one side there was a depiction of an animal being pulled in by a rope fastened with its neck. On the other side there was a picture of a deity. The deity was seated in lotus position wearing a horned headdress. The cake connected Harappan traditions of worship with animal sacrifice. Archaeologists and historians concluded that those fire-pits at Kalibangan were public worshipping place. Huge amount of ash was found at a nearby pit.

Fig. 5.3 A triangular terracotta cake from Kalibangan inscribed with a horned deity on one side and a man pulling an animal on the other side (Courtesy: ASI)

Some more similar types of fire-pits were excavatedat KLB-3 mound. It was mentioned at the beginning that KLB-3 was a happening place for Harappan religious activities and rituals. Five fire-pits were found in this site. We will study those fire-pits, at length. An upland, covering 3.45 meters in length and 2.90 meters wide was strewn with ash, triangular terracotta cakes and potsherds. All the fire-pits were made with clay bricks measuring 7.5 cm X 15 cm X 30 cm. The largest fire-pit had a diameter of 50 cm. Ash and loose burnt soil were found inside. The second fire-pit too, was round-shaped but smaller in shape. Its diameter was 40 cm. It contained a stele which was found broken. Inside, triangular terracotta cakes, loose burnt soil and ash were present. The third round-shaped fire-pit was of 30 cm diameter. The fourth fire-pit was different in shape. It was rectangular with a 0.65 meter length and 0.53 meter width. There was a 25 cm long steleinside. It also contained ash, triangular terracotta cakes and loose burnt soil. The fifth or the last fire-pit was oval-shaped. It held two steles inside. Between the fourth and fifth fire-pits, heaps of intact and broken terracotta cakes (mostly triangular), and potsherds were discovered. A north-south wall was erected at a distance of 4.65 meter from the fire-pits. Amidst the terracotta cakes, potsherds and ash, two clay models of sheep were discovered. All the pots found there were made by potter's wheel. After the excavation of all the mounds were completed, archaeologists thoroughly scrutinized the potsherds and concluded that about 7% of them belonged to pre-Harappan era while the rest were of matured Harappan period. This was an important revelation and attributed historic recognition to the fire-pits of being traditionally used for centuries. Many of the popular types of Harappan pots were missing at KLB-3. Only terracotta dishes, small jars and dishes-on-stand were found which was thought provoking and spoke of a specific purpose. In the context of colors, mostly red ware and buff colored ware were found. The gray ware, also known as "Fabric F Pottery", otherwise prevalent in Kalibangan was also missing at KLB-3. The fact that all those potteries were made by potter's wheel instilled considerable relevance in terms of later phase Vedic Yajna rituals that suggested use of handmade pots only.

Fig. 5.4 Five fire pits of KLB 3 of Kalibangan (Courtesy: ASI)

Another important aspect of the finds was the bone fragments. The study of the bones found around the fire-pits will help us understand the Harappans' choice of sacrificial animals for their worship rituals. The bones were identified as belonging to five types of animals. They were 1) Fish 2) Zebu 3) Gallus (Jungle fowl) 4) Goat/sheep & 5) Deer. One important feature of KLB-3 was the absence of well in the vicinity. Archaeologists found well near the altars at KLB-1. But the site at KLB -3 was completely devoid of any signs of human habitat. There were no residential dwellings in sight.

The necessity of establishing worshipping fire pits both inside the citadel complex and outside its boundary (at KLB – 3) gave rise to a controversy. According to related excavation report, the fire-pits inside the fort was for the elite class and distinguished persons who resided inside the fortified citadel - a contention without any substantive evidence!

Having studied the public fire worshipping sites, we will now enter the Harappan homes to inspect the fire-pits used indoor for fire worship. An excavated house (Trench ZD-10) presented one worshipping fire-pit which was round-shaped with 50 cm diameter. It held charcoal ash, small stele, terracotta cakes potsherds and bone fragments (not identified). Archaeologists got the idea of a busy city-center at Trenches D-4 and E-4 of KLB – 2. It was crisscrossed with grid-like streets and alleys intersecting each other at right-angles and also a few raised platforms, depicting a city marketplace. The houses had two or sometimes three entry gates facing the streets or alleys. Some of those houses held indoor hearths. The bricks used in the houses measured 30 cm X 15 cm X 7.5 cm. At Trench No. XD -9, another unique household fire-pit was found. The round-shaped fire-pit was 50 cm deep with a rectangular (20 cm X 40 cm) stele entrenched inside.It contained charcoal ash, potsherds and triangular terracotta cakes. Not all the Harappan houses had worshipping fire-pits. But surprisingly, one house at Trench No. D -7 of KLB – 2 came up with three fire-pits! The first one was a 20 cm square pit with a rectangular stele. The second one was oval-shaped with a small stele inside. No bricks were used for this fire-pit. It was plastered with clay. Further scrutiny revealed the presence of gravel in the material used for this fire-pit. It was excavated with ash filled up to its brim and concealed six round-shaped terracotta cakes, one triangular terracotta cake and a broken piece of brick. In the same house (Trench No. D -7 of KLB – 2), a large oval-shaped fire-pitwas found in a separate room. It was also clay plastered like the earlier fire-pit with a small amount of gravel. The fire-pit stretched from north to south. It was 1.75 meter in length, 1.5 meter wide and 50 cm deep. It also had a small stele inside and filled with ash and pottery sherds.

Another remarkable find was the large indoor fire-pit found in the same area. Completely made of clay and gravel, the unique oval-shaped fire-pit spanned a whopping 8 meters in length with 3 meters width and 3 meters depth. The presence of this great fire-pit inside a house was awe inspiring. It had two steles instead of one, both measuring 1 meter in diameter and 2 meters in height. It was the only one of its kind in the entire site. According to excavation report residual blue and black ash along with terracotta cakes were found inside the fire-pit. The range of fire and enormous heat generating potential of the fire-pit hardly justified its presence inside a residential building. Probably the structure was safely covered, while in use.

Undoubtedly, KLB -2 was the Harappans' lower town, inhabited by commoners who preferred to have their fire-pits at home and accordingly constructed dedicated rooms, big or small. A house surfaced at Trench No. E -8 with only a 50 cm square-shaped fire-pit of 40 cm depth. It was clay plastered and had a stele. Besides ash, a saucer-shaped terracotta cake and two broken clay-bricks were found inside the fire-pit. These bricks were slightly bigger (15 cm X 30 cm X 60 cm) than the standard Harappan bricks that measured 7.5 cm X 15 cm X 30 cm. The fundamental rule of measurement ratio 1 : 2 : 4 was retained. Even the bricks (10 cm X 20 cm X 40 cm) that were used to construct roads, fort-walls and sewage system followed the same principle. The common bricks (7.5 cm X 15 cm X 30 cm) were required for constructing houses. Although, many Harappan houses were built with bricks measuring 10 cm X 20 cm X 30 cm. Some archaeologists emphasized the utility of this ratio as being convenient for bonding while bricklaying. But the logic did not hold water when they found two bricks of 15 cm X 30 cm X 60 cm size inside one fire-pit. These two bricks had nothing to do with bricklaying or bonding with other bricks. They built the hearth and yet did not ignore the basic principle. This was the essence of Harappan culture which represented remarkable consistency and discipline. The quality of any civilization can be gauged by the homogeneity of its basic principles – and for the Harappans, those indicators were of paramount importance. Another house, near Trench No. E -8 possessed an oval-shaped, clay plastered fire-pit situated between two walls in the corner with a north-south stretch. It was 1.75 meters in length with 1.10 meters width and 40 cm depth. It was without any stele since no fragment of the stele was found. Only a broken brick was placed inside the fire-pit amidst ash and terracotta sherds. In one house at Trench E -8, a round-shaped fire-pit, made of clay and gravel was found with 1.35 meters diameter.

This too did not have any stele. Onlyash, potsherds and triangularterracotta cakes were found inside. One more house at Trench No. E -8 had an oval-shaped, clay plastered fire-pit situated between two walls in the corner with a north-south stretch. It was 1.2 meters in length and 1 meter wide with 1.5 meters depth. It was badly damaged preventing any assessment of its utility.

Moving across the descriptions of the fire-pits of Kalibangan which were most vividly discussed in the archaeology spheres, we will adopt an analytical perspective of those fire-pits (debatably fire-pits) for our comparative study. So far, we have drawn reference from actual excavation reports which unfortunately led to an array of arbitrary conclusions by mostly referring to the five fire-pits and analyzing the remnants and artifacts of KLB -1.

Imagine the Harappan city of Kalibangan in 3000 BCE,overlooking the Ghaggar riverbed of the Indian subcontinent, about 5000 years ago. Surrounded my thick mud-wall the early Harappan village were dotted with small one-storey houses made of bricks (10 cm X 20 cm X 30 cm; 1:2:3) *(Kalibangan A Harappan Metropolis Beyond the Indus Valley: Thapar B K)*. The prosperous habitat attracted outsiders, eventually expanded and further progressed with settlers with their skillset turning the village into a small settlement surrounded by a fortified wall. The citadel was at its center facing the river. Its gate was the main passageway to the city and the citadel. There were rectangular bastions at both sides of the entrance and few along the boundary wall. Flags flew atop long wooden flag posts behind the gate (pits for those flag posts were found). Trading vessels from distant places anchored at the riverside and merchants bartered a plethora of items. They brought special stones from Rohari mountain of Sindh from which blades and weights were made. Conches and shell bangles were brought from Kuch area of present Gujrat. Deep blue coloured Lapis Lajuli came from Afghanistan. In return merchantscollectedfood grains, cereals, Alabaster Bangles, painted pottery, toys and many other household and decorative items. Besides, influx of emigrants was order of the day. The fort complex accommodated one and all. On one side there was the citadel on a raised platform, abode of the elite class while common people resided in the other side (lower town).

It was mentioned that human settlement existed at Kalibangan even before the emergence of Indus people. After the excavation of Kalibangan, renowned archaeologist Dr. B.B.Lal wrote in his scholarly essay, *"A picture Emerges: An assessment of the Carbon 14 datings of the protohistoric cultures of the Indo Pakistan Subcontinent"* that initially human settlement took place at KLB - 1. The "cultural equipment" of that society did not adhere to Harappan norms, instead retained many characteristics of the chalcolithic age. Some types of pottery of this phase were typically reddish brown without any slip with white designs or slipped and bore black-colored designs. In the context of archaeological phasing, this pre-Harappan culture was more ancient (*As the stratification shows, this "Kalibangan culture" well preceded the Harappa, ibid.*). Potteries of those inhabitants were found contemporarily with pre-Harappan ceramics for a considerable period of time. Another archaeologist-excavator B. K. Thapar aptly discussed those settlements prior to the emergence of Indus Valley civilization in his essay: *Kalibangan A Harappan Metropolis Beyond the Indus Valley.* From the rocky evidence collected by them, we now understand that even before the Indus Valley civilization there was human settlements in the area who merged with the Harappan culture while cohabitating for a certain period. This happened in other places too. Among these non-Harappan societies some were able to retain a semblance of their separate identities addressed as "Phase" in archaeological terms. Accordingly, there were Kot Diji, Amri, Ravi and Hakra phases that reflected in their culture, customs, crafts and artistry.

Returning back to Kalibangan, we now have KLB -1 to be the first human settlement. Till 2700 BCE the fort city thrived with exponential human activities. Then a natural catastrophe befell on the people. An earthquake of disastrous magnitude completely destroyed the city and reduced it to rubbles. In fact, Kalibangan was the most damaged among the excavated proto-historic cities hit by earthquake. While the main city around KLB -1 was grounded by earthquake KLB -3 with its worshipping sites remained almost intact since it did not have much structured establishments or residential houses. Survivors abandoned the city but continued their religious activities at the worshipping places in and around KLB -3. Eventually, more and more Harappans resettled in the area and after almost 100 years, a new settlement, east of the earlier one was consolidatedthat we know as KLB -2. Following the trail of the past,the Harappans restored the old destroyed city that was probably chosen by the Harappan elites as their residential place. Common people resided at KLB -2 area.These conjectures were drawn on the basis of years of researches undertaken by scholars and archaeologists on the reconstructions of houses, potteries and other articles of the average Harappans' daily life.

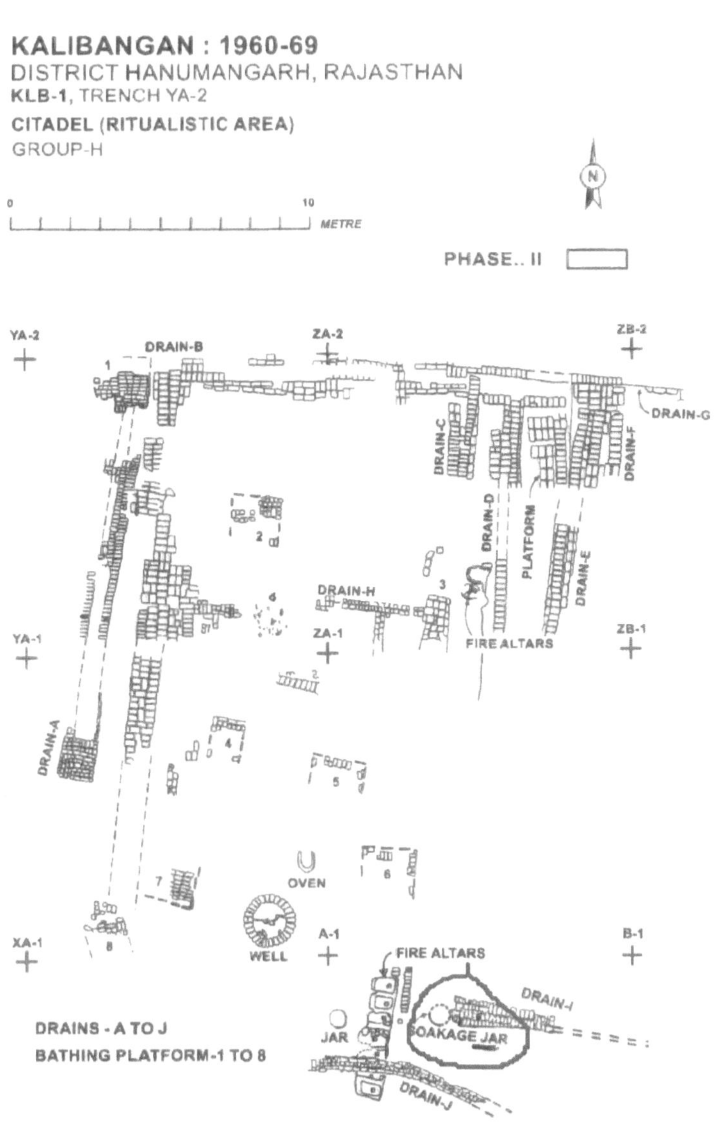

Fig. 5.5 *Site plan with five fire pits and wells found in the KLB 1 area of Kalibangan (Courtesy: ASI)*

Now, we will undertake an analytical comparative study of the altars of Kalibangan - our first case scenario being KLB -1. The

site presented five or seven fire-pits. The dilemma about the number of fire-pits arose from the fact that initially there were seven fire-pits placed in series. Later a drainage channel was constructed by demolishing two fire-pits making them five. According to related excavation report, those fire-pits were associated with public worship and social activities, since they were not inside houses but located outdoor on raised platform at the side of a walkway and accessible to a large number of people together. A well and so-called bathing platform was identified beside those fire-pits. In Vedic parlance, that type of communal fire-worshipping was mentioned as "Shrauta-Yajna" but those five fire-pits were not placed atop altars, instead they were dug underground. The Vedic Yajna fire altar was constructed by laying bricks on the floor with provision for a depressed area to hold the fire at its center. But at KLB -1, the fire-pits were unmistakably dug-out fire-pits. Although in Vedic era too, some Yajnas were performed with such fire-pits but the ancient scriptures strictly prescribed raised altars for Yajnas. The KLB-1 fire-pits were rectangular with rounded corners. They were like domestic bath-tubs, one meter in length, fifty centimeters wide and approximately twenty-five centimeter deep. All those five fire-pits had "stele", a pillar-like structure just short of 50 cm in length inside them, which was never a part of any type of Vedic fire-altars.Insidethose fire-pits,ash, terracotta cakes, especially triangular terracotta cakes and potsherds were found. The other fire-pit that was found at southside of those five fire-pits was larger than the five fire-pits (1.3 meters in length, 0.9 meter wide and 0.60 meter deep). Inside the
fire-pit,animal bones were found along with ash, terracotta cakes, and potsherds. The bones bore marks made by sharp weapons. This purportedly established the Harappans' ritual of animal sacrifice. In the Vedas, the "Ahavaniya" (invitational) Agni of the Yajna is induced by "Shrauta Agni" to be appropriated for sacrifice. We have seen in the related chapter that "Ahavaniya" Agni was invoked by preparing "Uttaravedi" on top of the "Mahavedi" (Pic 2.2) and initiating the fire at the center spot (naval point) of the Uttaravedi. As mentioned earlier, in the east of the "Ahavaniya"

Agni, another large Vedi was instituted, called the "Mahavedi" or "Soumik Vedi". This "Mahavedi" was a paved floor with the shape of a trapezium. Its eastern side being shorter (18 meters) than its western side (23 meters). They were parallel to each other. The northern and southern sides were equal (28 meters) but not parallel. Contrary to this, the five fire-pits at KLB -1 were placed on a single platform which was 76 meters long and 24 meters wide that was way different from the Vedic "Mahavedi". It may also be remembered that a "Mandap" was erected on the Mahavedi called *"Sadahsala"*, which held a number of Agnis. This Mandap was 8 meters long and 4 meters wide, hence cannot be identified with the KLB 1 fire-pits on a raised platform. Now, let us consider the shapes of the Agni fire-pits. According to Vedic principle, six Agnis were placed side-by-side under the Sadahsala which were called *"Dhishnya"*. These were square or circular-shaped. For square shape the sides were to be 18 finger or one arm's length which is 36 – 48 cm. In case it was circular, its area equalled to the equivalent area of the square. This gave a diameter of approximately 50 cm. The Ahavaniya Agni was square shaped with 1 "Aratni" length of its sides. One Aratni was the measure of the elbow to small finger of the Yajman, which was approximately 1.5 feet or 50 cm.

On the other hand, the fire-pits or supposedly fire-pits of KLB -1 were all rectangular and measured 1.5 meters X 0.5 meter. The number of Dhishnyas were six but here we find only five or seven fire-pits. Another anomaly is the presence of the drain through the fire-pits. In Vedic Yajna, the blood of the sacrificed animal was disposed at a place far from the Yajna area. But in KLB -1, the drain passed right through the fire-pits, which was odd from religious point of view. A drainage system at a place of worship raises doubts. The Harappans were quite hygienic in nature and conscious about cleanliness. Every household had drainage and sewage system for waste and garbage disposal. Based on this premise, the drain behind the fire-pits raises serious doubt about their intent and more so, as the drain was constructed at the cost of two fire-pits. Some presented the logic of bathing water from the well nearby being channelled out of the worship area through the drain. Connecting ablution with sanctity, Archaeologist B. B. Lal emphasized the need for the well and the platform for the worshippers who supposedly purified themselves before engaging in the religious rites. It sounded good. But the presumably noisy bathing place being so close to the holy fire-pits and not at a place far from it, did not make sense. Secondly, the hygiene-conscious Harappans could have made provisions for a well and drainage system prior to construction of those seven fire-pits instead of demolishing two of them at a later stage to make way for the drain and the well. Scholars and archaeologists who are familiar with Harappans' hydro-engineering capabilities knew that they regularly used soak pit (dug chamber for soaking excess waste water). Such a soak pit was found a few feet away from the drain at KLB -1 (Fig. 5.5). Evidently, the Harappan engineers could have solved the problem of waste-water disposal easily without having to demolish two holy fire-pits. Further, if the Harappans felt ablution essential for participating in religious practices, then why the confirmedly religious sites of KLB -3 were without such wells or bathing platforms. The principle of sanctity could not have been followed selectively. So, it compels us to turn our focus on the very purpose of the drain. In the chapter related to the Indus furnaces, kilns and hearths we have seen extensive use of "Stele" fitted double chambered updraft furnaces in Harappan industry. The stele was used to hold a dish on which beads, pottery and other objects were placed for indirect heating without coming in direct contact with the fire chamber. In Lothal, some double chambered updraft kilns, dedicated to metalworks were found with drains close by. The purpose of this drains was to supply water for the extraction of metal or other metalworks,especially for quenching where the metal or alloy is heated to a specific temperature, known as the austenitizing temperature and then subjected to rapid cooling by immersing it in a quenching medium - cold water. Usually near the metal working furnace, a provision of water is made for quenching purposes. *"This feature being close to the furnace can be identified as a water container. Usually near the metal working furnace a provision of water is made for*

Besides metalworks, Harappan also made provisions for water in their workshop for cooling of their heated objects and hardening the heated beads, stoneware and tools. Archaeologists found water supplying arrangements for their industrial kilns. For quenching those heated objects in water, the craftsmen required large vessels. We have seen such large storage of water in vessels, drums or barrels in the blacksmith's workshop where heated metals are frequently immersed in water for hardness, strength and wear-resistance. In order to stabilize the water resource, their vessel for this purpose is conventionally embedded in ground. Interestingly, behind (south) those KLB -1 fire-pits, a large pot, half-buried in the ground was discovered. Many historians, not without reason, believed those fire-pits were actually industrial kilns. Discovery of similar set-up at Lothal coppersmith workshops, involving fire pits and water storage reinforced the idea. A series of fire-pits accompanied by a drainage (pic 5.6) and lumps of copper and copperware were found strewn around those fire pits clearly identified them as industrial kilns. In another Indus archaeological site at Mitathal, a set of fire pits were excavated with drainage for supply of water (pic 5.7). In the workshop at Binjor 4MSR, three round-shaped industrial furnaces, a drain and a storage vessel for water were excavated (pic 5.8) in 2017. It is true that KLB -1 site at Kalibangan did not yield any metal object in and around the fire-pits. However, it may not be out of place to mention that metal, in those ancient time was an expensive commodity. Limited use of copper and bronze were known to the Harappans. Copper ore was obtained through rigorous effort or imported. So, the copper products underwent frequent recycling. Unlike stoneware or terracotta items that was nearly impossible to reshape for multiple objects, copper items were easily recycled to make different items.

This is one reason for people attempting to take away metal objects while leaving a place, which the Harappan probably did. Besides, looters and treasure-hunters ransacked those ruins for centuries. Their most valuable find would undoubtedly be metals. This may also account for the site being devoid of any metal artifacts. In many areas at KLB -1 site of Kalibangan, ancient bricks were looted by vandals. It was unlikely that they spared the remnants of metal artifacts, if they found any. The short north-south wall east of those five fire-pits meant sitting before the fire-pits at westside of it, facing east which was considered auspicious. But the disclaimer is, Vedic Yajna altars were never erected behind walls as opposed to walls essentially erected behind the fire sources in Indus sites to let the smoke billow over it and also for keeping implements and lamps in the alcoves of the walls. As for the direction, the isolated fire-pit found south of those fire-pits had seating arrangement for participants facing north and south, defying the eastwardly direction rule. Going by Vedic principles, all directions (there are ten) had their unique significance (and specific deity, too) and could be interpreted as holy depending on the contexts and the purpose of the Yajnas. Besides, the participating members of the Yajnas, like the Ritwik, Yajman, etc. had their prescribed seats as elucidated in pic. 2.2.

Fig 5.6 Furnace and drain from Karsola (Courtesy: ASI)

Fig. 5.7 Furnace and drain from Mithathal (Courtesy: ASI)

Fig. 5.8 Furnace, drain and earthen vessel in a workshop at Binjor 4MSR (Courtesy: ASI)

Let us consider the bricks, now. We have seen earlier those bricks used for the altars of Vedic Yajna had various sizes and even names. Their dimensions were determined by the measurements of different body parts of the Yajman. All the bricks of KLB -1 kilns were of same dimension – 10 cm X 20 cm X 40 cm. This specification of bricks was maintained throughout the city for general purposes also. But In the southern vicinity of the five fire-pitsdescribed earlier and depicted in picture 5.2, the lonefire-pitwas made of bricks that were wedge-shaped or trapezoidal. One side of these bricks measured 40 cm, while the opposing side waslimited to a length of 35.40 cm. Almost all the rectangular and round-shaped kilns excavated at KLB -1 had stele, which was a key feature at that time in most of the Harappan furnaces and kilns, including "Double Chamber Updraft Kilns" which we have studied earlier.

Table 5.1

fire-pits of KLB-1

#	Shape	Dimension	Stele Yes/ No	Terracotta cake	Pots herd	Remarks
1	Rectan gular	1m X 0.5 m X 1.25 m	Yes	Yes	Yes	Five fire-pits were found with terracotta cake with ashes.
2	Rectan gular	1.3 m X 0.9 m X 0.6 m	No	No	Yes	Ash, terracotta cake and animal bones were found

Now, we will study the oblations of the two periods. For Harappan sacrificial objects what is found in plentiful were the terracotta cakes, especially the triangular cakes. Not only in the fire-pits of KLB -1, those triangular cakes were dispensed in the fire abundantly in almost all other fire-pits found in and around the Kalibangan archaeological sites. This was a common feature for the Indus people. Regardless of the dimension or shape of the Harappans' fire-pits, kilns, furnaces or hearths, the presence of terracotta cakes of various sizes was ubiquitous. On the contrary, terracotta cakes were never included in Vedic oblation. In Vedic context, edible items were mostly preferred as offerings to the deities while animals were chosen for sacrifices. Earlier, we have seen "Satapatha Brahmana" dictum of humans, horses, oxen, sheep, goats and cereals being appropriate for sacrifices. No wild animal was named. In Indus fire-pits, archaeologists generally found bone fragments of two categories of animals – bovine fauna and antlers of the deer family (Cervidae), the latter being an untamed wild animal. The oxen found mention in the Vedas as sacrificial animal but their remains (like bones) were never found at Yajna sites, as in the Harappan sites. In this context, the Vedas gave clear instructions about not shedding blood in the Yajna area as it attracts the "Rakshashas (evil incarnate)".

In "Satapatha Brahmana", immediately after the *mantras* declaring the five animals for sacrifice, there is this commentary (2.1.3.9) about Human, when earmarked to be sacrificed, turned into "*Kimpurusha*", a mythical and elusive creature, (described randomly as some mythical being, aborigine, gnome or ape) while the horse and ox transformed into "wild Gour" and bison, lamb into camel and goat into "sarav" (another mythological beast). Those converted animals did not receive the essence of Yajna, hence prohibited for sacrifice while the deer was outright taboo!

After the animal sacrifice, the "Adhwaryu" sliced its belly to extract the fat (Bopa) from its navel area and placed it on Arani (wood used as fuel) and then heated it by the "Ahavaniya Agni". Then adding ghee to the heated animal fat, it was offered to the Agni. This Vedic ritual was called "*Bopastok Ahuti*". This was followed by "Pasangayag" or "Pashupurodash" during which only selected parts of the sacrificial animals were collected in a cooking vessel called "Pasukumbhik" and boiled by a fire ("Shamitra agni"), that was separately ignited at the slaying zone, located at northside of the Mahavedi. Nopart of the animal was to be brought in direct contact with the Yajna fire. The heart of the sacrificial animal was pierced through a skewer and subjected to the "Shamitra agni", before placing it in the "Pasukumbhik" with the other parts for boiling. After the boiling was over, the "Adhwaryu" offered the meat to Agni pouring small portions at a time with a ladle. It was unlikely that the cooked meat would contain large bones. In the event of the substance containing small bone fragments, it was again unlikely that one would be able to separately trace them in the charred remains after the Yajna fire was extinguished. In contrast, the sacrificial spot at Kalibangan was positioned to the south-west corner of the fire-pit and not north-west as prescribed in the Vedas. In Vedic Yajnas, only edible items as oblation for the deities or offering funeral cakes for the deceased ancestors were allowed and no inanimate object like terracotta cake was ever known to have offered. A related commentary in *"Yajyamantra"*, appeals to the Agni to carry the offerings to the deities – *"Agna Vrihi Vaushat"*. In all the fire-pits at Kalibangan sites, offering Terracotta cakes was traditional and unique. So, we may conclude that even in the context of oblatory or obsequies rites, there were more dissimilarities than likeness between the two great cultures.

The isolated fire-pit of KLB -1 was unique for the wedge-shaped or trapezoidal design of its bricks. Another kiln, found at Binjor 4MSR inside a beads-workshop was constructed with similar bricks. A drainage for supply of water (pic 5.9) was also found. The kiln was square shaped with 130 cm sides – same length as the rectangular fire-pit of KLB -1. This KLB -1 fire-pit that had a drain in the vicinity to its southwest, purportedly a channel to dispose of animal blood and waste water from the fire-pit had its outlet or exit point well above the fire-pit (pic 5.2) making it well-nigh impossible for blood or water to flow from the fire-pit against gravity. Rather, it was possible to supply water from above to the fire-pit. This theory, again negates the idea of the isolated KLB fire-pit being a worship place and turned the drain instead into a reservoir of water. Yet, the ash and bone fragments found in the fire-pit called for the benefit of doubt. The container, which was labeled as a jar in the excavation report, discovered to the south of the fivefire-pits, held ash and burnt charcoal. This jar was partially buried below the surface and was likely made using a potter's wheel. But, linking the jar to Harappans' religious rituals and comparing it with the Vedic ritual vessels would definitely be farfetched.

Figure 5.9 Kiln and Channel found at Binjor 4MSR (Courtesy: ASI)

One important aspect of our study would be the sitting arrangement. We have the five fire-pits of KLB -1 placed along north-south direction with a short wall to the west that also extended from north to south. This gave historians an idea that the worshippers had to face east while seating in front the fire-pits. Comparing this with the Vedic positioning becomes difficult. Because in Vedic Shrauta Yajnas there were more than one Ritwiks who also had their assisting members and facing a particular direction during the Yajnas was not mandatory as clearly depicted in pic 2.2. While the so-called worshippers at the five fire-pits of KLB -1 had to seat facing east, the isolated fire-pit nearby had raised seats both at the north and south side of the fire-pit, for participants. It gets more baffling when we study other fire-pits at

142

KLB -2 and KLB -3 where not only the seats but also the fire-pits themselves did not follow any Vedic guidelines in terms of measurements and directions.

Our purpose is not to prove that the Kalibangan fire-pits had nothing to do with religious practices, but it can be concluded that all the fire-pits cannot be ascribed to religious activities. The five fire-pits of KLB -1 and most of the fire-pits at KLB -2 appeared to be furnaces, kilns or reservoirs and since they were recovered partially without the top portions, we could not inspect the fuel supply mechanism with them. On the other hand, the lone fire-pit at KLB -1 and the fire-pits at KLB -3 were indicative of religious activities.

Having studied the fire-pits of KLB -1, let us move onto KLB -3. The table would help as a ready reckoner to assess the KLB -3 fire-pits.

Table 5.2
fire-pits of KLB-3

#	Shape	Dimension	Stele Yes/No	Terracotta cake	Potsherd	Remarks
1	Round	50 cm dia	No	Yes	Yes	Inside All the fire-pits, bones of five types of animals were found along with ash.
2	Round	40 cm dia	Yes (Circular)	Yes	Yes	
3	Round	30 cm dia	No	Yes	Yes	
4	Rectan-gular	0.65 mX 0.53m	Yes	Yes	Yes	
5	Oval	Less than 50 cm dia	Two	Yes	Yes	

It is mentioned earlier that KLB -3 mound did not yield any trace of human dwellings. It was identified as a communal worshipping site. During its excavation, the site was found to be sitting over a small hillock, which seemed natural. Throughout the Indian sub-continent, choosing hilltop and places not easily accessible for the purpose of temples, shrines and monasteries had been a common phenomenon since ancient times. KLB -3 offered insight into the unceasing religious activities from pre-Harappan period onward. In 2700 BCE when the city at KLB -1 was destroyed by a devastating earthquake,a group of Harappan people still fought for survival there. The worshipping site of KLB -3 showed evidence of that and it made the worshipping places special as public assemblage and congregational activities similar to the Vedic Shrauta Yajna venues.

A total of five fire-pits or fire-pits were excavated at KLB -3. All the fire-pits were constructed along north-south axes. The raised platform that held those fire-pits was 3.45 meters in length and 2.90 meters wide. Earlier we discussed Saumik Vedi or the Maha Vedi of Shrauta Yajna that had two sides measuring 23 meters and 18 meters and two equal sides of 28 meters. The "Sadahsala" on top of the Vedi was 8 meters long and 4 meters wide. So, the dimensions of KLB -3 fire-pits did not match with Vedic specifications. In Vedic Shrauta Yajna rituals, six Agnis were kindled in series along north-south direction beneath the Sadahsala Mandapa, while the KLB -3 had only one of its five fire-pits along north-south direction. Other fire-pits were set up in random fashion. Harappan Bricks of the platform and the fire-pits were of common dimension used in the rest of the city and measured 30 cm X 15 cm X 7.5 cm. All the five fire-pits yielded residual terracotta cakes as offerings along with bone fragments of five animals. The shapes of the fire-pits were quite different from their Vedic counterparts. The shape of the Vedic Ahavaniya Agni was a 0.5-meter rectangle. The six Agnis or Dhishnyas beneath Sadahsala were either round-shaped or rectangular with 0.5-meter sides or diameter. Here in KLB -3, three fire-pits were round-shaped with diameters 0.50 meter, 0.40 meter and 0.30 meter,decreasing in terms of area. Those five fire-pits at KLB -3 were not constructed side-by side like the Dhishnyas, they were constructed over a large area with no specific pattern. Only the second round-shaped fire-pit had a stele which was not present in the other round-shaped fire-pits. In Vedic rituals, the Garhapatya Agni altar was round in shape as also the Grihya Agni or Sthandil which was used for performing daily rituals at home. Understandably, the Sthandil Agni was never used for animal sacrifice or "Pasuyag". The diameter of Garhapatya Agni altar was essentially 50 cm that was never altered. One of the two remaining fire-pits at KLB -3 was rectangular (0.65 meter X 0.53 meter) with a stele and the other, oval shaped like the five KLB -1 fire-pits. Its dimensions were unavailable. But, as the related excavation report identified the first fire-pit as the largest, so the oval-shaped fire-pit must be smaller in size.This last fire-pit had two steles inside. This craft related fire-pit raised serious doubts about its utility. Around the fourth and fifth fire-pit, and in-between them, there was huge ash deposit, terracotta cakes, pottery and sherds. This indicated maximum use of those two fire-pits. Questions were raised about whether there were five separate social hierarchies. And whether those two fire-pits were categorically used by the marginal classes; ostensibly, more frequently than the other classes. But those were hypothesis based on a few physical features. Two terracotta sheep figurines were found between those two fire-pits (fourth and fifth), probably both were offered during worship. Those figurines resembled the terracotta "Chhalan" sculptures of Bengal and never found as offering in any other Harappan archaeological sites. Even if they existed, they could not have been identified as objects of offering unless found at a religious site as KLB -3. We can further infer that KLB -3 of Kalibangan may have been a unique cult worship place. Continued religious activities in KLB -3, since pre-Harappan era spoke volumes about its religious importance to the Harappans.

We have discussed about terracotta cakes found inside the fire-pits at Kalibangan archaeological sites, but only loose burnt soil was found inside the fire-pits at KLB -3. They might be the remains of "Mushtika" (discussed in earlier chapter), the terracotta cakes for general use. Mushtika cakes were abundant in any Harappan archaeological site. They were not properly baked, casually prepared and were brittle. Religious implements, pots, triangular cakes and bone fragments found around the KLB -3 fire-pits identified the place as a very active spotassociated with their rites and rituals.

As for the sacrificial animals, the terms "animals" and "bones" may not be appropriate when we scrutinize the remains. According to related excavation report, five types of animal bones were found: - Fish, Ox/Cow *(Bos Indicus)*, Jungle Fowl *(Gallus gallus)*, Goat/Sheep, and Deer. Some of the bones bore marks of weapon-strikes, confirming sacrificial killings. Fishbones were among the major finds in KLB -3. Fish were foremost in the Harappan menu and fishbones were found in plentiful in all Harappan settlements. The human tradition of sacrificing their most cherished object justified the presence of fishbones in the Harappan ritual site, KLB -3. Vedic traditions, however strictly forbade inclusion of animals that were wild and restricted to five domesticated animals only. Fish too, were not permissible.

Pottery from the Early Harappan Phase discovered at the Kalibangan archaeological site was systematically categorized to establish a foundational reference point for ceramic studies across the Indian subcontinent. This classification, known as the six fabrics of Kalibangan, groups Fabrics A, B, and D under the category of redware. Fabric C pottery, characterized by their violet and black hues, are identified as a subtype of black and red ware within this classification system.

The various pottery found at KLB-3 unfolded a few mysteries and offered much insight into the evolution of the Indus art and culture. But first we need to understand the salient features of Kalibangan potteries. All great civilizations had regional characteristics influencing their crafts, especially handicrafts like terracotta pottery. Archaeologists and historians identified different cultures by their unique pottery traditions, like Ochre Colored Pottery (OCP), Painted Grey Ware (PGW), Northern Black Polished Ware (NBPW), etc.

The term "Six fabrics of Kalibangan" pertained to the distinct features observed on pottery from the Early Harappan phase, marked by six categorized fabrics labeled A, B, C, D, E, and F. These fabric classifications were subsequently recognized at the nearby Sothi site, associated with the Sothi-Siswal culture, which were identified as a subtype of the Early Harappan Phase.Six fabrics of Kalibangan were:

Fabric – A: - Thin and light potteries of red or pinkish in color. Some had black designs on the surface. A few hadwhite designs on red surface.

Fabric – B: - Carefully crafted pottery. Before firing, potters applied red "slip" (A liquid mixture of clay and water) from its bottom to shoulder. Black horizontal stripes, designs or motifs were noticed as decorations.

Fabric – C: - Those were more durable than the Fabric – B pottery. The whole fine textured surface of the ceramic was covered with red or purple-red slip. Some displayed black designs.

Fabric – D: - Comparatively thick, having a ring-base. Markings of cord and some other designs were noticed.

Fabric – E: - Buff or reddish-buff in colored pottery. Some carried inscriptions in white.

Fabric – F: - Grey in color with inscription on the surface in white.

Excavation report of KLB -3 listed a total number of 840 Harappan pottery including fragmented remains, out of which 7% of the items were from pre-Harappan era discovered at the lowest level of Kalibangan excavation site. Two unscathed specimens of the pre-Harappan period, found at the site were a jar and a basin. Pottery of mature Harappan period, found intact were jars, bowls, dishes, dish-on-stand, basins, etc. There were many dish-on-stands, although another unique Harappan pottery item – the perforated jar, was not found. Beakers and pointed goblets were also missing. Another significant fact was, those pottery were not exclusively hand-made pottery as Vedic tradition permitted but ordinary kind of wheel made Harappan wares. Gray ware was found during excavation at archaeological sites of later period known as "Painted Gray Ware". This PGW had similarities with Fabric – F of the Harappan era. But KLB -3 yielded no Fabric – F wares. KLB -3 being a worshipping place, the Harappans preferred and continued to use primitive types of pottery, the Fabric – A to Fabric – E. Significantly grayware pottery were completely missing n KLB -3. This served the theological doctrine that religion beckons for adherence to traditions. So, buff ware was much less used during pre-Harappan era and later adopted during its mature stage.

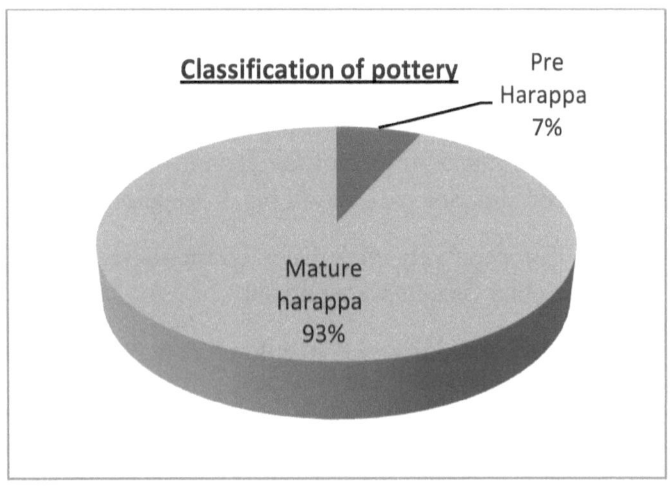

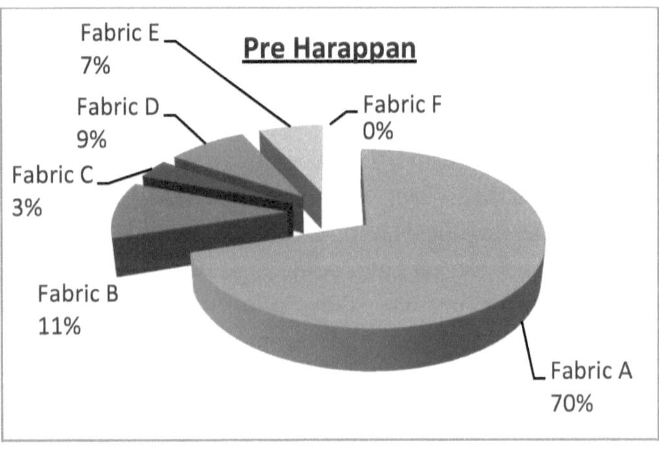

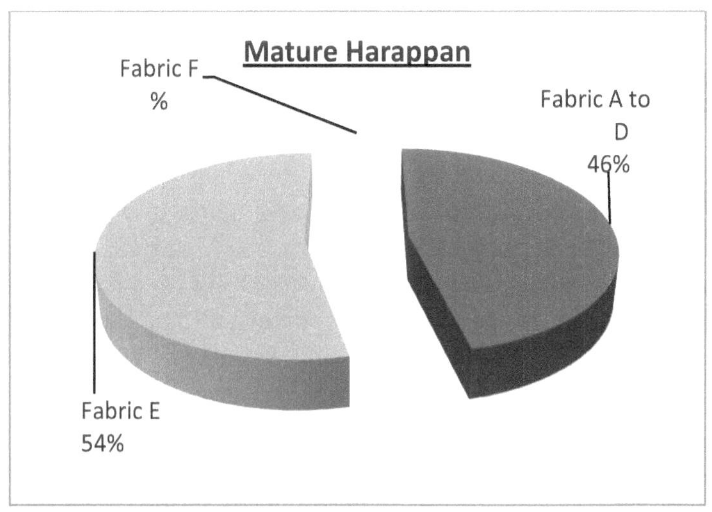

In the context of Vedic Yajnas, we studied the Grihya Agni also called the "Garhasthya" Agni, or "Smarta Agni", which was kindled indoor by the home-owner to perform household rituals. We also found that Grihya Agni was invoked in the morning and evening by the patron. This Agni was indispensable for domestic events like marriage, sacred thread ceremony, naming of newborn, house-building, sowing seed, recuperation from diseases, etc. Round or rectangular in shape, the Grihya Agni or the Smarta Agni was kindled in a "Garhasthya fire-pit". We find mention of Garhasthya Agni in "Khadira Grihyasutra". This structure was called "Sthandil" - a smaller fire-pit (not an altar), made of clay and sand and constructed at the eastern part of the house. It was made functional by a giving a coat of cow dung. The seat of the Ritwik used to be at south of Sthandil and so was the position of the "Praneeta" water.   For thousands of years, the tradition of using clay and sand/gravel for constructing domestic oven or fire-pits survived and found in rural Indian households even today. Sthandil was round in shape and constructed in a one arrow's length square space. (Ashvalayan Grihyasutra 1.3.1) The length of an arrow was approximately 74 centimetre, little more than two feet.

A comparative study of the fire-pits of KLB -2 is necessary here. KLB -2 was the lower township, dwelling place of the common Harappans. The settlement included farmers, and many types of artisans. They needed furnaces or kilns for their crafts that were mostly constructed in their home and workshop. Excavation report of KLB -2 recorded a total of ten furnaces. Three of those furnaces were found in the same house! They were no different from the KLB-1 fire-pits, in shape. The presence of three fire pits in a single house raised questions about their purpose as ritualistic fire-pits. From the domestic worship point of view, only one fire-pit could serve the purpose. According to Vedic guidelines, Garhapatya Agni was protected by the house-owner who was entitled to perform the fire rituals along with his wife. In case the father of the family was away, his son qualified as the patron but in the presence of the father, the sons only acted as subordinates before the same Agni. Multiple Agnis could also be justified if there were separate or split families under the same roof. It could be ascertained whether there were such descents. But societies in the Indian subcontinent rarely witnessed split in a family under one roof even one century ago. So, it was hard to believe that the Indus families suffered such condition during their times. This brings us to the final conclusion that not all the fire-pits were used for worship. Some of them were possibly industrial kilns. Out of those ten fire-pits of KLB -2, three were round-shaped. Two of them had diameters of 50 cm and the remining fire-pit was of 1.35 meters diameter. Two were square-shaped with 50 cm and 20 cm sides respectively. Rest of the five fire-pits were oval-shaped or rectangular with rounded corners. Oval-shaped fire-pits appeared to be mostly used by the Harappans. We have already studied the bath-tub-like fire-pits a KLB -1 and KLB -3 archaeological sites. Seven fire-pits held steles inside. In two of the fire-pits, the steles were replaced by brick structure. Ash, terracotta cakes and potsherds were mostly found in and around those ten fire-pits.

Table 5.3

fire-pits of KLB 2

#	Shape	Dimension	Stele Yes/No	Terracotta cake	Pot-sherd	Remarks
1	Round	50 cm diameter	Yes	No	Yes	No terracotta cakes were found here, but unidentified animal bones were found with ashes inside the fire-pit.
2	Round	50 cm diameter	Yes (oblong)	Yes (triangular)	Yes	
3	Square	20 cm side	Yes	Yes		
4	Square	50 cm side & 40 cm depth	Yes (round)	Saucer shaped	No	A brick was found which was much larger than the conventional brick of Kalibangan although its dimensions followed the conventional ratio (1:2:4).
5	Oval	1.75 m X 1.10 m X 0.40 m	No	No	Yes	No stele or pillar-like structure was found here but there was a brick placed in its place.

6	Round	1.35 m dia	No	Yes (triangular)	Yes	
7	Oval	1.20 m X 1 m	Not known	Not known	Not known	
8	Oval	Not known	Yes (square)	Yes (triangular and saucer shaped)	Yes)	There was a brick inside the fire-pit
9	Oval	1.75 m X 1.50 m X 0.50 m	Yes	No	Yes	
10	Oval	8 m X 3 m X 3m	Two steles each of 1 m dia and 2 m length	Yes	Yes	The shape of the fire-pit is gigantic and there were two steles or pillars inside it. Blue strained ash was also found inside the fire-pit along with normal ash.

Figure 5.10 Fire pit inside a room at KLB 2 (Courtesy: ASI)

Since all the fire-pits at KLB -2 were found inside houses, those were often addressed as Indus versions of the Vedic Garhasthya Agni that was round-shaped with a diameter of 74 cm. The diameters of the fire-pits at KLB -2 were quite different. The first, second and sixth fire-pits were circular but with different diameters. The third and the fourth fire-pits were square-shaped, hence could not be compared with a Sthandil. Even if we draw reference from the Vedic Ahvaniya Agni, the two round-shaped fire-pits were made of mud and gravel and not with bricks that constituted the Vedic Ahvaniya Agni. The fifth, seventh, eighth, ninth and tenth fire-pits were oval-shaped. No Vedic Yajna altar was ever found with this shape. Steles were found in all the KLB -2 fire-pits except the fifth and sixth fire-pits. We have their presence in KLB -1 and KLB -3 fire-pits also. The ninth fire-pit of KLB -2 even had two steles. This, again was a unique Indus feature and no Vedic altar appeared to have been equipped with this strange yet effective attachment.

As opposed to Vedic oblatory offerings that included edible items and cooked meat of specified domesticated animals, the Indus fire-pits presented the terracotta cakes especially the triangular terracotta cakes and potsherds within the charred deposits. Bone fragments found in a KLB -2 fire-pit did not adhere to prescribed Vedic procedure which was discussed in detail in the context of KLB -3 fire-pits. The small portions of meat offered by Ritwiks during the Yajnas did not contain bones that would endure the Yajna fire.

Readers' attention is drawn again to the three fire-pits found in one single Harappan house. We may assume this was connected with some form of cult or faith difficult to perceive by present day perspectives, yet the fire-pits pointed to some other implications than mere worshipping purposes. Note the dimension of the last fire-pit (Sl. No. 10). With a length of 8 meters, width of 3 meters and depth of 3 meters it appears too huge for domestic use. Imagine, fire being ignited to its full capacity under a single roof made of timber. An inferno would immediately follow and the house would have been incinerated in moments. Take the other indoor fire-pit at Sl. No. 9. That too, was enough to destroy the house if the entire fire-pit was ablaze. Those fire-pits were of course fired up, even if partially. The unavoidable question is why the Harappan instituted such huge fire sources, if it was not possible to utilize them to their full capacity? Why the atypical depth of 3 meters? The gigantic indoor fire-pit yielded bluish ash deposit about which no explanation was available in the related excavation report. So far, no chemical analysis was undertaken to ascertain its source unlike the bone fragments which were scrutinized and recorded. The blue colour of the residual deposit raises doubt about whether the fire-pit was a worshipping fire altar or an industrial furnace. There was an entry in the "Fire Altar" section where this fire-pit found mention. The lack of additional details regarding any other artifacts discovered inside the house, such as beads or copperware, did not help either. When geologists were consulted to explain such ash, considering the geology of the site, the metal/ores found there during the Harappan era, and the account of the Harappans' metallurgical activities, it was assessed that the residual ash likely originated from a copper-based compound, or copper ore, explaining its bluish tint.

The terracotta cakes discovered in Harappan settlements were classified by their distinct shapes. These identifying artifacts held great significance for archaeologists. These cakes were categorized into four types. The triangular terracotta cake stood out as a particularly intriguing find. Since the terracotta cakes were abundantly present in nearly all archaeological sites and extensively used at KLB -3, they were considered as a valued worship-related element of the Harappan era.

The KLB -2 fire-pits that were identified as worshipping altars in the excavation report and other archaeological articles and journals were mostly double chamber updraft kilns since, at least seven of them had steles inside. Some even had two steles for increased production using multiple suspended surfaces inside the fire chambers. In some fire-pit the stele was replaced by brick platforms. No explanation for those alterations was available in the concerned report. The brick pillars functioned in the same way as the stele to create compartmentation within the fire chamber with an upward transmission of heat. Gaps between the bricks allowed the heat to pass through and evenly heat the objects. In the chapter on Indus furnaces and kilns, we have seen this type of heat treatment (Pic 4.19) that explains our complications. There was no explanation for the presence of those multiple fire-pits with extraordinary dimensions under a single roof, unless the setup was actually a house cum workshop instead of a religious household. Secondly, the mystery of having such massive fire sources and grossly under-utilizing them for safety concerns could only be explained, by assuming that Harappans controlled the fire by covering the top of those fire-pits by a dome or ceiling, again following the dual-chamber method.

Finally, the bluish residual ash that confirmedly established the presence of copper derivatives, as no other metal was in use in that period. The positions of those ten fire-pits of KLB -1 (one in pic

5.10) were always at the corner of a room or behind a wall. Worshipping fire-pits and altars never allowed walls erected behind for prevention of smoke. Even at present day rural kilns and ovens are placed at a corner or behind a wall to keep away or re-direct the smoke. The ten fire-pits of KLB -1 were more likely used for industrial purposes than worshipping fire-pits.

Chapter - 6

FIRE WORSHIP OF LOTHAL

The confluence of Sabarmati and **Bhogavo** rivers of present Indian state of Gujarat ran about 30 km before they emptied into the Gulf of Khambhat and the Arabian Sea. It was the eclipse of the neolithic age and inception of the chalcolithic era when a group of people settled within this *"doab (meaning -two rivers)"*. They were skilled boatmen. Year after year, the inhabitants struggled to protect their village from flood. They constructed mud houses and surrounded them with an earthen embankment that even in present time is the first line of defence for the rural riverine habitat of Bengal. The alluvial plain yielded rich harvests like cotton, wheat and paddy that attracted societies beyond its boundaries, like the Indus people. The indigenous terracotta of those earliest settlers were the *"Lustrous Micaceous Red ware"*, *"Coarse Grey ware"* and the *"Red and Black Ware"* which were much different from the contemporary Harappan pottery craft in terms of shape, fabric and firing process. Their trade links with the Indus settlements subsequently resulted in large-scale migration of the Harappans, who peacefully cohabited with those original inhabitants. The easily accessible waterways, prospects of constructing a dockyard and the fertile land enticed the Harappans to settle there permanently. External trade being the core factor of Harappan economy, they needed to further extend their outreach to as many places and people as

Mesopotamia (Sumerians) and countries in the Arabian Peninsula, the modern-day Bahrin, UAE and Oman. This region was known to Sumerians as Magan and Dilmun. The Sumerians had trade links with the people of Magan, and Dilmun and they referred to it in their texts. Harappans also establishedtrade links with Magan and Dilmun.Magan was known for its copper resources, which were highly sought after by the Harappans for various purposes. Lothal was ideal as a trade transit point for its strategic position. Besides, Lothal was strategical to procure semi-precious stones for their famous beads industry and conch shell and ivory as raw materials for Harappan artisans.Forprocurement, and transportation of those items to other Indus regions, Harappans realised the importance of Lothal's strategic position and permanently settled there during 2450 BCE. From historical point of view, in such cases more powerful outlanders always turned invaders and vanquished the inhabitants. Furthermore, the Harappans were superior in their technology and metal related knowledge. But no violence ever took place and in 2450 BCE, the Indus people started living in peace with the indigenous people, without any attempt to establish Harappan style of settlement-plan. Readers may question the veracity of this inference and exactness of the period of Harappan migration. This can be argued by the fact that from the later stage of that very period, typical Harappan-style terracotta pottery surfaced in Lothal. The theory of peaceful coexistence also had merits. A fusion of indigenous and Harappan craftwork left impression in the terracotta pottery of that period. Not all potteries were subjected to those experiments but many of them bore mixed artistry like the indigenous Lustrous Micaceous Red pot with a Harappan stud-handle. On the other hand, Harappan vessels displayed indigenous graffities, design and motifs on their pottery fabric. This was a clear sign of collaborative living. We may identify this development as an example of "soft skill" during the formative periods of the human race.

Historians classified the foundation and developmental stages of the Indus people in Lothal by the yardstick of intermittent devastation caused by floods. The Harappan settlement of Lothal witnessed many flood situations and after every onslaught, they brought about remarkable changes in the process of restoring and reconstructing the settlement. Immediately after the advent of Harappans in 2450 BCE, a catastrophic flood presented the first opportunity for the Harappans to exert their working skill. The Harappans employed their technological expertise and constructed a circular embankment surrounding their territory. This was the beginning of Indus civilization at Lothal. The next flood came 200 years later. In 2200 BCE. After this disaster, the Harappans showed their mettle once more and went on to build an ideal Indus city. Harappan Houses and buildings came up on the ruins. This well-planned city expanded threefold compared to their earlier settlement and was divided into blocks within its confines. Like other Harappan cities, an Acropolis was built by its side, representing the citadel of power. The famous dockyard of Lothal with warehouse was constructed during this time. The governing power behind this massive project, the unique ideas, perfect planning and execution led historians to believe that perhaps architects and skilled labours were brought in from other cities. And that was the reason for the city's expansion and accommodate the migrant workforce, administrators, aristocrats, traders, sailors and craftsmen. In congruence with other greater Harappan cities, a thorough sewerage system, underground drains, manholes and public bath were built. But the most amazing feat of the Harappans was an architectural marvel – the Lothal dockyard! In building the dockyard, they exercised maritime engineering, much ahead of their times. The project was made successful with active collaboration from the indigenous inhabitants.

Imagine this Herculean task, performed more than four thousand years ago. The dockyard covered an extensive area of impressive dimensions. The main dock at Lothal was a massive structure measuring approximately 710 feet (216 meters) in length, 120 feet (36 meters) in width and 8 feet (2.4 meters) depth.The entire area was encircled with a 14 feet wall. The entrance to this dock was about 121 feet (37 meters) wide, allowing seafaring vessels to enter and exit with ease. A complex system of docks, warehouses, sluice gates, berths, and channels managed the flow of tidal water and removing silt, mud, and debris from water bodies to maintain navigable waterways for seafaring and inbound ships. Mudbrick berths were built for loading/unloading of goods and merchandise. Another remarkable feature of the dockyard was its warehouse. It was positioned on an elevated platform of 165 feet length, 145 feet width and 12 feet height and connected to the main dockyard through a long wharf.

The warehouse held twelve brick blocks raised 2.5 above ground for storage of commodities, mainly crop. They were accessed through a maze of passages for loading and unloading merchandise or goods for shipment. The goods were piled on timber planks placed on those Brick structure. During excavation, many Harappan seals were found around the place. Some had the imprint of sacks implying that the storehouse played an important role in Indus trade and commerce. Archaeologists found husk as evidence of paddy and rice stored there.

This was the phase -II revival of the Indus settlement at Lothal. But disaster struck again in the form of another devastating flood that recurred in 1800 BCE.This unprecedented flood pushed the Harappans to the brink. Yet, instead of giving up, the Indus people embarked on the Phase -III reconstruction of their city. After 100 years, the Harappan city of Lothal was destroyed by flood in 1700 BCE once more and resurfaced, stepping into Phase -IV. The cataclysm was complete and decisive when the final deluge in 1400 BCE (Phase -V) hit the city of Lothal and wiped it out.

Having the brief history of Lothal narrated, we will now inspect this Harappan city from the archaeologist's perspective keeping an eye on its fire worshipping places. The city that overlooked the banks of Sabarmati river of Gujarat, and its tributary, lasted from 2200 BCE to 1700 BCE. The resilient Harappans reconstructed their city after every onslaught of the flood. Their meteoric progress based on periodic floods were categorized in five phases by archaeologists. Phase I to Phase -V are representative of the following chronology: -

Phase I - 2200 BCE to 1900 BCE

Phase II - 1900 BCE to 1800 BCE

Phase III- 1800 BCE to 1700 BCE

Phase IV- 1700 BCE to 1600 BCE

Phase V - 1600 BCE to 1400 BCE

The Block -A area of Lothal was identified as the "Lower Town" and consisted of market area for the common people. But in early period i.e., in Phase I and Phase II nothing except a few mud-huts existed there. Obviously, they belonged to the pre-Harappan indigenous people of Lothal. An embankment built by the indigenous people, left its mark during this time (Phase -II) suggesting that the struggle against flood was deep seated prior to Indus footsteps. Since periodic destructions and phoenix-like revivals went on side by side, many structures were erected on the ruins of their earlier skeletal remains. Some old establishments assumed new forms. So, we must go by the phases while studying the sites.

At B-19 of Phase -II, two enclosed rectangular spaces were identified as fire-altars. One of those rectangular pits (henceforth referred as fire-pits) measured 46 cm in length, 30.50 cm in breadth and 28 cm in depth. It was constructed with clay and bricks. The dimension of the bricks (28 cm X 14 cm X 7 cm) were similar to the common bricks found at other sites. Ash was foundinside the fire-pits. The other fire-pits measured 61cm in length, 46 cm in breadth and 13 cm in depth. One more fire-pits was found inside a house in this site but could not be measured, as it was badly damaged. Another rectangular fire-pits was found from a house at 86-B location.The artefacts found in this house suggested that it was the house of a merchant, involved in foreign trade as beads, gold, ornaments etc. of Sumerian culture. The house displayed the taste of a wealthy owner. The dimension of the fire-pits was 1.07 meter in length and 0.84 meter in breadth, stretched along the northeast -southwest direction, the two ends marking the seats for operators or worshippers. Besides ash, other items were found inside the fire-pits included burnt remains of bovine jaw-bone, golden pendant, a carnelian stone-bead and sherds of a painted pot.

A Harappan house of Phase -IV (1700 BCE) presented three fire-pits; two of them were round-shaped and one rectangular. One of the circular-shaped fire-pits had a diameter of 61 cm while the other measured 74 cm. The rectangular fire-pits had a 46 cm X 31 cm dimension. Ashes were found in all the three fire-pits but the rectangular fire-pits also had triangular terracotta cakes and earthen balls.In the vicinity, a large jar was discovered. Related excavation report mentioned engravings on the surface of the jar but no description of its motif or design was available.

Next was Block –B, that revealed the most amazing architecture of the Harappans. The underground drainage system, broad streets in grid pattern well-planned sewerage system, compelled the archaeologist to visualize the bastion of elite class – the Acropolis!

The Indus architects showcased another impressive engineering achievement in this context. They effectively separated wastewater and sewage, including actual contaminants, using a "runnel" – a small, shallow channel or trough designed for transporting wastewater from the Harappan residences, baths, and buildings. The runnel was designed to direct the flow of wastewater towards the drainage system. The waste sewage was collected in soakage jars through manholes connected to the drains, where it would later undergo decomposition and absorption by the surrounding earth. The Acropolis was subjected to several makeovers during different phases. After every catastrophe, new roads, buildings and sewerage were constructed. But Lothal's Block B was always a stronghold of the elite class of Harappan society. The devastating flood during Phase-III (1800 BCE) destroyed the city including the Acropolis after which the city again underwent a restoration process during Phase -IV. Although, at this time it was experiencing an eclipse. Common people took refuge in the citadel. The two square-shaped fire-pits found in two adjacent Harappan houses in Block -B were indicative of the inflow of commoners into the Acropolis area. The dimensions of those two fire-pits could not be ascertained.

Block C was the famous granary/warehouse of Lothal while Block D was a large paved courtyard. Its utility for the Harappans is still unknown.

During Phase -I and II, houses were scarce in Block E and only a few indigenous mud-houses existed. At the end of Phase II, few more mud-houses with some reinforcements like beams etc, and the use of terracotta cakes, earthen balls for flooring purpose were noticed. Fired bricks were introduced in Phase -II but it was only during Phase – III when they were used extensively to build houses and buildings. Indus architecture was superbly employed in those constructions. The floors were reinforced with "Mustika" and had cavities signifying supporting timber beams. Walls had marks of roofing beams being attached. Big "Grain silos" were found inside those houses for storing grains and cereals. By Phase -IV, Block E had many houses that were built on the flood-washed ruins of their earlier constructions and gained a natural protection from future floods. Inside one Harappan house, an oval-shaped fire-pits was found. It was approximately 2 meters in length and 1.25 meters wide. A small earthen altar was found inside. Excavation report identified it as a worshipping fire-pits as its brick wall was well-burnt. But, since no ash or other worshipping implements were found around, it is hard to imagine it as a worshipping fire-pits.

Our next destination is Block F, situated in the western part of the citadel. Similar to Block E, it underwent periodic renovation from Phase I to Phase III, with only a few mud houses remaining. However, during Phase IV, a significant structure was erected: a prominent bead-making factory within a spacious courtyard, measuring 38 feet in length and 23 feet in width. The residential quarters of the Harappan artisans were lined up behind the factory. This type of workshops are still found in present day Rajasthan, Gujarat and Haryana. Approximately 600 finished and a substantial quantity of unfinished carnelian beads were found from this factory site. The necessary implements and raw materials like semi-precious stones, lapidary drill, ordinarykilns for firing the beads were found in the factory.But no fire-pits or fire-altar was located there. Block G was located near the burial ground. In the beginning (Phase I and II), there were hardly any residential building in this area but as more immigrants joined the Harappan settlement of Lothal, they added new areas for people to live. During Phase -III, clusters of Harappan houses were built in Block – G area, despite the area being prone to flood. Block G was connected to the main city by a wide street (No.9). Beside this street (SRG 2, D 27-D 28)a big fire-altar (public worshipping fire-pits) was excavated. It measured 2.75 meters in length, 2.60 meters in breadth and 30 cm in height. The centre of the north and south flanks of the fire-pits had depressed surfaces apparently to place pots or jars. While the shape of the north side depression was rectangular, the southside spot was semi-circular. Those depressed spots were not a result of repeated use but carefully constructed with bricks for specific purposes. Dr. S.R. Rao,one of the excavating archaeologists assumed that the hollows were made to accommodate worshipping pots of specific shapes and measures. On the northeast side a post-hole was discovered where a pole was erected during the events. On the southwest side an "S"-shaped jar was found, beautifully crafted in Harappan style with black design on a red fabric. It was considered to have played an important role in the Harappans' rituals. A shell ladle for pouring oil or ghee in the fire was also found nearby. Besides ash, some triangular terracotta cakes were found. Inside a house near the intersection of street 1 and street 9, another fire-pit was excavated. Not much detail about its dimensions were available but it was reported to have constructed by ten layers of bricks, which made it at least 1 meter deep, hence it was a sizable fire-pit. A pile of clinker, ashes and terracotta ball/lump (probably Mustika) were found inside the fire-pits. A jar was found beside the fire-pit. An intriguing aspect of this house, constructed in Phase III, is that during Phase IV, another house was built directly on top of this partially ruined building, without much consideration (or paying respect) to the earlier fire-pit, which was violated by the new structure. No other fire-pit of Phase IV or V was found in the area. The last Block comprised the dockyard. Thus, it is beyond the scope of our study as no fire-pit could possibly have existed in the area.

Before we embark on the analysis of the worshipping fire-pits found in Lothal, a table with the relevant content would prove useful.

Table 6.1

fire-pits of Lothal

	Area	Time period	Shape	Dimension (cm)	Goods found inside the fire-pits	Remarks
1	Block A	Phase II	Rectangular	46 X 30.5 X 28	Ash	
2	Block A	Phase II	Rectangular	61 X 46 X 13	Not known	
3	Block A	Phase II	Rectangular	107 X 84 X not known	Bull/ox/cow jaw bone, gold pendant, carnelian stone bead, potsherd	The expansion of the fire-pits is in the NE-SW direction
4	Block A	Phase IV	Round	61 dia	Ashes, triangular terracotta cakes and Mustikas	
5	Block A	Phase IV	Round	74 dia		
6	Block A	Phase IV	Square	46 X 31 X Not known		
7	Block B	Phase IV	Square	Not known	--	
8	Block B	Phase IV	Square	Not known	--	
9	Block G	Phase III	Rectangular	275 X 260 X	Ashes, triangular	There is a rectangular

| | | | | 30 | terracotta cakes | depression in the northern arm of the fire-pits and a semi circular depression in the southern side, a flag hole in the north-east corner, a large earthen jar found in the south-west of the fire-pits. |
| 1(| Block G | Phase III | Not known | Not known | Ash, loose burnt earth and Mustikas | |

Fig 6.1 A domestic fire altar found at Lothal (courtesy: ASI)

166

FIRE ALTARS - PLAN

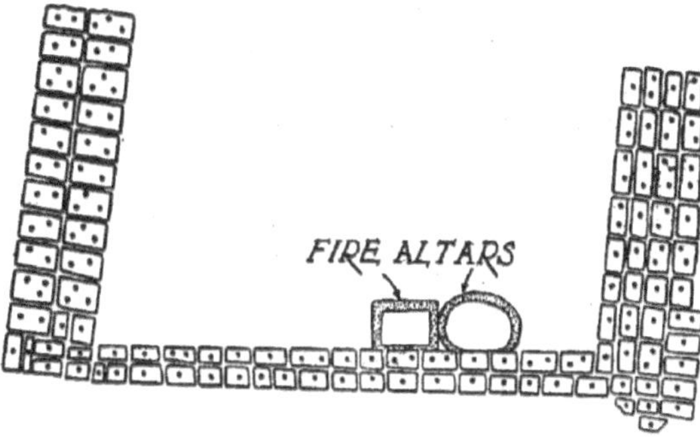

Fig. 6.2 Plan of a domestic altar found at Lothal (courtesy: ASI)

Having studied the history of the findings of Lothal, we will take a look at the significance of those fire-pits and attempt to relate the facts with our already acquired knowledge of Vedic fire worship or the Yajnas. It emerged that all ten fire-pits except two, found at Lothal's archaeological sites were from the lower town areas. The citadel or the upper town area where the aristocrats and the upper echelon or administrators resided, did not have a single public fire worshipping place. The 10th fire-pits in the above table did not have sufficient details to contribute to our study. We will also set aside the 9th fire-pit for now, as it was a public worshipping place and will be analysed later. First, we will consider the domestic or household fire-pits (1st to 8th in the table).We gathered basic information about six of the household fire-pits from the report and so let us discuss them first. All of these fire-pits were unearthed from the Block-A site, which was located in the lower townthat primarily housed common people. Thosefire-pits came in various shapes, including rectangular and circular, but they did not adhere to specific Vedic dimensions. The dimensions of the round-shaped domestic fire-pits, or Garhasthya fire-pits, used by the Harappan

167

people did not follow the specifications outlined in the Vedic texts for round-shaped Vedic fire altars, which were expected to have a diameter of 74 cm. The diameter of the 5th fire-pits (in the table) was an exact match to that of the Vedic Garhasthya Agni. The 1st, 2nd and 3rd fire-pits were rectangular with different dimensions. No Vedic altars were prescribed to be rectangular in shape. They were either round, square or semi-circular.According to Vedic principles, the shape of the Oistik Vedi was suggested to be "Krishamadhya," akin to a "Damaru," (a concave percussion instrument). But it was not exactly rectangular. Furthermore, the Oistik Vedi was used for Vedic rites for which fire was not needed. The 3rd fire-pits deserved special attention.The fire-pit's dimensions measured 1.07 meters in length and 0.84 meters in width, extending in the northeast-southwest direction, with the two ends serving as seating areas for the participants. In contrast, the Vedic position (Garhasthya Yajna) for the worshipper (Yajman and Ritwik) was south of the Garhasthya Agni. Furthermore, a charred bovine jawbone was found in the fire-pit that defied Vedic procedures of animal sacrifice.According to the Vedic practices, animals were slayed at a designated area known as "Shamitradesh," which was situated north – west of the Vedi. Thereafter, a ritual called "Bopastokahuti" took place during which the "Adhwaryu" sliced in the animal's abdomen to extract the fat (Bopa) from its navel region. This fat was then placed on an Arani (a wooden piece used for fuel) and cooked over the "Ahavaniya Agni" (sacred fire). Ghee was added to the cooked fat, and it was offered to the Agni.Subsequently, the "Pasangayag" or "Pashupurodash" ritual occured. In this ceremony, only eleven specific parts of the sacrificial animals were collected in a cooking vessel called the "Pasukumbhik" and boiled over a separate fire, the "Shamitra agni," which was ignited at a pre-arranged location north of the Mahavedi. Notably, no part of the animal came in direct contact with the Yajna fire.The heart of the sacrificial animal was pierced with a rod (likely ironskewer) and briefly fired in the "Shamitra agni" before being placed in the "Pasukumbhik" with the other parts for boiling. After the boiling process was complete, the "Adhwaryu" offered the meat to Agni by pouring it in small portions using a ladle. It is improbable that the cooked meat would contain large bones, especially a jaw bone. In the rare event that it did contain small bone fragments, it is also unlikely that one could separate them from the charred remains in the ashes after the Yajna fire was extinguished.

Apart for the animal bones, a goldenpendant anda carnelian stone-bead were found inside the fire-pit. Archaeologist and excavator Dr. S. R. Rao inferred that since Vedic rites allowed for gold offerings, the 3rd fire-pit could be connected to Vedic practices. In order to examine the claim, let us consider the related Vedic Yajnas in which offerings of gold were permitted.

In Vedic Agnicayan, five layers (*chiti*) of brick-laying for the altar was mentioned and it made provision for gold offerings. There was a story behind this precept. In the chapter on Vedic Yajnas, we have already seen that Vedic Agnicayan Yajna altar required brick-laying in five layers. The first layer was (symbolically) water as Prajapati created the earth from water. According to Satapatha Brahmana, He created the land on a lotus-leaf (Satapatha Brahmana 8.4.1.1 – 20). In similarnarrative, Rigveda says that

tvām agne puṣkarād adhy atharvā nir amanthata |
mūrdhno viśvasya vāghataḥ ||

Rig Veda 6.16.13

The sage, Atharvan, extracted you from upon the lotus-leaf, the head, the support of the universe.

The term "Pushkara" (mentioned In the actual Sanskrit Mantra) found its meaning in the interpretation of "*Sayanacharya*" that Agni was churned out of "Pushkara" which was defined as lotus. In Taittirya Brahman (1.1.3.5-7), another commentary described that Prajapati assumed the form of wild boar and brought earth from the seabed then sprinkled it on the lotus leaf, creating the universe. That was the Vedic explanation of the first layer of Agnicayan bricks, dedicated to water or "Apa" and the bricks were accordingly named "Apasya" (refer chapter on Vedic Yajnas). During the second layer brick-laying, a golden lotus was ingrained which was called "Rukma". The 21 petals of "Rukma" represented

169

21 rays of the sun. This too was mentioned in Satapatha Brahmana:
-

atha rukbhamupadadhāti | asau vā āditya eṣa rukbha eṣa hīmāḥ sarvāḥ prajā atirocate roco ha vai taṃ rukbha ityācakṣate paro'kṣam paro'kṣakāmā hi devā amumevaitadādityamupadadhāti sa hiraṇmayo bhavati parimaṇḍala ekaviṃśatinirbādhastasyokto bandhuradhastānnirbādhamupadadhāti raśmayo vā etasya nirbādhā avastādu vā etasya raśmayaḥ

- Satapatha Brahmana 7.4.1.10

"He then puts the gold plate thereon. Now this gold plate is yonder sun, for he shines over all the creatures here on earth; and 'rocas' (shine) they mystically call 'rukma' (gold plate), for the gods love the mystic: he thus lays down yonder sun (on the altar). It is golden, and round, with one and twenty knobs, —the significance of this has been explained. He puts it down with the knobs pointing downward; for the knobs are his (the sun's) rays, and his rays (shine) downwards."

The Vedic deities addressed this golden lotus as "Rukma", with reverence. So, the worshipper invoked the distant sungod on the Agnicayan Vedi. It was also clear that the second layer of Agnicayan "Uttar Vedi" positioned on top of water or "Apa" represented by the first layer (Apasya) and having the sun on top, symbolized the universe. So, the Indus fire-pit (supposedly fire-pit, third in the table) with a mere gold pendant and without the vital golden lotus with 21 petals raised serious doubts about it having anything to do with Agnicayana rites.

Another Vedic ritual that had provisions for gold and silver "Rukma" was "Pravargya" which was a part of "Som Yajna". "Pravargya" was repeatedly performed on the second and third day of "Som Yajna". In a way, the "Pravargya" was a 'ceremony' that was performed concurrently with the primary "Soma Yajna". The oblatory item of the ritual was "Gharma". It was made of warm ghee, cow milk and goat milk and prepared in "Mahavira", a Yajna vessel mentioned earlier (Yajna vessel Pravargya was for different purpose). For "Pravargya" ceremony, "Purodash (oblatory cakes)" of cereals also called "Rouhina Purodash", were required. For its preparation, a separate clay-oven called "Khar" was prepared at a distance from the Som Yajna Vedi. A silver plate (Rukma) containing "Manju" grass was placed on top of the oven and ignited by the fire of Garhapatya Agni. The fire was kindled with 13 pieces of fire-wood (*Flacourtia indica*). Then the "Gharma" was prepared by heating the Mahavira vessel with ghee in it and adding cow and goat milk to the heated ghee. A golden "Rukma" covered the Mahavira vessel. The prepared "Gharma" was offered to the Gods, Ashwani brothers and Agni.To sum it up, the silver and golden "Rukmas" were used in separate rituals from the main Agni fire-pit of Soma Yajna.

Even if we ignore the religious angle and resort to common knowledge, it stood out, that an ignited fire-pit, 1 meter long and 0.80 meter wide, would be too large for a delicate golden pendant to retain its features. And the exquisite red Carnelian bead nestled within the fire-pit would likely transform into silica ash when exposed to the extreme heat that the fire chamberwould produce.

The presence of these cosmetic items within the fire-pit can only be explained by their deposition at a later stage when the fire-pit was no longer in use. This fire-pit was originally from the Phase II period, but it underwent flood damage, destruction, and subsequent renovation. The structure that once housed the fire-pit belonged to a prosperous merchant and yielded various valuable artifacts. It is reasonable to assume that the golden pendant and the bead found their way into a hollow area like the fire-pitby rain or by flood water.

Architects discovered triangular terracotta cakes and "Mushtika" in the two round-shaped fire-pits. Details of these Harappan oblatory items were discussed in the chapter on Kalibangan. The Vedas had never prescribed such inedible and inanimate substance as offerings. Earth in any form could not be oblatory in Vedic practices.

Another noteworthy feature of the household fire-pits in Lothal was their placement behind walls (as seen in pic 6.2) or in the corners. It's important to note that Vedic Yajna altars were never positioned behind walls or in corners. Additionally, much like the arrangement in Kalibangan, three fire-pits were found within a single house in Lothal, with two of them situated adjacent to each other (as shown in pic 6.2). This intriguing observation was previously discussed concerning the presence of multiple worshipping fire-pits under the same roof. It is more likely that these fire-pits served as industrial kilns.

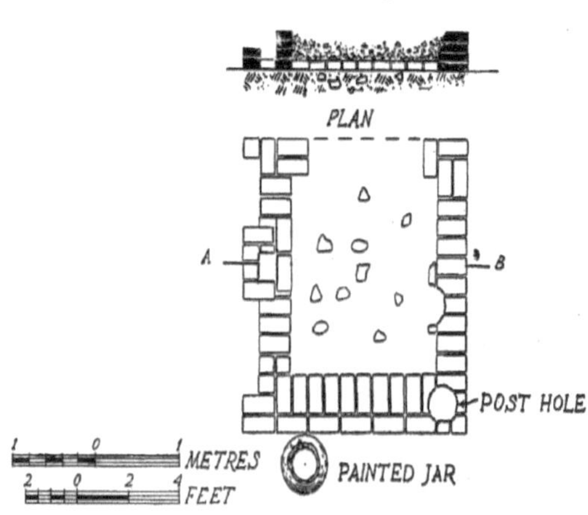

Figure 6.3 Community fire altar and vessel found at Lothal
(Courtesy: ASI)

Next, we will examine the outdoor fire-pit listed at number 9 in the table. Its close proximity to a Harappan street strongly favoured the idea that it was easily accessed by ordinary people. This fire-pit was positioned in Block - G, in the vicinity of the Harappan burial site situated at a distance from the settlement which existed during the Phase III period in Lothal. The houses indicated that people of marginalized class of the society resided here. The fire-pits was a well-constructed rectangular structure with sides exceeding 2.5 meters in length. Its sturdy brick walls, measuring 0.5 meters in thickness, added to its durability. However, it cannot be associated with the Vedic "Shrauta Yajna" altar because Vedic Yajna altars were never designed in rectangular shapes. The "Uttar Vedi," thatwas built upon the "Mahavedi" or the "Saumik Vedi," was traditionally square in shape. The "Ahavaniya Agni" invoked on the "Uttar Vedi" required a square area with 0.5 meters sides, whereas the Lothal fire-pits' dimensions far exceeded this requirement, measuring more than 2.5 meters on each side.

Earlier, we learnt about a finely crafted jar, discovered on the southwest side of the Lothal fire-pits and designed in the distinctive Harappan style, with black patterns on red fabric. This artifact was believed to have held a significant role in the rituals of the Harappan civilization. In contrast, Vedic worshipping vessels were invariably black. During the preparatory stage, after drying those vessels, they were exposed to black smoke generated by burning horse manure before firing. So, the designed Harappan vessel did not match the Vedic Yajna vessel. We have also known that on the northern and southern flanks of the fire-pits, there were recessed areas positioned at the central points, seemingly designated for placement of worshipping pots or jars. The northern recess took on a rectangular form, while the southern spot had a semi-circular shape. It meant Harappan worshipping rites demanded vessels suitable for placing on those two varying shapes to be placed at those exact spots. Another vessel was found on the southwest side of the fire-pits. In Vedic practices the indispensable water container, "Pranita" was always positioned on the right side of the Yajna Vedi. This aspect was discussed in the Vedic Yajna chapter. But here, in the Indus worship method, we find the vessels positioned on the north, south and southwest of the fire-pits. It is true that many other pots were required in Vedic rituals, but only the "Pranita" had a specified positional dictate. On the other hand, specified positions were allotted to multiple, or at least two vessels if those sunken spots were as a result of placing the pots, as mentioned in the excavation report. This again, was in complete contrast with Vedic precept.

A hole for erecting poles were discovered on the northeast side of the fire-pits. Did any Vedic Yajna have such poles? The answer is "yes". We have studied about "Sadahsala", a canopy that was constructed on the west of the "Soumik Vedi" and contained six small Agnis called "Dhishnyas". On the backside of the Dhishnyas a strong and thick log of fig tree was entrenched in the ground, called "Udumvari". The Udgata and his assistants chanted "Samagana", touching this "Udumvari". This gave us the position of the Vedic post on the west of the Vedi. But the Harappan post was erected on the northeast.

Although, the outdoor Harappan fire-pits did not display any criterion of Vedic rituals, we may still consider the fire-pits of Block – G as a worshipping fire-pits and not an industrial furnace. It was established that the fire-pits were mostly found in the general areas and not in the citadel or upper town where the elite class resided. Only two fire-pits were found in Block-B that belonged to phase -IV period. But the presence of those two fire-pits was in congruence with the fact that during phase -IV, when Lothal was on the verge of decline, many ordinary Harappan citizens encroached upon the citadel area and constructed houses. The structures that housed those two fire-pits were most ordinary and too dilapidated to protect those fire-pits. Hence their actual shapes and dimensions of the two fire-pits remained unknown.

Chapter - 7

FIRE WORSHIP OF RAKHIGARHI

Following our study of Lothal, our next destination is Rakhigarhi. Unfortunately, the archaeological sites subsequent to Lothal did not present extensive details. They lacked comprehensive excavation reports. Our primary sources of information regarding these sites, such as Banawali, Kunal, and Rakhigarhi, were the "preliminary excavation reports",and the treatises and articles published on these excavation sites.

Rakhigarhi was located at a distance of 25 kilometers from the present Ghaggar River in Haryana. In ancient times, the river flowed alongside the settlement. On itsother side, the river Chautang flowed, serving as a tributary to the Ghaggar River. Prior to Indus footprint, those areas were inhabited by an indigenous planter community that belonged to chalcolithic era. They lived in the alluvial plain between the two rivers which is presently segmented as Anta, Morkhi, Beri Khera (Safidon tahsil) Balu (Narwana tahsil), Hatho, Rani Ran (Bata), Pahlwan, Dhakal (Narwana tahsil), Ritauli, (Safidon tahsil), Birbaraban, Barsana, Jind (Bir) Pauli, Karsola (Jind tahsil), etc. Subsequently, the soil-rich territory nestled between the two rivers attracted the Indus people, who conceived the creation of a grand city, (by the standards of their times). The excavations of these sites revealed the remnants of a city that extended across a vast expanse of 5.5 square kilometers.

175

At the RGR-1 excavation site, archaeologists unearthed artifacts dating back 5000 years. The natural topography of the area had a slope from west to east. Preceding the arrival of the Harappan civilization, the indigenous inhabitants opted to inhabit the elevated terrain, where they constructed circularhuts to shield themselves from floods. These circular dwellings left traces at multiple locations, including L 5, P 11, N 10, AX 1, X 5, Y 5, and A 5 cuttings.

Existence of such a house was discovered at the K 3 site, featuring structural support through both horizontal and vertical wooden logs using the wattle and daub building method. The vertical posts were extended to form a conical roof structure. In the courtyard of such a house at R 3 site, a round-shaped fire chamber, resembling a present-day Tandoor was found with a diameter of approximately 1 meter.

The earliest settlement of Rakhigarhi did not have a perimeter wall like the Harappans. In the preliminary excavation report, carbon dating for this period was recorded as 3640 BCE.

As observed in Lothal, the arrival of the Harappans in the Rakhigarhi plains did not lead to conflict. In the primary stage, the Harappans introduced their advanced measurement system with balances and weights, and engaged in barter trade as their primary mode of interaction with the indigenous population. Over time, they introduced essential civic amenities such as drainage systems, roads, and fortified water wells. This suggested that the Indus people had an excellentroadmap in place before they settled in the region.They constructed splendid courtyards, roads, drainage systems, wells, and designated workshops for their artisans. The organized arrangement of residences, granaries, and a fortified perimeter wall further underscored the meticulous planning of this city subsequently making it one of the most prominent Harappan settlements of the Indus civilization.The artifacts unearthed from the Rakhigarhi sites were of high quality, including exquisite beads, painted pottery, industrial kilns, weights, seals, ivory ornaments, conch-shell items, and toys. This thriving Harappan city endured damage byperiodic events of flood. The settlement, which lay under the RG-1 moundwas destroyed by a devastating flood that occurred between the pre-Harappan period and the inception of the mature Harappan stage. From the mature Harappan period onward, the city witnessed a persistent cycle of reconstruction and expansion.

In the course of analyzing the fire pits discovered at Rakhigarhi, it was essential to refer the initial excavation reports that provided a concise overview of those excavated sites. The reports did not include extensive information such as maps, illustrations, or detailed measurements and dimensions of the excavated structures. We may also lack the specific measurements of the fire pits, the dimensions of the bricks used, and information about the remaining implements.

The first fire pit was discovered at mound RGR-1, the most ancient settlement where the Harappans collaborated with the local inhabitants to commence their construction efforts. According to the report, this fire pit was shaped like a female reproductive organ (Yoni). In all probability, it was a round-shaped fire pit with a stoking passage/tunnel.The report said – *"In RGR-1, Yoni-Linga style fire altars have been noticed. It is circular and one end having oblong structure and in the centre of the structure, one linga type, which is more hard and most probably made out of Kankarise soil and it was destructed during collapse (of) the building"*.

The following picture of this fire pit depicts its structure (Pic 7.1).

Fig. 7.1 so called "vagina-shaped fire altar" which is actually a double-chamber updraft kiln with a pillar in the middle

(Courtesy: ASI)

This structure could be identified as a double-chamber updraft kiln with a peer-shaped configuration. Now we know that such kilns were widely popular throughout in Harappan Civilization, and numerous similar kilns were discovered at various archaeological sites. An almost identical kiln was found in Rakhigarhi (see pic 4.19), with minor alterations involving the placement of bricks at the place of the central stele.

The exact diameter of the fire pit at RGR -1 mound remained unknown. This particular fire pit was situated on anelevated platformand utilized as an open outdoor fire pitwith easy publicaccess. It was erected on aplatform of unspecified dimensions and located adjacent to a wall. We are acquainted with these peer-shaped fire pits and have also seen images of them in

178

previous chapters. Another double-chamber updraft kiln that was very similar to the so-called "Yoni-Linga style" fire pitofRakhigarhi was discovered at another place near Tarkhanwala, Rajasthan (see figure 7.2).

Fig. 7.2 A double-chamber updraft kiln with a central pillar (stele) at Tarkhanwala Dera (Courtesy: ASI)

The nextfire pit was also uncovered at the RGR-1 mound, situated on an elevated platform with public access. In the preliminary excavation report, it was described as *"anthropomorphic,"* signifying its human-like form (see Pic 7.3). This fire pit had a T-shaped design, with the shorter upper arm curving in a bow-like manner and extending in an east-west direction. Both ends of the arms were open. The longer third channel extended to the south and had an open end. Inside the fire chamber, a small stele made of clay and gravel was noticed.

179

According to the preliminary report, in the vicinity of these fire pits, there were four sacrificial chambers, located on those elevated platforms and used for animal sacrifices. Two of the chambers were on the south and westside of a fire pit, the smaller one measured 0.65 meter in length and 0.45 in width. Inside this chamber, bone fragments (of unknown animal) were found. Measurements of the other larger chambers were unknown but they revealed bones of sheep/goat, terracotta cakes, charcoal, pottery sherds and charred seeds. No detail was available on the two other chambers that were found on the second platform. We may presume that they were not much different in terms of shape, position and measurements from the former chambers. Let us tabulate the information we have gathered, so far: -

Table 7.1
Communal fire altars in RGR-1 Mound area

#	Period	Shape	Dimension	Inside the altars	Remarks
1		Pear shaped	Not known	There is a central stele or small pillar	Both the altars are located on a high platform. The small arm of the T-shaped altar is extended east-west direction and the end of the big arm is towards south
2	Pre Harappa	T shaped	Not known		

Animal sacrificial chambers found in the same area

#	Period	Shape	Dimension		Remarks
1		Rectangular	0.65m X 0.45m	bones of sheep/goat, terracotta cakes, charcoal, pottery sherds and charred seeds	Located at west and south of the fire altars of each platform
2	Pre Harappa	Rectangular	Not known		

180

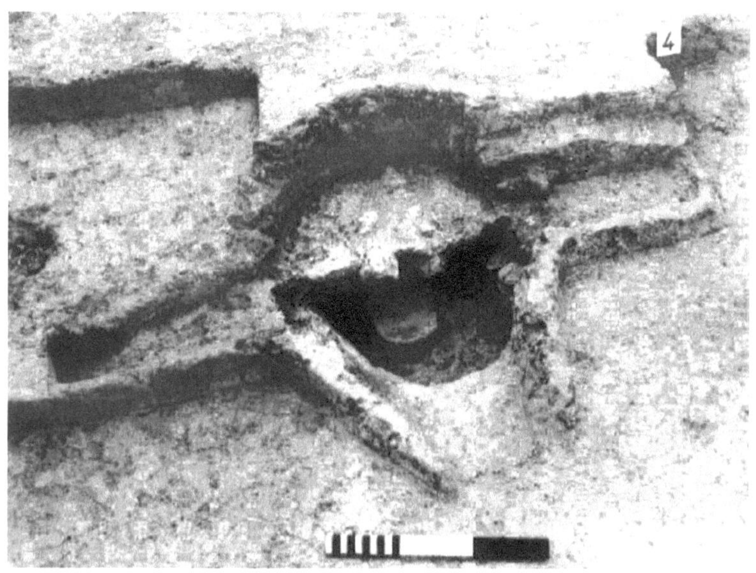

Fig. 7.3 'T' shaped fire altar of RGR-1 mound area (Courtesy: ASI)

In examining the fire pits of Rakhigarhi, we must once again focus on one aspect of the community- Yajnas of the Vedic practices. Multiple Agnis were invoked on the principal foundation which was the Maha Vedi or the Soumak Vedi. On the two platforms at RGR – 1 mound, we do not find the presence of such subsidiary Vedis thus ruling out the possibility of considering the platform as the Maha Vedi. First, the Vedic "Mahavedi" was a paved floor with a trapezium shape. Its eastern side (60 feet) was shorter than the western side (75 feet), even though they ran parallel to each other. The northern and southern sides were equal in length (90 feet), but not parallel. The shape was envisioned to resemble the torso of a male human figure, with one part of the Vedi being denoted as the "Angsa," and the other as the "Shroni," symbolizing the shoulder and waist. The measurements of the four sides were determined based on the body measurements of the "Yajman." These measurements were calculated using the unit of "Prakram," which amounted to approximately two and a half feet or thirty inches.

Secondly, oblatory rituals, in Vedic practices were performed with the Ahvaniya Agni. During community-Yajnas, an "Uttar Vedi" was constructed on the Maha Vedi and Agni was invoked from the fire of the Prachinavamsasala which then became the Ahavaniya Agni, appropriate for accepting offerings and at the same time the earlier Ahavaniya Agni of Prachinavamsasala changed to "Saladhwarya". The Ahavaniya Agni altar was square-shaped regardless of whether it was the original or invoked on Soumik Vedi.

In contrast, the two fire pits at RGR-1 mound were different – one was round-shaped, the other, "T"-shaped. The latter could not be identified as having anthropomorphic form. Its arms were not symmetric and one perpendicular side could not be accepted for two legs. The report went on to name it as "Vastu-Purusha" or "Chiti". In this context, we will refer our earlier study on the Agnicayan Yajna. The "Purusha" form of Yajna altar or "Chiti" was part of the Agnicayan rituals that, like the "Soma Yag", involved "Maha Vedi" or "Soumik Vedi". The three Agnis – "Garhapatya", "Ahavaniya" and "Dakshinagni" also accompanied the "Oistik Vedi" in Agnicayan Yajna, which was known as "Prachinavamsasala". Earlier, we learned that a few "Mandaps" (canopies) were made on the Vedi with the help of wooden poles. The one at the centre was called "Havirdhan Mandap" and another at the western side on the "Mahavedi" was called "Sadahshala" or "Sadogriha". In Agnicayan, on the eastern part of the Maha Vedi, a new Vedi was instituted replacing the Uttar Vedi, and Ahavaniya Agni was invoked at its centre. Among the various shapes (discussed earlier) of this Vedi, most popular were the Hawk form and the tortoise form. The only human forms of Vedis found were after two sages "Nachiketa" and Arunaketu". But whether they were one-legged as represented in one of the Rakhigarhi fire pits, raised doubts.

The "Chiti" was the process of construction of the Vedis where the brick levels were of religious significance. They had different names and measurements. A minimum of five levels were prescribed in the Vedas. But picture of the fire pit (7.3) clearly showed that it did not meet the Vedic specifications. All three edges of the "T" shape were rounded and displayed the signs of a peer-shaped double chamber kiln with its extended parts capable of accommodating multiple vessels leaving enough stoking passages to minimize fuel consumption. In the rural areas of Bengal boiling of Date juice for evaporation is done by such clay-ovens with multiple openings, sometimes holding eight vessels at a time while spaces created at the sides worked as flues.

The so-called sacrificial chambers found with the fire pits at RGR - 1 mound with ash, charcoal, potsherds and bone fragments called for some analysing too. A number of unanswered questions could be addressed if we consider those chambers, not as place of sacrifice but as a 'dumping place'! The two chambers, as can be seen from table 7.1, were located on the west and south sides of the fire pits. Vedic Yajna rituals never included two sacrificial spots at one Yajna site. Animal sacrifices and other violent acts were strictly prohibited within the Yajna area. Instead, a separate location known as the "Shamitra desh," located north (not west or south) of the "Pashuk" Vedi, was designated for such activities (pic 2.2). In our previous study, we examined a fire pit in Kalibangan (KLB-1) where the sacrificial spot for animals was situated to the southwest of the fire pit. We can be certain now, that the so-called sacrificial chambers were not related to Vedic rites. Furthermore, considering that the bone fragments found at most Harappan archaeological sites belonged to bovine species, it appears improbable that they could be sacrificed in a cell measuring only 0.65 meters (approx. 2 feet) in length and 0.45 meters (1.5 feet) in width. Even if we were to assume that the larger chambers were used for this purpose, the preliminary report would likely have mentioned it. Additionally, there was no evidence of any drainage systems that would be necessary to drain out the blood from the chambers. Table 7.1 also provided information about other remnants found inside these chambers, including charcoal, potsherds, and burnt seeds embedded in charcoal. While the presence of bones may support the idea of sacrificial rites, thepotsherds and charred seeds raised questions about their purpose within the chamber. The only answer was that the chambers were actually garbage dumps and the items found were disposed of as waste. The charcoal and seeds were probably the remains of agricultural waste and ordure used as fuel.

The other finds of RGR -1 mound included an excavated Harappan building at K5, L5 and J5 cuttings. It was quite large and had ten rooms surrounding an open courtyard. The preliminary report recorded it as a house but it is possible that the building was actually a Harappan factory. The comparatively smaller fourth room was square-shaped with its one wall 2.30 meters (7.6 feet) long. Two hearths and one T-shaped (anthropomorphic) fire-pit with a central stele was found inside the room. The first hearth was square-shaped and attached to the wall. The other was triangular, containing ash and terracotta cakes. The three extended channels of the third pit were open-ended. Its measurements were unavailable but it had the appearance of the peer-shaped double chamber kiln.

The archaeological excavation at the RGR-1 mound also unearthed a bead factory dating back to the mature Harappan period. In close proximity to the factory, a horseshoe-shaped furnace was also discovered, which was purportedly employed in the production of beads. Within the furnace, residual ash and terracotta cakes were found, and numerous Mustikas were scattered in the vicinity.

Table 7.2

Domestic altars in RGR -1 Mound

#	Period	Shape	Dimension	Inside the altars
1	T shaped	Not known	There was a central stele or small pillar	The Altar was found in a small room with two other hearths or furnaces

So far, we have examined the indoor Harappan fire pitsand thoroughlydiscussed the Vedic Garhasthya fire pits. We ascertained that the T-shaped fire pits were not associated with any Vedic rituals. Furthermore, another aspect of these fire pits supports this notion from a more general perspective.Consider a 7.6 feet square room containing three fire pits,onecircular, one square and one T-shaped. If one of those fire pits were used for worship while the other two remained blazing, it would hardly create the appropriate atmosphere for worshipping. We havestudied the differences between hearths/kilns and worshipping fire pits. The former were designed to hold vessels or containers and essentially equipped with provisions for fuelling, while the latter were enclosed from all sides except the top. All the excavated fire pits at RGR-1 mound had arrangements for stoking, and even the fire pits with public access had open sides. The two fire pits mentioned in table 7.1 had one or more side openings thatfundamentally contradict the principles associated with worshipping all-side-open fire pits and, by extension, Vedic fire altars. Further, the positions of the so-called (animal) sacrificial chambers and their contents did not comply with any Vedic tradition. One peer-shaped potter's kiln was found in Rakhigarhi that was reported as "conch-shaped".

The RGR-2 mound was an important public place for the Harappans. The presence of a large granary and all signs of a marketplace identified this site as a public square. In the vicinity, a few fire pits were discovered, situated on two raised platforms. The first platform was larger, measuring 22 meters by 12 meters. According to the report, two animal sacrificial chambers were found on top of that platform, though the report did not specify their exact locations. One of the chambers measured 2.40 meters in length and 1.50 meters in width, while the other was 1.80 meters in length and 1.20 meters in width. Both chambers contained charcoal and bone fragments.

In the northeast section of the RGR-2 mound, four fire pits were located on a raised platform. Archaeological reports identified these four fire pits as public worshipping places. They were placed side by side in a north-south direction, leaving a gap of 25 cm between them. They were rectangular in shape and measured 50 cm in length and 48 cm in width. All four had brick steles. At the center of the platform, an animal sacrificial chamber was found with dimensions of 1.70 meters by 1 meter by 0.80 meters in depth. Inside the chamber, bones of sheep/goat, charcoal, and potsherds were discovered.

At the same site, RGR-2, two indoor fire pits were discovered during the excavation of a Harappan house. The first fire pit was T-shaped, and the second, despite bearing similarities with the fire pit (depicted in pic 7.3) of RGR-1, was not identified as "anthropomorphic" and was recorded as *T-shaped with curved ends*. The report also mentioned another fire pit that was semi-circular, but no further details were available about these fire pits.

Table 7.3

Multiple fire-pits at RGR-2 Mound

S N	Period	Shape	Dimension	Inside the altars
1	Rectangular	0.50m X 0.48m	There is a central stele or small pillar	On a high platform, Four similar pits are located in a row.

Animal sacrificial chambers found in the same area

1	Rectangular	1.70m X 1m X 0.80m	bones of sheep/goat, terracotta cakes, charcoal, potsherds	Located at the centre of the platform

1	Rectangular	2.40m X 1.50m	Animal bone & charcoal	Two chambers on a platform
2	Rectangular	1.80 m X 1.20m		

Fig. 7.4 Four fire altars in RGR-2 Mound (Courtesy: ASI)

At this point, we have deduced the rationale for dismissing the possibility that those four altars of RGR -2 were associated with Vedic worship traditions. Vedic fire altars were consistently non-rectangular, regardless of whether they were employed for individual or community purposes. While some Vedic altars, such as the "Oistik Vedi," "Soumik Vedi," or the "Pashuk Vedi," may not strictly adhere to a square shape and instead appeared somewhat rectangular, those altars were not directly associated for invoking Agni. They served different ritualistic purposes.

The Indus fire pits, on the other hand did not align with these exceptions, as they were all ignited with fire for distinct purposes. The four identical altars discovered at the RGR-2 mound and placed in a series, could theoretically be linked to the Vedic "Soma

Yajna." But in the Soma Yajna, a "Sadahsala" was constructed on the west side of the "Mahavedi" or "Soumak Vedi," and a series of six smaller Vedis, each measuring 0.5 meters square and known as "Dhishnya," were constructed too. Nevertheless, there were only four fire pits at RGR-2, and those fire pits were both rectangular and larger in size.

None of these four fire pits yielded animal bone fragments, which were only found inside a chamber at the center of the raised platform that contained bones, charcoal, and potsherds and measured a mere 1.70 meters X 1 meter X 0.80 meter. It was more likely that the site may have functioned as a location for social festivities or, perhaps, as the kilns found in Kalibangan and Lothal for craftwork.

Furthermore, the fire pits' unusually close proximity, with gaps of only about 10 inches, gave the impression of either a community kitchen or collective workers' kilns, rather than a place of worship. All these fire pits contained steles, a distinct characteristic of double-chamber kilns. Similar cooking arrangements for communal use were also discovered in archaeological sites at Mohenjo Daro, as depicted in picture 7.5.

Fig. 7.5 cooking ovens in the open place at Mohenjo-daro

(Courtesy: ASI).

The assertion, that the sacrificial chambers could be waste disposal chambers was, in earlier occasion, compared on the basis of the preliminary excavation report that led to the dismissal of the notion of the structures in question being (animal) sacrificial chambers. Here, we have applied common sense in establishing them as unfit for sacrificial rites and instead appropriate as waste disposal chambers. We may further refer the related Vedic practice of waste disposal, mentioned in the chapter on Vedic Yajnas, in the context of "Soma Yaj" rituals. We have studied earlier that two pits "Chatwalak" and "Utkar" were dug on the northeast side of the "Mahavedi". "Utkar" was the waste disposal pit (Pic 2.2). So, there was indeed a specified waste disposal pit in Vedic Yajna where most of the disposable parts of the sacrificed animal, including blood were disposed. The chambers excavated at site RGR -1 were located on the west and south of the fire pits while the chambers at RGR -2 were at the center of the raised platforms. So, even being waste disposal chambers, they did not conform to their Vedic counterpart.

We will now turn our attention to the excavation site at RGR-6 mound. It is important to note that the excavation at this site followed the "Trench" method, meaning that the entire area was not completely unearthed. Instead, large trenches were dug to gain insight into the layout of the territory. Three such excavations were conducted using this method.

Evidence of human settlements dating back to the pre-Harappan period was discovered at this site. Among the findings were the most ancient round-shaped dwellings, signifying the site's long history of habitation. During the mature Harappan period, the site revealed a well-planned urban layout with organized roads and an advanced drainage system. A housing complex also was discovered, which consisted of seven Harappan houses. It was later transformed into a marketplace towards the end of the Mature Harappan period.

Unfortunately, RGR-4 could not be excavated due to its present religious significance, and the same applied to the present village of Rakhigarhi, located at the RGR-5 site, which also remained largely unexcavated. RGR-7, on the other hand, served as a burial ground, drawing relatively limited archaeological interest.

With these inputs from Rakhigarhi, we will now shift our focus to another intriguing archaeological site – Banawali.

## Chapter - 8

FIRE WORSHIP OF BANAWALI

Ancient Banawali was located in present day Fatehabad district of Haryana, on the bank of river Ghaggar. This was the same river that was called as "Saraswati" in Vedic era. Also, the archaeological site of Kalibangan was situated on the same river valley. Although a team led by Dr. Ravindra Singh Bisht undertook the excavation of this place in 1974 and it continued in subsequent years, a complete excavation report was never published. We need to rely on various articles and documents available from other resources in the academia.

For every archaeological site, evaluation of its phases is determined on by its historical and cultural span and its heritage. In Banawali, remnants from the pre-Harappan to Late-Harappan period was explored. Indus people settled in this area in 2500 BCE and according to Dr. Bisht they came from Kalibangan which was at a distance of only 120 Km. Kalibangan, around this time suffered a devastating earthquake. In the chapter on Kalibangan we learned about the earthquake that forced the Harappans to abandon their city. Pottery and other artifacts found at Banawali archaeological site supported the observation. It was also established from the findings that prior to the arrival of Harappans from nearby Kalibangan, a small settlement of indigenous inhabitants existed in Banawali. During this pre-Indus period, pottery made by those inhabitants bore designs by nail-marking on the lower surface of the pots and vessels. Pottery found during this period were similar to Fabric -A of Kalibangan. The same type of pottery were also found in the pre-Harappan archaeological sites in Baluchistan and Afghanistan *(Excavation of Banawali: 1974-77 By Dr. R. S. Bisht)*. Pre-Harappan (Kalibangan) culture existed in Banawali for about 200 years, from 2500 BCE to 2300 BCE.

Like other Harappan cities, Banawali also underwent historical and cultural evolution categorized by phases. The first settlers dwelled in an open colony without any fortification which was a primary feature of the Indus settlements. So, this period predating the inception of Harappan culture could be termed also as "pre-defence" phase. The populace, however, did not live without defence for long and they built a 1.40 thick wall encompassing their settlement. This period was labelled as "defence phase". But the wall did not last long and within a few years it began to tilt. They tried to prevent its fall by building supporting columns, but it did not work. Later it was replaced with Indus-style brick wall with thickness of 2.50 meters to 3.20 meters extending to 3.50 meters at some places. The bricks of the wall maintained a 1:2:3 ratio. This oval-shaped perimeter wall was protective for most of the settlement, except on the riverside. High-waters and alluvial soil erosion damaged its foundation, and subsequently it collapsed. Archaeologists found a moat alongside the wall. During the mature Harappan phase an Acropolis was built within the walled town. It was solidly built on higher ground in the upper town than the rest of the township (lower town). Besides the lanes and alleys in the residential areas, three major 5.5 meters wide roads were the major communication lines of the settlement. The average Harappan houses were large and spacious and generally had courtyards adjacent to a series of rooms. Some Harappan houses belonged to rich merchants, lapidarists or traders. Valuable etched carnelian and Lapis lazuli beads, seals and weights were found inside those houses. Hidden alcoves too, were found inside a house, probably used as a vault for safekeeping valuables. Only one figurine of a "Mother goddess" was retrieved from a Harappan house in Banawali. In contrast with other Indus township, Banawali did not have a centralized sewerage system. Every house had its own disposal zone and the waste water was drained out through soak jars. Following the mature Harappan period, the later Harappan phase lasted till 1400 BCE before it suffered a rapid decline.

Another interesting aspect of the excavation was the recovery of multiple hearths, domestic ovens and fire pits from one single house. The fire pits were round-shaped but of different sizes. They were dug underground and paved with clay-bricks the interior of the fire pits were plastered with mud. Inside the fire pits, blueish ash and charred grains were found. The floors of the house were burnt red due to excessive heat generated by those pits. But the interior walls of fire pits bore no sign of firing. Dr. Bisht wrote, *"Most of these pits yield fine bluish ash, occasionally mixed with charred grains; although the pits themselves show no sign of firing. These might be the storage silos or bins. The paucity or near absence of large storage jars lends further credence to this surmise."* (Excavations at Banwali: 1974-77 by Dr. R S Bisht)

The possibility of those fire-pits being worshipping fire pits, was ruled out. Instead, as Dr Bisht wrote: "Surely, *it should be a workshop, plausibly that of a metalsmith."*, they may have been storage silos or bins to collect charcoal and ash.

We may also relate those fire pits and the bluish ash with the hearths found at KLB -2 mound and the associated fire-pits in the vicinity. The bluish ash, of course indicated the presence of copper derivatives. Famous archaeologist Jonathan M Kenoyer wrote in his essay *(Metal Technology of the Indus Valley tradition in Pakistan and Western India: Kenoyer et all)* on the subject that the copper ingots found around the hearths clearly made them furnaces for metal related works. Another Harappan building housed two fire pits, probably for similar purpose.

In the citadel area, a square-shaped fire pit was found inside a house. *"Another dig in the citadel has yielded interesting walls, in the shape of a cross apparently belonging to a house. But certain short and thin walls, with hardly a thickness of 8 cm and height of 16 to 24 cm, radiate from the central point of the cross. One of these thin walls makes a triangle, albeit truncated at the apex, by*

The square fire pit was dug at that spot and a vessel buried half in the ground was found beside it. A conical earthen stele (similar to Kalibanganfire pits) was erected inside the fire pit. Similar fire pit with the conical stele was found from a neighbouring Harappan house where it was located behind the kitchen. The measurement of those fire pits were unknown. If at all they were worshipping fire pits, they must be for domestic use. According to Dr. Bisht, they were household fire places and had no resemblance with the Vedic Grihya Agni or the Smartya Agni. The Vedic Grihya Agni was generally round-shaped with a 74 cm diameter. But the fire pits of Banawali was square-shaped and they had conic steles inside. In rare cases the Grihya Agni could be square-shaped but would never have any type of pillar inside its fire chamber. Undoubtedly, the fire pits of Banawali were double chamber updraft kilns which were attached to a dish with perforations creating a suspended plane. The conical stele fitted into the hole at the center of the dish provided stability for the combustion and firing chambers. Another important aspect of those two fire pits were their positions. Either, they were adjacent to one of the intersecting walls or at the corner of their intersection. Worshipping fire pits never occupied such position. In the chapter on Indus furnaces, we learned about similar kilns positioned between intersecting walls at Hulas and Harappa. The materials found at the spots confirmed the nature of the fire pits as kilns, and the walls had specific purposes. Banawali was no exception and its fire pits were industrial kilns.

Table 8.1

firepits at Banawali

#	Shape	Dimension	Objects found inside the altars	Remarks
1	Square	Not known	Conical stele	Domestic
2	Semicircular	Approx. 6m dia	Round pillar like stele	Community

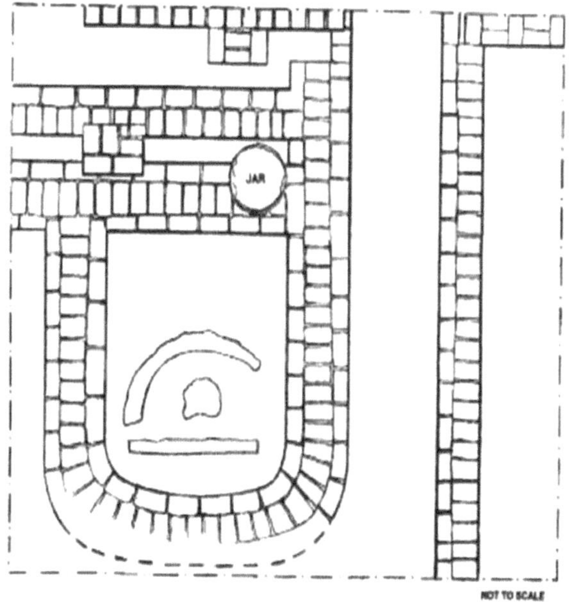

*Fig. 8.1 Plan of the apsidal temple at Banawali and its fire pit
(Courtesy: ASI)*

One great discovery at Banawali excavation site was the apsidal temple that housed a semi-circular fire pit (pic 8.2). Before we go into the description of the apsidal temple of Banawali, we need to know a few things about apsidal temple. An apsidal temple, also known as apse temple, is a type of religious or architectural structure characterized by having a semi-circular or apse-shaped design at the rear end of a hall. The apse is a curved or semi-circular recess, typically with a domed or vaulted ceiling. Such architecture is found in some Buddhist temples and Christian churches. The Durga temple of Aihol, Karnataka is one such apsidal temple. During another excavation at Sonkh near Mathura, a multi-temple urban complex was found dating to 1st and 2nd century CE. Most are apsidal temples on raised platforms. Contemporary temple structures were also found at Vidisha and Nagari, Chittorgarh. The Banawali Apsidal structure may be the forerunner of subsequent apsidal sanctums constructed in the subcontinent. The worshipping fire pit inside the Banawali apsidal hall was also semi-circular. The structure was considered to have constructed by local Harappan architects for worshipping purpose. This Apsidal temple and the associated fire pit were unique in themselves as no other such worshipping hall or semi-circular fire pit was found anywhere in the Indus archaeological sites. Measurement of this fire pit could not be ascertained but it also had a small vertical pillar structure inside. *"At Banawali, District Fatehabad, Haryana, in the Harappan levels, a structure having an apse was found which has a circular terracotta stump impression in the centre and some ash. This could have been a fire temple"*. *(Joshi: 2020)*

Some ash was found inside the fire pit and it was perceived that since the fire pit was found inside a temple-like Hall, it was used for social activities that could be compared with the Vedic Shrauta Agni. From the picture (pic 8.2), the fire pit's diameter could be determined as 2 meter or 6 feet. In Vedic Yajna, only the Dakshinagni took a semi-circular shape and stood between Ahavaniya Agni and Garhapatya Agni. Garhapatya Agni, Oistik Vedi and Ahavaniya Agni were placed along the east-west axis.

Dakshinagni position was south of this axis and also south of Garhapatya Agni and the Oistik Vedi. All these three Agnis measured one "Aratni (measure of the elbow to small finger of the Yajman or religious host)". Which was approximately 1.5 feet or 0.5 meter. By that standard, the semi-circular fire pit of Banawali was much larger in size than the Dakshinagni. Besides, there was no provision for a stele or pillar structure inside the Dakshinagni altar, that was present in the semi-circular fire pit and other fire pits found at Banawali. Existence of a long (water) cistern like structure behind the fire pit and the stele inside defined it as a furnace or kiln. But we will give this fire pit, the benefit of doubt because of its surroundings and the social aspect.

Figure 8.2 The apsidal temple at Banawali and its fire pit

(Courtesy: ASI)

197

Chapter - 9

FIRE WORSHIP OF KUNAL

The Kunal archaeological site, recognized by archaeologists as one of the oldest pre-Harappan settlements, was a notable fixture on the Indus map since its initial excavation in 1992-93. Over the course of several successive excavation efforts, running until 2019(1992-93, 1996-97, 1998-99, 1999-2000, 2001-2002, 2002-2003, 2016-17, 2017-18, 2018- 19), the site unveiled three successive phases of pre-Harappan indigenous culture in the plains of the Ghaggar (Saraswati) River. Carbon dating of the site has indicated that this Indus settlement dated back to as early as 6000 BCE, making it around 8000 years old.

The excavation process at Kunal involved the use of the trench method, in which artifacts were carefully unearthed from extended trenches. Regrettably, a comprehensive archaeological report on Kunal is yet to be published. Our exploration of the site relied on resources provided by articles, journals, the archaeological archives of Haryana, and assistance from the concerned departments.

During the first phase of Kunal's history, the indigenous inhabitants fashioned makeshift houses and erected canopy-like shelters over quarried ground. Some of these pits measured approximately 2 meters in diameter and featured mud walls supported by wooden posts. They employed the "wattle and daub" construction technique, connecting together wooden strips to create a lattice or framework. These strips were surely crafted from local plants available in and around the site. The conical wattle structure formed the framework for the walls, with the spaces between the woven wooden strips filled with a mixture of mud, clay, straw, and other organic materials known as "daub." The resulting houses had conical roofs, reminiscent of a teardrop shape. Similar structures that were discovered at Rakhigarhi.

In this pre-Harappan phase, the indigenous inhabitants were already skilled in making pottery, chert blades, and fishing-hooks. It wasn't until around 3300 BCE that Indus influences began to impact their way of life and skills, and they adopted the features from Harappan craftsmanship. This period also saw the introduction of Hakra Ware pottery. Additionally, they were involved in the production of fired and sun-dried bricks, adhering to the typical Harappan ratio of 1:2:3 for brick measurements. They switched over to brick floored houses by laying bricks over the pits they dug for clay and soil, usually selecting pits more than three meters in diameter.

Indus seals made of steatite, with geometric inscriptions were found in this phase. The third and the last phase was the pre-Harappan period when the Harappan bricks changed their ratio to 1:2:4 and they built more planned houses with roads and sewerage system and sullage jars/soaking jars.

At the archaeological site of Kunal, a fire pit of substantial sizecouldbe partially excavated due to the limitations of the trench method (See sketch, pic 9.1). Two-fifths of this massive fire pit remained buried in the ground. It had a diameter of at least 4.5 meters. The mud plastered interiorwas built with fired or sun-dried bricks. The shape of this fire pit resembled a funnel, gradually going narrower at the bottom from the top. It was determined to be round-shaped. Residual ash and unidentified animal bone fragments were discovered inside the fire pit.

Our knowledge about this unique and intriguing fire pit remained limited as it was not fully exposed. The concealed part may unveil significant features such as a stoke-hole for the supply of fuel, the existence of a central stele, and other residual elements like copper slag etc. This would promptly associate the great fire pit with an industrial furnace or kiln rather than a worship fire pit. The presence of the bones also remained inconclusive, as they are yet to undergo forensic investigation, radiocarbon dating, and other examinations.Presently, opinions differ as regards to their presence. They may have been offerings made by Harappans, or it was also possible that the bones ended up inside the fire pit naturally, carried by water and gravity. The size of the fire pitwas a key factor in the debate over whether it was used for worship or social rituals. On the other hand, the tunneling of the fire pit with decreasing width shaping it like a funnel indicated some other purpose than merely generating fire.

The rationale against the fire pit being related to Vedic Yajna is grounded in the fact that a fire pit of such immense size, with a diameter of 4.5 meters, was never utilized in any Vedic Yajna. In the Shrauta Yajna, the Maha Vedi featured another Vedi known as the Uttar Vedi, and the Ahavaniya Agni was invoked at the center or navel area of the Uttar Vedi. The Ahavaniya Agni itself was square in shape and measured one "Aratni" in size, which was approximately 1.5 feet or 0.5 meters. The Dhishnyas (which could be either round or square) — altars placed on the Uttar Vedi — measured from 36 cm to 48 cm (1.25 feet to 1.5 feet). The Garhapatya Agni, while round in shape, was never isolated and was always accompanied by the Oistic Vedi, Ahavaniya Agni, and the Dakshinagni. The Garhapatya Agni altar was approximately 0.5 meters in size. Finally, the Grihya Agni which was round or square had 74 cm sides or diameter.

Therefore, no plausible comparison can be made between the Vedic altars and the large circular fire pit at Kunal, as it significantly exceeded the size of any of the known Vedic fire pit.

Figure 9.1 Sketch of Kunal fire pit (Courtesy: Department of Archeology and Museums, Haryana)

Chapter - 10

NAGESHWAR, VAGAD AND BINJOR

There existed two relatively small Indus settlements (now archaeological sites) Nageshwar and Vagad in the Indian state of Gujarat where Indus fire-pits were found and another place Binjor 4MSR, in Rajasthan.

The discovery of Nageshwar on the southern shore of the Gulf of Kutch, at Jamnagar district in Gujarat revealed valuable new information about the expansion of the Harappan civilization in that area. The present archaeological site is located next to a freshwater reservoir called Bhimgaja Talao,connected to an ancient temple of Nageshwar Mahadeva, a Hindu god. The temple is approximately 17 kilometers northeast of the Dwarka-Gopi bus route.During excavations at this site, the focus was on removing soft organic soil for building a dam, which left behind large collections of pottery fragments, shell pieces, grinding stones, and stone foundations in their original positions. This unique situation allowed researchers to study important architectural features.

In Nageshwar, a small Harappan settlement flourished during the mature Harappan period i.e., from 2450 BCE to 1900 BCE in. The settlement was centered on the Harappan conch-shell artistry and its inhabitants were primarily skilled artisans. The tiny Indus community engaged in extracting marine shell from the seabed and crafting shell objects. Those artisans produced many different decorative as well as useful objects using different kinds of shells. In fact, shell objects enjoyed a special status in Harappan society and traditions and also considered as something "magical" by the Indus people. Archeologists found a fire-pit in this Harappan industrial settlement. It was round-shaped with one side open where a long duct, that renowned archaeologist J P Joshi identified as "Pranala" or a channel to dispose waste water from the worshipping place. A conical stele was erected inside the fire-pits whose bottom was of 90 cm diameter. The diameter of the open end of the fire-pit was 165 cm and it was 65 cm deep. The duct channel measured 120 cm in length. Only some ash was found inside the pit.

During excavation of Nageshwar, shell objects, weights, copper objects, triangular cakes and potsherds were recovered amidst the remains of the settlement. Many bone fragments, found at the site gave archaeologists an idea of Harappan eating habits.

Table 10.1

Fire pit at Nageshwar

#	Shape	Dimension	Objects found inside the altars	Remarks
1	Pear shaped	Dia of the round portion is 165 cm	Inside the Altar there is a conical stele with a bottom diameter of 90 cm	One side of the circular portion is open and there is a duct of 120 cm long and 50 cm wide.

Many Historians and archaeologists declared the fire-pit of Nageshwar as an industrial kiln. The open side was an inlet for supplying fuel-wood and stoking. A worshipping fire-pit is closed from its sides as it is not used for heating purpose. The fire-pit of Nageshwar was a peer shaped double chamber updraft kiln about which we have studied earlier.

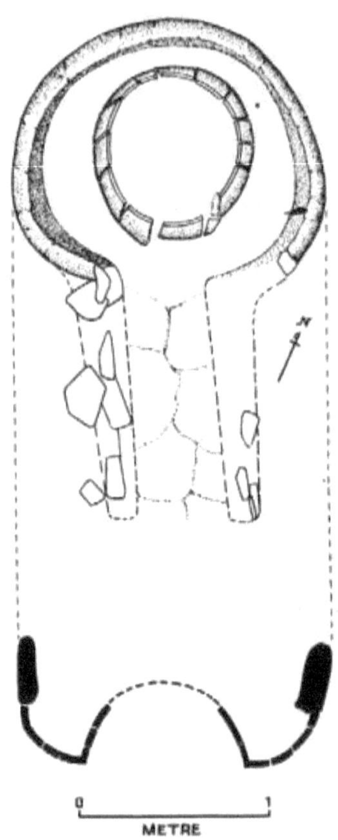

Fig. 10.1 Fire pit (pear-shaped furnace) at Nageswar

(Courtesy: ASI)

Archaeological site, Vagad is also located in Gujarat in the district of Ahmedabad. It was a hamlet of the Harappans that existed during mature and later phase of Indus Valley Civilization. Here, four fire-pits were restored from one Harappan house. Besides the fire-pits, terracotta objects and stone weights were found inside the house. One type of popular Harappan terracotta ear ornament found inside the house. It was a pulley shaped delicate adornment, wide at two ends with a narrower central part. Several such terracotta ear- studs were found in the house. In addition, partially ground celt (tool), and potteries were also discovered from the house.

The four fire-pits were located on a courtyard attached to the Harappan house. Three of them positioned in the north, south and west direction made a triangle while the fourth pit was between the north and west side pits inside the imagined triangular area. The three fire-pits (forming the triangle) were placed at a distance of 90 cm from each other and they had diameters of 1 meter, 1.45 meters and 1.20 meters respectively. The fourth fire-pit was conical in shape having a diameter of 40 cm to its circular top. The depth of those fire-pits could not be ascertained. There was one odd aspect that made the archaeologists curious. The interior walls of all the fire-pits were plastered with clay and cow-dung. A related report read: - *"All of them were internally neatly plastered with cow-dung paste mixed with fine clay. These pits contained ash, possibly of cow-dung cakes - J P Joshi"*

Table 10.2

Fire pits at Vagad

#	Shape	Dimension	Objects found inside the altars	Remarks
1	Round	1 m dia	Ash	Interior of the pits were plastered with cow dung and no trace of charcoal or charred bone was found
2	Round	1.45 m dia	Ash	
3	Round	1.20 m dia	Ash	
4	Cylindrical	0.40 m dia	Ash	

The odd aspect was that, no charcoal was found in any of the fire-pits and the interior walls did not show any signs of being exposed to fire. Those unique fire-pits of Vagad, occupying the vertices of a triangle and round in shape (except the fourth) were compared with Vedic Garhasthya Agni by some historians. Now, the Vedic Garhasthya Agni or Smarttya Agni was round or square in shape. They had a diameter (or sides) of 74 cm. None of those three round-shaped fires-pits followed this principle. One more curious point was the cow-dung plastering which was never appropriate for interior plastering of any firing chamber. Interior plastering of such fire chambers was usually done with heat resistant materials only and not with something inflammable. Cow-dung plastering is a practice in rural areas in India on the exterior of the hearths and also for earthen floors, in order to strengthen them and keeping them clean. But, inside those fire-pits of Banawali, cow-dung would easily have been burnt and loosen the clay wall and we could not have found any trace of cow dung in the interior of the used fire pit. So, we may conclude that those pits were never meant for kindling fire. The fourth fire-pit could be excluded from consideration as a firing device because of its very shape. Closed from all sides, it is quite impossible to ignite fire inside those deep dug pits as inadequate supply of oxygen would prevent any such effort. One cylindrical fire-pit was found in Harappa. But it had provision for supply of oxygen at the bottom as well as smoke exit flues. That leaves us with only one explanation. Those pits were storage silos or bins, as explained by Dr. R S Bisht on the subject of fire-pits excavated at Banawali. The ash found in the pits were reported as fine burnt cow-dung cake-ash without any clumps. The use of cow dung cake ash, for polishing/grinding stone-beads, tools, metal objects and ornaments has been traditional since ancient times. The half-ground celt found in the house explains the existence of the silos with cow dung cake ash. Ash was used by the Harappan as a major cleaning agent and also as a material to control heat. So, its storage was probably in order with its utility. Finally, the presence of four fire-pits in one single room strongly negated the possibility of any worshipping activity taking place there.

The Binjor 4MSR archaeological site is in the district of Sri Ganganagar, Rajasthan. A fire-pit was excavated there (Pic 10.2). It had a pillar-like structure with octagonal shape at the center of the altar. Some historians described this fire-pits as an ancestor of Vedic Yajna fire-pits and the pillar as 'yasti": *A remarkable discovery is the octoganal brick which is a yaṣṭi.in a fire-altar of*

Figure 10.2 Binjore 4MSR Fire Altar (double-chamber updraft kiln)
(Courtesy: ASI)

In previous discussions, we studied that Vedic Yajna kundasdid not permit any additional structure within their fire chambers. The primary purpose of the Yajna fire-pit was to kindle fire, not generation of heat. Besides, many historians made reference to the Vedic YupaKashtha or Yasti, the timber post which was used to tie the sacrificial animal. In the Vedic tradition, the "Yupa" was typically made of wood, not stone or terracotta and the "Yupakashtha" was positioned outside the Yajna fire-pits, not inside it. But in the case of the fire-pits at Binjor, a small octagonal pillar was constructed using terracotta. It served as a central stele for supporting a suspended floor, consistent with the features of a double-chamber updraft kiln. The broken suspended floor was clearly visible (see Pic 10.2). Several industrial kilns were discovered at the Binjor 4MSR archaeological site, indicating that the location was an important industrial township during the Harappan period.

Chapter - 11

MYSTERY UNRAVELED

R eaders are now acquainted with the physical characteristics and their utilities of the Harappan fire-pits that were associated with worship or industry of the Harappans. It was worth noting that all of those Harappan fire pits were not exclusively used for religious or worship purposes. Only some of them, particularly the open, outdoor fire-pits found at KLB-3 in Kalibangan, displayed distinct signs of collective ritualistic activities.

Several significant aspects came to light during our examination of the Harappan fire pits. The majority of them featured a central pillar or stele constructed from fired bricks and clay filler. Their function was centered on a "double chamber updraft technology," which emphasized the heat generated within the combustion chamber and the firing chambers rather than just burning of fire. A grate or suspended floor, supported by this central pillar (or stele), held the objects for firing, preventing their direct contact with the flames. This particular characteristic of the Harappan fire-pits led archaeologists and historians to surmise that they were, in fact, industrial kilns rather than religious altars. Famous anthropologist and historian Heather M. L. Miller offered clarity over this perplexing aspect of Harappan fire-pits. He wrote: - *"For example, a group of structures found at numerous Indus sites are all described as shallow ovate pits (ranging from 0.35 to 1 m in length), showing traces of firing, with a cylindrical or rectangular block/pillar in the centre (sometimes made from a single brick coated with clay), and usually containing terracotta cakes or lumps as well as ash and charcoal fragments. These apparently identical structures are variously interpreted as ritual "fire altars" at Kalibangan (Lal 1979:77; Thapar 1973:101), as "cooking hearths/ovens" at Harappa (Meadow & Kenoyar in press), and as "fire-pits" related to domestic use (but also compared to pottery kilns) at Naushero (C. Jarriage 1994:288)"*

Our examination of the fire chambers at Kalibangan, Lothal, and Banawali primarily relied on excavation reports. We explored the potential significance of these fire pits as fire altars and their possible links with their Vedic counterparts. Thereafter, we carefully analyzed the available information to determine whether they supported or contradicted the prevailing premises. We did not face difficulties in separating the fire-pits/kilns from the ritualistic altars/Yajna kundas.

In this concluding part of our study, we must accentuate the ritualistic precepts of Vedic Yajna practices in the context of the fire-pits/kilns/furnaces of the Indus people and obtain a relative assessment. We must be able to independently draw inference from available information that may be available in future, justifiably comparing them with the established Vedic principles. It is imperative to refrain from making hasty judgments based on selective conjecture while interpreting the findings. For instance, one might assume that since all five fire-pits of Kalibangan (KLB-1) faced east, which held significance in Vedic rituals, those fire-pits must be linked to Vedic practices. Such an inference would be a speculative leap without supporting evidence to justify the claim. We need to accept that the Harappans might have chosen an east-facing orientation for simple reasons related to the natural phenomena of the sunrise and moonrise. Even Paleolithic people positioned their deceased with their heads facing east. Furthermore, not all fire-pits at Kalibangan conform to this east-facing arrangement. Additionally, the construction of a drain that required demolishing of two assumed fire-altars and its passing through those functional altars raisedserious question as being odd against a backdrop of a supposedly religious atmosphere. Alternatively, we have seen such infrastructure with the industrial kilns found in many archaeological sites like Lothal, Karsola and Mithathal.

Certain historians alluded to the presence of charred cereal or fruit-seeds, accompanied by ash and charcoal inside some pits, suggesting that those might be residual offerings (Ahuti) as seen in Vedic Yajna rites. We must acknowledge that not all Harappan fire pits, which are definitively known to have been used for worship, exhibited such trend. Moreover, undigested seeds are commonly found in dung of the domestic animals. Agricultural waste could also contain these seeds. In this particular instance, the strong possibility of these seeds being transported through the use of cow dung or agricultural waste as fuel was apparently ruled out. We, however do not intend to completely dismiss any aspect connected with worshipping components within the Indus civilization. In Kalibangan, Lothal, and Banawali, we have identified certain pits that satisfy the criteria for being regarded as sacred worshipping altars or Agni fire-pits.

The common denomination among all the Indus archaeological sites is the antiquity of the settlements, with their origins predating the arrival of the mainstream Indus people. Settlements sustained from later neolithic age already existed in Kalibangan, Lothal, Kunal, Banawali, and Rakhigarhi long before the arrival of the Indus merchants in the regions. Remarkably, there was no conflict when the Harappans subsequently settled in those areas and introduced their culture.The indigenous and Indus cultures and traditions seamlessly blended, creating an extraordinary fusion that thrived in perfect harmony. In the Ghaggar-Chautang river delta. The Sothi-Siswal culture was one of those regional cultures that left their distinctive impressions which the historian called "Phase". The influence of those phases can be noticed in the Fabric – A potteries of Kalibangan. There were other regionalization phases like Ravi, Hakra, Amri, Nal, Kot Diji. Etc. During the late stage of the Indus civilization, cultures like Cemetery H, Jhukar phase and Pirak also influenced contemporary Indus crafts. People who belonged to those phases and cultures had origins traced back to the Microlithic and Neolithic period.

Connecting the dots between the Neolithic Age and the advent of the Indus Civilization at the beginning of the Chalcolithic Age, the name of Mehrgarh inevitably emerged as a crucial link in the genesis and further progress of the Indus culture, which subsequently spread across distant regions of the Indian subcontinent. Mehergarh, located at present-day Baluchistan in Pakistan, served as an essential archaeological site and provided insights into the transition from early agricultural practices to the development of urban centers and complex civilization. This transition marked a significant step towards the rise of the Indus Valley Civilization and its expansion to other parts of the region. Many hitherto unknown facts about the great Indus valley civilization and myriads of fresh insights kept being integrated with our existing understanding, prompting us to believe that the immense nurturing and "gardening" of this complex transition did not happen overnight. It was the result of various seeds of beliefs and faiths, cults, cultures and traditions that developed and left their impressions in the societies' rites, rituals as well as infrastructures and artifacts.

The Kachhi plains near Mehergarh was not far from Iran. The river Bolan contributed to its fertility. Harvesting was easy. The Bolan Pass in proximity with its traffic of faraway travelers and seasoned traders made the place attractive to some indigenous hunters-gatherers. So, 9000 (7000 BCE) ago, those foragers settled in the area (later came to be known as modern Mehrgarh) and engaged in animal farming, agriculture as well as handicrafts like weaving baskets and making ornaments and figurines. Study on their figurines and burial indicated presence of faith and ritual in that society. On the eastern side of the civilization, the tract covering present day Gujarat, Rajasthan and Haryana were also not uninhabited. In Kalibangan, Lothal, Kunal and Banawali, settlements of indigenous inhabitants existed even before the pre-Harappan era. Remnants of paleolithic people were found at Puskar, Didwana, Tilwara, Baghar, Kota, Luni River basin,

Chittorgarh (Gambhir riverside), Negarai (Berach riverside), Mewar (Wagon and ḷ riverside), Mogra hill area (near Jodhpur) in Rajasthan, The Indian state of Gujarat too, had its share – a few places beside Sabarmati and Mahi rivers, Bhandarpur (beside Orsong river), Bhadar and Narbada River basins (Sundari creek) bore signs of paleolithic existence of the human race. Amidst the Aravali ranges in lower Haryana, near the fringes of Indus settlements a series of sites have recently been discovered. In 1991, an archaeological site was excavated at Anangapur in Faridabad district of Haryana where many paleolithic tools were found.Such artifacts continued to surface in Delhi and adjacent Haryana. Those precious artifacts were destroyed on a regular basis by rapid urbanization and human activities in these busy cities.

According to an archaeological survey conducted by D. K. Chakravarty and Nayanjyot Lahiri in 1985-86, a total of 43 archaeological sites of paleolithic era were identified in Delhi and Haryana. In recent times, another big archaeological site has been identified in the vast hilly area of Aravali range, adjacent to villages like Kot, Manger in Haryana. The author worked with them in three phases and found numerous petroglyphs, cupules and about 35/40 tools. "In Western India, microlithic sites of all kinds abound everywhere except in the most arid central parts of the desert. As in the peninsular India, they take the form of small camping places, semi-permanent settlements and multi-activity sites, usually on old fixed dunes or small hills; and quite large factory sites to which nodules of chert and agate must have been carried many kilometers from their sources. The brilliant colors and delicate workmanship tell us that the stones were heat-treated' (*Origins of a Civilization: The Prehistory and Early Archaeology of South Asia by F. R. Allchin & Bridget Allchin*). This Harappan attribute of heating stone to impart color and hardness was discussed in the chapter on their kilns and crafts.

When early humans first learned to stand on two feet, they looked skyward as if the origins of all natural powers lay above. From the very first sunbeam to the gentle touch of moonlight, and from the life-giving rain to the thunderous storms, they saw the sky as the source of these awe-inspiring forces. Fire, to them, represented a transcendent energy, a conqueror of the most fearsome beasts and the ultimate victor over powerful adversaries with its devastating might. At that time, we see that all over the world, animism pervaded their belief system, a deeply-held conviction that all living creatures, inanimate objects, and natural elements possessed a spiritual essence or soul.

Humans felt a profound desire to appease those seemingly formidable forces, ensuring the safety and prosperity of both individuals and their communities. According to social scientists, early humans sought to establish connections with the inanimate and lifeless entities, drawing lessons from the living that ended upon death. Over time, they harnessed the power of fire, deeming it the most potent weapon against external threats.Despite their apprehension regarding the destructive potential of fire, they sought solace in its warmth amid harsh cold and protection from the dangers posed by wild beasts.With the assurance of safety it provided, fire gradually obliterated fear and insecurity from the human psyche. It came to be regarded as a divine gift, a belief that resonated universally, as fire was seen as a heavenly or celestial bestowal from the sky as lightning struck and created devastating wildfire.

Early humans recognized the need to control fire and ultimately itwas harnessed. They strived to keep it burning continuously through the nights. This responsibility primarily fell upon those who did not venture out for hunting – the womenfolk, especially the pregnant and mothers. In the course of ensuring an unceasing fire, they unwittingly inaugurated another groundbreaking source of sustenance – agriculture. It was as if the fire had embraced fertility within its realm. While the women gathered fruits and cereals during their foraging, the seeds often found fertile ground to disperse and grow, germinated by rainfall. The early humans comprehended the significance of this phenomenon and embraced farming as a means to secure a consistent food supply. The transition to farming represented a shift from a nomadic, hunter-gatherer way of life to a more settled one. The concept of family was developed inside of the community. Inter-family and intra-family mutual support and protection brought principles of generational hierarchy, property ownership and inheritance over the years.Sustaining the firewas of paramount significance, representing the most sacred duty that transcended through generations and retained a permanent place in all religious convictions.The supreme sanctity of fire was a recurring theme in the Vedas, underscoring its profound significance. Furthermore, not only in Vedic traditions but also among the Zarathustrians, as well as within the Sintashta and Andronovo cultures of the Bronze Age and among the Greeks, Romans, ancient Judaism and Christianity we observe a comparable fervor for the veneration of fire.

Our study has advanced smoothly in the context of nature worship, in which fire played a significant role. Nature worship has found its place in the fields of history, social science, and anthropology. Fire worship was widely practiced and popular in various parts of the world. The examination of Indus archaeological sites not only revealed distinct remnants of pre-Harappan times but also affirmed a strong cultural assimilation. This was evident in contemporary pottery, artwork and the use of agate/chert tools (the microlithic method of firing stone before shaping it into a blade persisted into the Harappan era). Similarly, the religious beliefs and worship practices of entities dating back to the period before the pre-Harappan era certainly influenced the people of the Indus region.

Throughout history, we have seen blending of such cultural traits, where the distinctive features of ethnic ideas, beliefs, and religions have remained prominent despite the passage of time. Therefore, the notion of an ancient tradition of fire worship existing alongside the Harappan culture did not seem implausible.

Now, let us focus on one of the most intriguing aspects of Indus worship – the offering of terracotta cakes, particularly the triangular terracotta cakes. This seemingly unassuming object of Harappan oblation has deep-rooted anthropological implications.

We have encountered the use of terracotta cakes for controlling the heat of the Indus furnaces and kilns. We also discussed four types of terracotta cakes. The presence of these cakes was also found in the open fire-pitss (as in KLB-3) dedicated to worshipping purposes. The triangular cakes drew special attention as they were extensively found in the worshipping fire-pitss. It interests us to reason, why a craft-related item would be placed in a worshipping fire and not used as fuel or kiln-settler! There is only one answer to this question: the triangular cakes were objects of oblation in Indus traditions.We have previously learned about the discovery of a triangular cake at a Kalibangan excavation site, featuring religious and ritualistic engravings. On one side, there was a depiction of an animal being pulled in by a rope fastened around its neck. On the other side, there was an image of a deity seated in the lotus position, adorned with a horned headdress. This cake served to bridge Harappan worship traditions with animal sacrifice. These depictions of horned deities were uncovered at various Harappan excavation sites. Engraved triangular cakes strongly suggested that such cakes were the objects of worship for the Harappans. Some historians speculated that the representation on the terracotta cake was the Harappans' visual interpretation of their ritualistic animal sacrifices. The interconnection of the deity with a horned headdress, the triangular cake, and the depiction of animal sacrifice made it clear that these common terracotta triangular cakes held great significance in Harappan worshipping practices. Many historians noticed signs of Harappan worship or religious rituals with this artifact. *"The mushtika and the triangular terracotta cakes have mostly been associated with rituals. From the early sixties the terracotta cakes were supposed to have been used in the performance of 'fire altar' rituals during the mature Harappan period as at Kalibangan (IAR, 1962-63: 30)"*. Later, the presence of terracotta cakes, ash and the cylindrical blocks in fire places were reckoned as the usual contents of 'fire altars' (IAR, 1968-69: 31). Sankalia (1974: 350) also mentions that 'in the center of the pit was a cylindrical or rectangular (sundried or fired bricks)' and around this central stele of 'fire altar', 'flat triangular or circular terracotta pieces, known hitherto as terracotta cakes' were placed.

Further, according to Rao (1979: 121 & 1985:15,24,26,27) these ovoid balls and triangular cakes 'were used for ritualistic purposes' and found in different types of 'fire altars'. The triangular terracotta cakes and mushtikas were noticed as offering in 'fire altars' at Rakhigarhi (Nath, 1999: 48). Terracotta cakes have also been reported from Tarkhanewala Dera as part of a square 'fire altar' (Trivedi & Patnaik, 2004: 31). Thus, mushtikas and triangular cakes now have been reportedly associated with the phenomenon of 'fire altars' for well over four decades. Pertinently, besides its association with fire, triangular terracotta cakes were earlier reported to have 'special significance in connection with ritual bathing or other ablutions' by several scholars including Gordon (Allchin, 1993: 235).*(The Enigmatic Mushtikas and the Associated Triangular Terracotta Cakes: Some Observations by J. Manuel)*

To establish the triangular terracotta cakes as "sacred artifact" exclusively used in religious or ritual contexts, it's important to consider their various functions. Besides being offered as oblations and used in religious ceremonies, these cakes were also used in *"ritual bathing or other ablutions*." The sacred nature of these cakes can further be justified when they were placed in industrial furnaces or kilns, symbolizing a token of sacrifice with the expectation of unhindered success of the project.

However, it's crucial to investigate whether these terracotta triangular cakes had any other utility that didn't carry religious sentiments.

Archaeologists have uncovered a multitude of "miniature artifacts" at Indus excavation sites, many of which are smaller renditions of their full-sized counterparts. Most notably, those sites yielded reduced-scale versions of pottery, sparking differing interpretations regarding their purpose. Some regarded them as mere playthings, while others proposed that they served as items for religious worship.

Miniature pots, bowls, and dishes are still found in use in household worshipping place, often within the small confines of the alcove. Harappan people fashioned terracotta toys for their children. So, they may have also produced miniature pottery for a similar purpose. But the considerable production of certain specialized miniature pottery items pointed at a probable connection to religious practices and rituals.

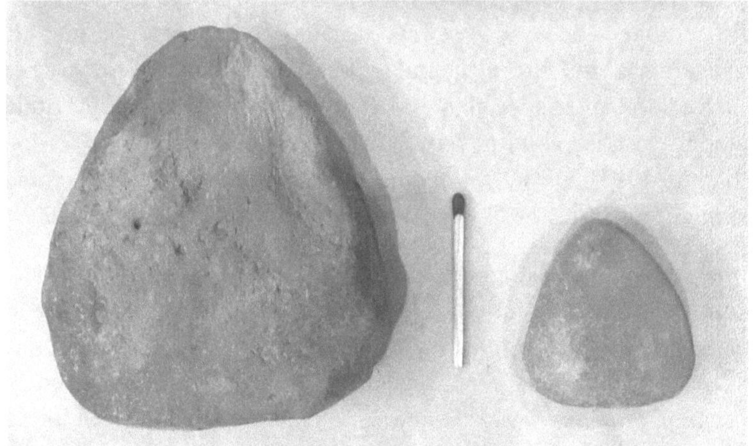

Fig. 11.1 Miniature triangular terracotta cake and a normal triangular terracotta cake (Collection and photo by author)

Similarly, miniature versions of triangular cakes, although quite rare, have also been discovered at archaeological sites (see Figure 11.1 from the original author's collection). If these cakes were intended as playthings for children as kiln related object, one would expect to find miniature kilns or small furnaces among the artifacts, uncovered at the same sites. Moreover, the shape of the miniature triangular cake, as depicted in the picture, is quite larger than what would be typical for a conventional toy. Such a toy-cake could have been easily crafted by shaping potsherds. The creation of this cake required significant attention to detail and passed through various ceramic production stages. Lastly, the absence of miniature cakes in any other form raises doubts about their identification as toys. The perplexity could only be resolved by inferring that even the miniature triangular cakes were part of Harappan rituals.

An essential question arises at this point: Why did the Harappans and their predecessors find this particular triangular shape in terracotta so appealing and chose as oblation for their deities? To answer this question, we must delve deeper into the evolution of human thought and faith, tracing the path from nature worship to gender dynamics, and from customs and traditions to a belief system rooted in fertility cult orientations.

With the emergence of human comprehension of the universe, the concept of the male-female duality and the notion of complementary opposites have profoundly influenced our belief systems. The male and female were perceived as productive and balancing forces or principles that came together to create and sustain the natural world and all living beings. Reproduction was the dynamics that prevailed among the progenitors, and was essential for the survival of the community and the subsequent generations, as well as for the harvest of crops and the fruits produced by the trees. The cave's shelter was embraced as akin to a mother's lap. The enigma of creation was envisioned in the embodiment of "Mother Nature," and the practice of "Mother worship" became ingrained.

During the archaeological expeditions and excavations, we find such motifs, symbols, idols and images that depict the idea of reproduction. The "Ring stone", "Mother Goddess", "Female nude sculpture" and "Expectant mother" are all part of the mother Goddess worship ormaternal deity worship.

It is relevant to note that, alongside the genitalia motif, numerous symbols and motifs of the male phallus (Linga) are also found in plentiful. But we will restrict our study to the supremacy of maternity and its symbol – vulva, the female genitalia (Yoni). And the Yoni is the primary motif of the "fertility cult". The strong connection of the Yoni and copulation with fertility manifests into the depiction of a full-breasted (or many-breasted) figure, a child in her arms and exposed Yoni. Among numerous such artifacts the bronze "Dancing girl" of Harappan civilization was a nude anddisplays the Yoni.

Fig. 11.2 Triangle symbol at the center of tantric Yantradiagram (from Brihattantrasa text)

Another widespread motif/symbol representing female genitalia was the triangle. Its relevance with fertility prompted the Indian Government to use it (with one of its vertices pointing downward) in its family planning campaign. An Indian postage stamp with the triangle symbol was also printed for this purpose (pic 11.3). Hindu rituals have adopted the symbol at many stages and this symbol of fertility found its place in Judaism, Christianity, Buddhism and Jainism. But the symbol of triangle was extensively used in "Tantra", an esoteric and mystical branch of Hindu religion. An integral part of Tantra was "Yantra", a geometric design or diagram that was used as a meditation tool and a visual representation of a specific deity or spiritual concept. Yantras were considered sacred and are an integral part of Tantric rituals and practices. They were used for various purposes, including meditation, worship, and as aids for focusing the mind on spiritual or metaphysical principles.Triangles, especially equilateral triangles, held symbolic significance inTantra, the triangle (pointed downward)was often used to represent the feminine principle, the divine feminine energy (Shakti), and the upward-pointing triangle symbolizes the male phallus, the masculine principle. When these two triangles intersected, they formed the symbol of a six-pointed star or the Shri Yantra, that represented the union of masculine and feminine energies, responsible for creation. The tantric Sri Chakra cult also gave special importance to the yoni. *"The main iconic emblem of the Goddess, the SRI YANTRA, is composed of interlocking triangles. Five of these, symbolizing the yoni, point downward; the other four, symbolizing the LINGAM, point upward, in reference to the union of feminine and masculine qualities and representing the mysteries of creation and destruction"* (Encyclopedia of Hinduism by Constance A. Jones and James D. Ryan)

Fig. 11.3 Stamps of India with triangular symbol

The enigma of life and death, the fusion of masculine and feminine energies, and the fecundity of nature ingrained the symbolism of the triangle in the human psyche. However, as time passed, its fundamental significance evolved within their culture and customs. Similarly, within the realm of Tantra, the triangular symbol underwent various transformations, giving rise to a multitude of concepts, and its core significance was elucidated through a wide array of theories. Thus, the symbol of triangle which was once considered as the supreme deity, transformed into the supreme energy that created the universe, or elsewhere, as the "divine nature". Even the sides of the triangle were interpreted as having several implications.

Not only in India, the same faith associated with the symbol of triangle (or delta) spread independentlyin different parts of the world. A stone was unearthed at Stonehaven (a neolithic archaeological site) in Scotland that bore an engraving of triangle and a fish (which was a recognized symbol of the male phallus). *"The meaning of these symbols can easily be gauged, because, as already noted, they are often not far removed from what they actually signified. Thus the significance of a Delta or a Triangle is quite obvious: it stands for the supreme Female Principle. But the Tantras slightly differ among themselves as to its exact interpretation, some taking it for "Shakti, while creating the Universe", others for "the Eternal prakriti", while still others even attribute meaning to each of its sides. The primitive man, while regarding the Female Principle as both eternal and creative, might not have gone to the length of identifying each side of the triangle. ...The connection of a triangle with the cult is, however, vouchsafed by its occurance on a stone at Stonehaven, where it is accompanied by a fish symbol".(The Mother Goddess by S K Dixit)*

There are numerous examples of using triangle or delta in other cultures, a few are noteworthy as the Egyptian ritualistic bull, described by Greek historian Herodotus. In Herodotus' account, the bull was not an ordinary one but a sacred and revered animal. It was typically chosen for its purity, and the Egyptians believed it to be an embodiment of the god Apis, a deity associated with fertility and strength. The bull was selected based on specific markings, such as a distinctive white triangle on its forehead and other unique characteristics. Some bronze statues of the deity Apis with silver triangle on their forehead, were found at Memphis, in Greece. In India, there is a tradition of branding the foreheads of cows and buffaloes with such symbol. In Hissarlik, which was the ancient city of Troy, an idol of goddess was found with a distinct triangle in her pelvic region. A similar goddess with a triangle replacing her genitalia was found from the archaeological site at Phaistos in Crete.

All these surmises, arguments and examples validate the idea that the fire worship of the Indus valley people did not have any link with Vedic religious practices. Like the Vedic Yajnas, the Harappan fire worship too was deeply rooted in ancient nature worship and its phenomena (oblation, shape, accessories, etc.) differed entirely from their Vedic counterparts. The argument was further strengthened with the revelation that all those archaeological sites presented distinct signs of human existence since microlithic / neolithic era. So, their progenies would carry and protect their ancient belief, was an obvious and logical conclusion.

We also did not find any evidence of a homogeneous form of religious belief system throughout the vast expanse of the Indus civilization. One particular altar of a certain phase at Lothal was completely shelved with disrespect by Harappan people of a later phase while renovating the old structure. Presumably, the altar was part of a cult worship that was pejorative for their successors. As offerings to their deities, those worshippers preferred the triangular terracotta cakes related to another ancient worshipping ritual and representing the fertility cult. So, there was an existence of Harappan Fire Worship Cult that was incorporated through their predecessors from the Stone Age. The hypothesis however, is open to debate as long as we are unable to produce more concrete archaeological evidence. We would only be left with a mere prediction, that the stone age (Paleolithic, Mesolithic and Neolithic) traditions of fire worship, mother goddess cult and fertility cult survived through the Harappan civilization just like the stone scraping, stone knapping and stone carving.

The pivotal question now is - were there any hard evidences of the stone-age people engaging in fire worship and that they revered the triangular cakes and offered them as oblation? For answer to this question, we needed to visit a particular stone-age archaeological site in India in pursuit of our quest for the "Holy Grail" in Indian history.

Baghor is an upper paleolithic archaeological site in the Son River valley near the village of Medhauli, in the Sidhi District, Madhya Pradesh, India. The Baghor site, that turned out to be a treasure of lithic artefacts, was dated between 9000 BCE and 8000 BCE. The site was first excavated under the direction of archaeologists G. R. Sharma of Allahabad University and J. Desmond Clark of University of California, and assisted by Jonathan Mark Kenoyer and J.N. Pal. They published a paper on the existence of the site *(An Upper Paleolithic Site in India? By J M Kenoyer et al)*. Many "rock shelters" was unearthed within the river valley. Inside, cave paintings dating from the Paleolithic to the Mesolithic era were found. Those remarkable rock artsdepicted the lifestyles of the ancient hunter-gatherers and displayed enigmatic designs. The region was inhabited by indigenous tribes such as the Gond, Kol, and Baiga, who, adorned their bodies with intricate designs during ceremonies. A recurring feature in those designs was the presence of a series of concentric triangles, one within the other, in a diminishing order of shape. But presently, our quest is for, a distinct artifact, although those components of the excavation were interconnected.

It was January, 1982. The second excavation of Baghor -1 was underway. Within a vast area, scattered remnants of artifacts left behind by Stone Age people were being uncovered. They included debitage or waste stone flakes, the byproducts of the process where one stone was struck by another to create sharp-edged fragments, as well as Chalcedony nodules, Chert blades and other tools. Readersmay recall that those types of stones were also favored by the Harappans. After clearing the earth and the stones, a sandstone platform was discovered. On the platform, tools and fragments were neatly stacked. It seemed that they were laid down by individuals or families before their deity. Possibly there were other perishable oblations like cereals and fruits too that decomposed over time. Between the protruding piles there were depression with lesser quantity of rubbles. At that very spot, archaeologists found our most 'sought after' artifact – a fire-pit. *(and a possible hearth: ibid Kenoyer etal)*. The sandstone platform was 85 cm in diameter and held a few stone fragments at its center. Stone fragments on the central platform attracted the attention of the team, so the platform was further explored.

The excavation team realized that they were on the verge of uncovering an extremely important artifact assemblage. They looked for and discovered ten pieces of the same stone that had fragmented away from the central piece. Like a jig-saw puzzle the pieces of stone challenged the archaeologist who, after some effort assembled the pieces and lo! The great idol of the stone age took shape before their eyes – a 15 cm high, 6.50 cm wide and 6.50 thick triangle!

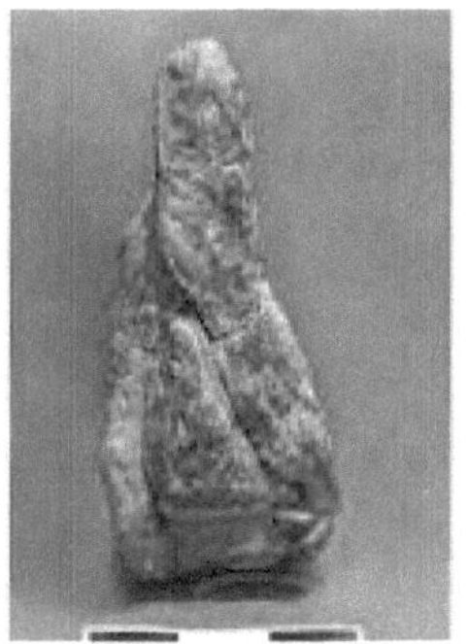

Fig. 11.4 Triangular stone of Baghor (courtesy: Kenoyer et al.)

The position of the idol was determined as exactly at the center of the platform, since seven out of ten stone pieces were located at that very spot. Another aspect that drew attention of the team of excavators was that the complete formation of the idol evolved a complex architectural pattern that was "concentric geometric laminations". A mathematical and geometric concept that involved arranging shapes or patterns in a specific way, with each successive layer or level containing similar or related elements and nested within the previous layer. The great idol held such concentric triangles in diminishing order (pic 11.4). Weathering added spectacular hues to its surface. Similar layered sandstones were available at a distance of 2/3 kilometers. The idol was originally made of a natural stone, probably chosen by the inhabitants for its triangular shape. The sandstone platform and the piles of tools clearly indicated that the arrangements were made on purpose.

The triangular stone and the fire-pit! The stage was now set for a corroboration of the fire worship-fertility cult theory. Further anthropological proof of transmission of the faith and the cult over the centuries was found among the tribals, the Kols, the Bhils and the Baigas who still held on to hunting and gathering. Archaeologists learned that those tribals had a female deity, "Mata" or "Mai". The tribals used the same type of colorful natural stone with concentric geometric laminations, often in the form of triangles which symbolizes their "Mai" known as "Kerai Mata".

Fig. 11.5 Triangular stone on the open shrine of Angari Mai or Fire Goddess (Courtesy: Kenoyer et al)

The open-air shrine of the Kerai Mata was 1 km northeast of the site. Upon visiting, the archaeological team found a roughly circular platform composed of sandstone and limestone rubble blocks on which six natural pieces of triangular and ellipsoidal stone were placed. In addition to those natural stones, a headless figurine, also called Angari Devi (pic 11.5) was located. *"In addition to these natural stones there is a headless figurine of what one informant called Angari Devi (the Goddess of Burning Coals) who is probably the same as Angar Matti, a Goddess worshipped by the Agaria. The six stones of the centre of the shrine all have triangular or ellipsoidial laminations ranging in colour from*

226

yellowish red to reddish brown and are identical nature to the one found in the excavations. These stones are said to represent the Goddess and are smeared with vermilion, while the area around the shrine is littered with broken coconut shells, shorn locks of hair, potsherds and fragments of clay figurines" (ibid Kenoyar et al)

Now, we can rule out the possibility that the Baghor stone happened to be there by chance, as similar stone-slab was being worshipped elsewhere. The placement of the one-piece natural stone was also at the center of a sandstone platform and the constituent stone-pieces were also geometrically shaped. During the excavation, local people (some of them even Muslims) recognized and revered the excavated stone at Baghor as their own deity. They even accused the team of breaking it! But later prostrated before the stone structure.

Baghor is not the one and only pre-historic site where triangular stone was found. Two stones were found at Burzahom in Kashmir from a neolithic archaeological site. One was rectangular with a hunting scene engraving; the other smaller stone was triangular in shape with a tectiform engraving *(B M Pandey:1969)*. The stones were attached to remains of stone slabs and sand, implying that they were placed on a platform.

Evidence, so far concealed in the rugged remnants of the paleolithic era at Baghor -1strengthened my belief that much before the Harappans, paleolithic tradition of offering triangle-shaped oblation by the fire to a mother Goddess not only existed but also found its way into Indus civilization over different regions of   the
Harappan dominion especially in the eastern part. The fact that the same tradition of worship was being followed by the local inhabitants to this day at Baghor left no doubt that it prevailed during the chalcolithic Indus period too. The triangular-shaped stone chosen by the paleolithic worshippers of Baghor was later replaced with terracotta cakes by the Harappans since their settlements, mostly close to the alluvial riverbanks did not yield

stones in abundance. Ubiquitous presence of triangular terracotta cakes in and around the Indus fire-pitss finally could be accounted for.

A socio-religious allusion also could be derived with regard to the use of triangular cake having relevance with fertility and the female reproductive organ. In present day Tantra practices, we find the triangle motif connected to womanhood. One would be curious about whether the Indus people ever thought of instituting a stone triangle for their worship, retaining the tradition of their ancestors. It was natural for them to have at least one or two stone carved triangular effigies at their community worshipping places, in addition to their common terracotta cakes.

"During an important Indus archaeological field day at Mithathal in 2022, I (author) found a stone-made triangular artifact. It was black and possibly made of Basalt stone. Since black Basalt stone was not native to Mithathal, it was indeed brought in from some other place and carved to obtain the desired shape. It is quite popular   in India to sculpt statues with black stones especially Basalt, popularly known as "Kastipathor". Recovery of this triangular stone-carving was a significant find. Thorough scrutiny also confirmed that it was man-made and not formed by natural causes. It was carved with precision to get an equilateral triangular form, and then polished to produce a smooth surface. I can visualize the triangular stone, the symbol of the mighty Harappan fire goddess, seated under Ficus Religiosa, the sacred Peepal tree of the Indus people.

Fig. 11.6 Traingular stone found at Indus site

(collection and photo: Author)

We have reached the end of our study. In this journey, we have encountered the Yajna hearths, the Indus archaeological sites, the Harappan kilns and furnaces, pre-Harappan culture and finally the pendant of the chain of subjects – the Goddess of fire and the quest for her triangular stone. After this study it is felt that during the Indus civilization the mantle of fire worship was passed on to the Harappans, by the descendants of indigenous inhabitants that existed in a period prior to pre-Harappan era or the indigenous elements retained and protected their ethnicity through cult worship, during the Harappan phases.

The Vedic Agni was a powerful male deity. In contrast, the Indus fire worship was dedicated to an embodiment of a maternity principle, a female deity. The triangular terracotta cakes were her oblation, and so was earth or clay, as representation of a cult worship similar to the fertility cult. Within a vast territory there existed several streams of faith or cults in the realm of the common religion. They were prevalent on regional basis. In Bengal, there

229

were the Vishnu cult (Vaishnavites), the Mother Goddess cult (Shaktism), Shiva cult (Shivaite) etc and the locally popular deities emerging through myths and urban legends. Other religions too had their share of such sub-denominations. In Islam, there were the Sufis, the Salafis, the Malikis and the Hanafis and the Zaidis. In Christianity – the New Apostolic, the Jehovah's Witnesses, the Quakers and the Unitarian Universalists.

The Harappans could not be free from such diversities. Despite the extensive presence of female deities in most sites, the absence of female goddess in the river plains of Ghaggar-Chautang was awe-inspiring. Fire worship took precedence over other faiths in this area. Clearly, the Indus Valley Civilization comprised of a diverse culture and faith.

Om purnamadah purnamidam purnat purnamudachyate

purnasya purnamadaya purnamevavashisyate

Om Shaantih Shaantih Shaanti.

What is visible is the infinite. What is invisible is also the infinite.

Out of the Infinite Being the finite has come, yet being infinite, only infinite remains.

Peace in my heart, peace with each other, peace in the cosmos.

Stone Age Chronology

(Area wise may differ)

Phase	Approximate timescale	Tools	Ways of gathering food
Lower Paleolithic	100 thousand years from today	(Pebble & Core Tools	Hunting & gathering
Middle Paleolithic	Between 100 thousand and 40 thousand years from today	Introduction of flake tools	Hunting & gathering
Upper Paleolithic	Between 40 thousand and 10 thousand years from today	Making of blades & Burin	Hunting & gathering
Mesolithic	Between 10 thousand and 8 thousand years from today	Microlith	Hunting, gathering, fishing, animal domestication (in some areas)
Neolithic	Between 8 thousand and 4 thousand years from today	Polished and ground tools	Hunting, gathering, fishing, animal domestication & agriculture

Measurements related to Vedic Yajna were mostly based according to the Yajman or sacrificier's body.. The values of those units of measurement are mentioned in various scriptures. Here is a concise list of them:

1 Anguli (finger)		= 14 Anu
		= 34 Til (sesame seed)
		= 8 Yab (barley seed)
1 Khudra pada (small foot)		= 10 Anguli
1 Pada (foot)		= 15 Anguli
1 Pradesha		= 12 Anguli
1 Pritha or Uttaryuga		= 13 Anguli
1 Isha		= 188 Anguli
1 Aksha (axis)		= 104 Anguli
1 Yuga		= 86 Anguli
1 Janu (Thigh)		= 32 Anguli
1 Shamya (arm)		= 36 Anguli
1 Prakrama	= 2 pada	= 30 Anguli
1 Artni	= 2 pradesh	= 24 Anguli (18 inches)
1 Shay		= 24 Anguli
1 Purusha or Vyam = 5 Aratni		= 96 Anguli
1 Prakrama		= 2 Padas (Istiyaga)
		= 3 padas (in PashuYag)

	= 2 ^ 1/2 Pada (in SomaYag)
	= 5 Pada (Sagnik yajna)
1 Rathaksha (axis of a chariot)	= 4 Aratnis (Anagni Yajna)

First Physical Evidence of Vedic Maha-Yajna

After studying the Vedic Yajnas with its myriad nuances and procedural precision over the rites, readers would naturally be curious about whether there was any physical evidence of the Vedic Yajnas described in this book. There exist conflicting theories among experts and scholars on the subject. But our research had established that the Vedic Yajna sites and the associated paraphernalia were all perishableitems like bamboos, grass, timber, etc. and used to build in temporary fashion. But the brick altars of the Vedic period needed to be explored. We have found some of such brick altars especially Ashwamedh Yajna. Archaeological record of 1000 BCE showed that after the decline of the great Indus Valley Civilization, remnants of the oldest Vedic Agnicayan Yajna was found at Kaushambi, in present Uttar Pradesh, India. By its shape, historians identified it as a "Cyena (hawk) citi" Yajna altar. The majestic bird with its outspread wings faced the southeast direction.

There were pits dug initially to erect the Yajna Vedi with the minimum depth measuring 6 feet 10 inches below ground level. A layer of loose gravel spread over the pits yielded bovine bone fragments. Another 5 feet 3.5 inches square-shaped pit with 1 foot depth was found behind the gravel pit that was paved with fired bricks. Those bricks came with different shapes and sizes, they were triangular, rectangular, hexagonal, etc. Dimension of the largest brick was 19.5 inches X 11.5 inches. They were special bricks made for specific purpose. A three inched thick sand layer covered the foundation on which the actual Vedi was constructed layer by layer with stone, pebbles, sand, clay and gravel. Most part of the altar were destroyed. A part of the top-most layer at a height of 8 feet resembled the Uttarvedi. The dimension of the entire vedi was 49.8 feet in length and 33.6 feet in breadth. The figure of hawk covered an area of 19 feet 6 inches long and 13 feet breadth. The extended wing span measured 14 feet 3 inches. The right wing, mostly found intact, measured 9 feet 10 inches. The wings comprised bricks as large as 18 X 11 inches and as small as 3.5 X 3 inches. A considerable part of the vedi that contained bricks was vandalized by miscreants. On the east, west and center of the Vedi, Yajna vessels were found containing unknown oblatory materials.

A human skull that lay in between two Yajna vessels was found near the tail-side of the Hawk. The vessels were turned upside down. A terracotta figurine of a woman was also found. She had six long braids in which trident, whip, etc. were embedded.

The first layer of the Maha Vedi held a peculiar item. A mound of gravel with cavities. It was neatly surrounded by ten special bricks. One trapezoid brick attracted the attention of the excavators. It had two equal sides of 3 inches. While the unequal sides were 7.5 and 4.5 inches. It lay at a distance of 1 foot 9 inches from the gravel mound. The 2-inch thick red brick was made by clay and bone chips. A few bones were seen protruded from the brick. The most important aspect of the brick was the image it carried. It was the image of a man tied up with the sacrificial pillar (Yupakashtha). The human figure was depicted with wobbly legs, hands helplessly dangling and ready to be slaughtered. It was tied at three parts of its body, with the pillar. The picture included the weapon to be used in the sacrifice. Three lines were drawn on the surface of the brick. Besides, on the first layer of the Mahavedi, a horse-skull, an elephant bone, tortoise bone, jawbone of boar, and bones of Indian humped cattle were found on the first layer of the Mahavedi. An iron-made snake was also found on that layer. On the second layer and above the gravel mound, a jaw-bone of bull was found amidst bricks of various sizes. Numerous bone fragments were found from the third layer, comprising a total of 234 bones. Some of them bore marks of slaughter. Out of those 234 bones, three unscathed human skulls and ten skull bones including the human jaw were found. The fourth and fifth top layers were damaged considerably by antiquities-looters and natural causes over the centuries. Yet 30 bone fragments were recovers from those two layers out of which seven were human skeletal remains.

Sketch of Cyena (hawk) citi excavated at Kaushambi

(Courtesy- Sharma:1960, University of Allahabad)

THE SACRED TRIANGLE OF BAEL LEAVES

Aegle Marmelos, commonly known as Bael, also referred to as Bengal quince, golden apple, Japanese bitter orange, stone apple, or wood apple, is a species of tree, native to the Indian subcontinent and Southeast Asia. It is found in India, Pakistan, Bangladesh, Sri Lanka, and Nepal as a naturalized species. This tree is considered sacred by Hindus and Buddhists.

Phallus-shaped artifacts were discovered in many Harappan archaeological sites. It is a well-established fact that the "Shivalinga" represented the primitive fertility cult, symbolizing the union of man and woman. The tradition of using the three-leafed Bael plant as a representation of the three eyes of Shiva continued to the present day. While there were other gods with three eyes, the three-leafed Bael became the primary motif for the worship of the Shivalinga. By joining the tips of the three leaves, one can create an imaginary triangle. It was possible that the recognition of the triangle influenced the choice of Bael leaves by ancient religious minds.

The sacred triangle of Bael leaves

Bibliography

- Acharya Sriram Sharma: Rigveda Samhita (4 volumes)
- Agarwal D P & Chakrabarti Dilip K: Essays in Indian Protohistory
- Allchin F. R. & Bridget Allchin: Origins of a Civilisation: The Pre-History and Early Archeology of South Asia: 1987
- Allchin Bridget and Raymond: Birth of Indian Civilization: 1968
- Allchin Bridget And Raymond: The Rise Of Civilization In India And Pakistan: 1996
- ASI: Indian Archeology 1983-84-A Review: Nageshwar excavation
- ASI: Indian Archeology 1985-86-A Review: Kutch area excavation
- ASI: Indian Archeology 1987-88-A Review: Banawali excavation
- ASI: Indian Archeology 1998-99-A Review: Kunal excavation
- ASI: Indian Archeology 2006-07-A Review: Kanmer & Mithathal excavation
- ASI: Indian Archeology 2007-08-A Review: Shivsagar excavation
- ASI: Indian Archeology 2008-09-A Review: Shikarpur excavation
- ASI: Indian Archeology 2009-10-A Review: Khirsara excavation
- ASI: Indian Archeology 2010-11-A Review: Karsola excavation
- ASI: Indian Archeology 2012-13-A Review: Khirsara excavation
- ASI: Indian Archeology 2013-14-A Review: Karanpura excavation
- Avari Burjor: India: The Ancient Past A history of the Indian sub-continent from c. 7000 BC to AD 1200: 2007
- • Anirban: Bedmimansa (three volumes): 1975Banerjea Jitendra Nath: The Delvelopment of Hindu Iconography: 1941 (Beng)
- Bhan Kuldebp And Kenoyer Jonathan Mark: Nageshwara: A Mature Harappan Shell Working Site On The Gulf Of Kutch, Gujarat: 1984
- Bhattachrya Sripadasharmna: Kathak Samhita

- Bisht R S: Excavations at Banawali in Possehl Gregory L: Harappan Civilisation A recent perspective: 1982
- Bisht R S: Excavations at Dholavira: 2015
- Buhler Georg: The Sacred Laws of the Aryas, as taught in the schools of Apastamba, Gautama, Basishtha and Baudhayana: 1882
- Basu Dr. Yogiraj: Beder Parichay: 1980 (Beng)
- Bhattacharya Narendranath: Dharma o Songskriti, Prachin Bharatiya prekkhapot: 2013 (Beng)
- Bhattacharya Harinarayana: Sankhayana Brahman: 1377 (Beng)
- Bhattacharya Vidhusekhara: Shatapatha Brahman (Beng)
- Vidyabhushan Avalucharan: Amulyacharan Vidyabhushan Rachnabali (Part I): 1982 (Beng)
- Brahmachari Dr. Mahanambrata: Veda-Vedanta Uttarkhand Veda Vichintan: 1999 (Beng)
- Caland Willem & Lokesh Chandra: Sāṅkhāyana-śrautasūtra: 1953
- Chakrabartri Dilip K & Lal Makkhan: History of Ancient India Volume I & II: 2014
- Chakrabarti Dilip K: Who Owns the Indian Past?The Case of the Indus Civilization: 2009
- Chakrabarti Dilip K: india-An Archaeological History
- Chakrabarti Dilip K: The oxford Companion of Indian Archeology: 2006
- Chakrabarti Dilip K: The Archeology of Ancient Indian Cities: 1997
- Chakrabarti Dilip K(ed): Indus civilization sites in India new discoveries: 2004
- Chanda Ramaprasad: Survival of The Prehistoric Civilisation of the Indus Valley (MASI No. 41): 1998
- Chase Brad, Rajesh S V, Ambika Patel & Bhanu Prakash Sharma: Materializing Harappan identities: Unity and diversity in the borderlands of the Indus Civilization: 2014
- Chwalkowski Farrin: Symbols in Arts, Religion and Culture: The Soul of Nature: 2016
- Cortesi E, Tosi M, Lazzari A And Vidale M: Cultural Relationships Beyond The Iranian Plateau: The Helmand Civilization, Baluchistan And The Indus Valley In The 3rd Millennium Bce
- Chattopadhyay Amarakumar: Ashvalayan Shrautasutra: The Asiatic Society (Beng)
- Chattopadhyay Amarkumar: Vedic Yagna: 2003 (Beng)
- Chattopadhyay Rasikamohan and Chandrakumar Tarkalankara: Brihat Tantrasara: 1369 (Beng)

- Dales F George: Civilization and Floods in the Indus Valley: 1965
- Dangi Vivek: Current Situation on the Indus Civilization: 2011
- Dangi Vivek & Manmohan Kumar: Pre-Harappan Culture of Ghaggar Basin: Recent Perspective in Harappan Studies: 2017
- Danino Michel: The Harappan Legacy
- Danino Michel: The Lost River, On the Trail of the Saraswati
- Dibyopama Astha And Vasant Shinde: Early Historic Archaeology Of Rajasthan: Recent Perspectives
- Didier Aurore, David Sarmiento Castillo, Pascal Mongne, Syed Shakir Ali Shah: Resuming excavations at Chanhu-daro, Sindh: First results of the 2015-2017
- Dikshit K. N: Excavations At Hulas (1978 – 1983) (From Harappan Times To Early Medieval):2020
- Dikshit K. N: Rise of Civilisation in the Saraswati Valley and Adjoining Indus Region:
- Dikshit S K: The Mother Goddess:
- Dwivedi Amitabhvikram: Gṛhya Sūtras: 2018
- Datta Rameshchandra : Hindu Shastra Four Volumes: 1303 (Beng)
- Datta Rameshchandra : Rigveda Samhita (two volumes): 1358 (Beng)
- Eggeling Julius: Satapatha Brahmana: 1894
- Fleming Andrew The myth of the mother-goddess : 1969
- Forizs Laszlo: Apāṁ Napāt, Dīrghatamas and the Construction of the Brick Altar Analysis of RV 1.143 Conference Paper: January 2003
- Fairservis Jr. Walter A: The Roots of Ancient India
- Frenez Dennys: The Lothal Revisitation Project. A Fine Thread Connecting Ancient India to Contemporary Ravenna (via Oman): 2014
- Frutiger Adrian: Signs and Symbols Their Design and Meaning: 1989
- Gabre Richard: The Srautasutra of Apastamba: 1883
- Gabre Richard: Vaitana Sutra: 1878
- Ghosh A: An Encyclopedia of Indian Archeology: 1989
- Gosden Chris, Barry Cunliffe, and Rosemary A. Joyce: The Oxford Handbook of Archaeology
- Green Adam S: Killing the Priest King: Addressing Egalitarianism in the Indus Civilization: 2020
- Ghosh Jagadishchandra: Srimad Bhagavad Gita (Beng)
- Gupta Nalinikanta: Veder parichay: 1966 (Beng)
- Harari Yuval Noah: Sapiens: A Brief History of Humankind : 2015

- Haug Martin: Aiterya Brahman of the Rigveda and Rites of the Vedic Religion Vol I: 1863
- Haug Martin: Aiterya Brahman of the Rigveda and Rites of the Vedic Religion Vol II: 1923
- Hawthorne Nathaniel: Fire Worship: 2020
- Heather M.-L. Miller: Pottery Firing structures (Kilns) of the Indus Civilization during the Third Millennium B.C.: 1997
- Hillebrandt Alfred: Sankhayana Srautasutra: 1888
- James E O: The Cult of the Mother Goddess: 1959
- Jansen Michael: Mohenjo-Daro, city of the Indus Valley: 1985
- Jansen Michael: Forgotten Coities of Indus: 1991
- Jarrige]ean-Francois and Richard H. Meadow: The Antecedents of Civilization in the Indus Valley: 1980
- Jones A Constance and Rya D James: Encyclopedia of Hinduism: 2007
- Joshi J P: Excavation at Surkotada and exploration in Kutch: 1990
- Joshi J P: Harappan Architecture and Civil Engineering: 2020
- Kak Subhash C: The astronomy of the age of geometric altars. Quarterly Journal of the Royal Astronomical Society, vol. 36, 1995
- Kak Subhash C: The astronomy of the Vedic altars: 1993
- Kalyanaraman S: Export processing zone of Sarasvati civilization, metal workshops at Binjor 4MSR and Indus Script Corpora
- Kashikar C G: Baudhāyana-Śrauta-Sutra
- Kenoyer Jonathan Mark, Clark J D, Pal J N & Sharma G R: An Upper Paleolithic Shrine in India?: 1983
- Kenoyer Jonathan And Mark Richard H. Meadow: Excavations at Harappa 1994-1995: Perspectives on the Indus Script, Craft Activities and City Organization:
- Kenoyer Jonathan Mark: Birth of a Civilization: 1998
- Kenoyer Jonathan Mark: Cultures and Societies of the Indus Tradition
- Kenoyer Jonathan Mark: Early City States in South Asia
- Kenoyer Jonathan Mark: Early Developments of Art, Symbol and Technology in the Indus Valley Civilization: 2001
- Kenoyer Jonathan Mark & Heather M.-L. Miller: Metal Technologies Of The Indus Valley tradition In Pakistan And Western India
- Kenoyer Jonathan Mark: The Indus Valley Tradition of Pakistan and Western India: 1991
- Kenoyer Jonathan Mark: Uncovering The Keys To The Lost Indus Cities: 2003

- Khan Aurangzeb and Carsten Lemmen: Bricks and urbanism in the Indus Civilization: 2014
- Kharakwal J. S: Kanmer : A Multicultural Site in Kachchh, Gujarat, India: 2009
- Kharakwal Jeewan S & Shruti: History Of Science And Technology –A New Perspective
- Kintaert Thomas: On the Role of the Lotus Leaf in South Asian Cosmography Article: 2012
- Knipe David M: Vedic Voices Intimate Narratives Of A Living Andhra Tradition: 2015
- Krishnan K. and Sneh Pravinkumar Patel: The Art and Technology of Reserving a Slip. A Complex Side of Indus Ceramic Tradition in Walking with the Unicorn Edited by Dennys Frenez, Gregg M. Jamison, Randall W. Law, Massimo Vidale and Richard H. Meadow
- Kumar Ashish: Sonkh: A Tale Of Two Shrines, Journal Of History & Social Sciences Volume Vii: December 2017
- Kumar Manmohan et al: Excavations at Mithathal, District Bhiwani(2011)A Preliminary Report:
- Kumar Nitin: Tantra : The Art of Philosophy: 2009
- Kumar Manmohan: Settlements in the Ghaggar –Yamuna Divide in current studies on the Indus Civilisation: 2011
- Kyoko Amano: A Non-Srauta Ritual in the Oldest Yajurveda Text. Maitrayani Samhita (Gonamika Chapter: 2019
- Kundu Sagarchandra: Agni Brahmer Tattwa and Ahuti Prakaran: 1926 (Beng)
- Lal B.B., Jagat Pati Joshi A.K. Sharma Madhu Bala K.S. Ramachandra: Excavations At Kalibangan, The Harappans Part – I&II
- Lal B.B., B K Thapar, Madhu Bala: Excavations At Kalibangan, The Early Harappans: 2003
- Lal B B: A Picture Emerges: An Assessment of the Carbon 14 Datings of the Protohistoric Cultures of the Indo-Pakistan Subcontinent
- Lal B B & S P Gupta: Frontiers of the Indus Civilisation, Sir Moieemaer Wheeler Commemoration Volume
- Lal B B: The Earliest Civilisation of South Asia: 1997
- Larios Borayin: Embodying the Vedas:2009
- Lahiri Durgadas: Yajurveda Samhita: 1358 (Beng)
- Lahiri Durgadas: Samveda Samhita: 1358 (Beng)
- Mackay E J H: Further Excavations at Mohenjodaro Vol I & II

- Macron Vincent & Mutin Benjamin: Shahi-Tump: Results of the Last Field-Seasons (2001-2003: 2005
- Mahalik Er. Nirakar: Worship Of Mother-Goddess: 2009
- Maisels Charles Keith: Early Civilizations Of The Old World: 1999
- Mallory J P & D Q Adams: An Encyclopedia of Indo-European Culture
- Manuel J: The Enigmatic Mushtikas and the Associated Triangular Terracotta Cakes: Some Observations: 2010
- Marbaniang Domenic: History of Hinduism: Prevedic and Vedic Age: 2015
- Marshall Sir John: Mohenjo-Daro And The Indus Civilization (3 volumes);
- McIntosh Jane R: The Ancient Indus Valley New Perspectives: 2008
- Meadow Richard H: Harappa Excavations 1986-1990 A Multidisciplinary Approach to Third Millennium Urbanism
- Menon M Srikumar: The "Round Mound" and its Structural Requirements: A Possible Scenario for the Evolution of the Form of the Stupa: 2016
- Munshi K. M., R. C. Majumdar, A. D. Pusalker: The Age Of Imperial Unity: 1960
- Majumdar Narendrakumar: Yajnavedi and Yajnagni (Beng)
- Nandagopa Prabhakar: Evolution of Early Human Settlements in the Sarasvati River Basin: Archaeological Evidence and Site Distribution Analysis (paper): 2020
- Nandagopal Prabhakar & Randal Madiso: Mitathal: New Observations based on Surface Reconnaissance and Geological Provenance Studies Article: 2010
- Nath Dr. Amarendra: Excavations at Rakhigarhi: 2014
- Ninan Prof M M: The Development Of Hinduism: 2008
- Oldenberg Hermann: Āśvalayana Grihya Sutra
- Oldenberg Hermann: Ankhayana Grihya Sutra, Asvalayana Grihya Sutra, Paraskara Grihya Sutra, Khadira Grihya Sutra: 1886
- Oldenberg Hermann: Gobhila Grihya Sutra, Hiranyakesin Grihya Sutra, Apastamba Grihya Sutra
- Olivelle Patrick: Between the Empires: Society in India 300 BCE to 400 CE: 2006
- Otto Bernd-Christian, Rau Susanne and Rüpke Jörg: History and Religion:2015

- Pande B M: Neolithic Hunting Scene on a Stone Slab from Burzahom, Kashmir: 1969
- Parpola Asko: The Roots of Hinduism The Early Aryans and the Indus Civilization: 2015
- Pathik Pratishtha: The Historical and Philosophical Exegesis on Yagya in Ancient India: 2019
- Patra Dr.Benudhar: Beginning of Agricultural Life in India
- Petraglia Michael D and Allchin Bridget: The Evolution and History of Human Populations in South Asia Inter-disciplinary Studies in Archaeology, Biological Anthropology, Linguistics and Genetics: 2007
- Piggott Stuart Prehistoric India To Iooo B.C.
- Possehl Gregory L: Ancient Cities of the Indus: 1979
- Possehl Gregory L: Harappan Civilisation A recent perspective: 1982
- Possehl Gregory L: Harappan Civilization and Rojdi: 1989
- Possehl Gregory L: The Indus Civilization A Contemporary Perspective: 2002
- Pottentavida Ajithprasad: The Pre-Harappan cultures of Gujarat: 2002
- Pracchia Stefano & Vidale Massimo: The Archaeological Context of Stoneware Firing at Mohenjo Daro
- Pradhan S. V: The Indus Valley Cones, Cakes And Baffles: 1999
- Pal Vimalakrishna: Vedasar Sanchayana: 2013 (Beng)
- Raczek Teresa P: Subsistence Strategies And Burial Rituals: Social Practices In The Late Deccan Chalcolithic
- Ranade H G: Latyayana Srauta Sutra (3 Vol)
- Rao V.D.N: Essence Of Aapastamba Grihya Sutras: 2019
- Rao S. R: Lothal A Harappan Port Town 1955-62 Vol I & II: 1985
- Rao S. R: Excavation at Rangpur and other explorations in Gujarat
- Ratnagar Shereen: Enquiries into the Political Organization of Harappan Society: 1991
- Ratnagar Shereen: The End of the Great Harappan Tradition: 2000
- Ratnagar Shereen: The Other Indians Essays On Pastoralists And Prehistoric Tribal People: 2004
- Ratnagar Shereen: Understanding Harappa
- Rawat Yaduvir Singh: The Coastal Sites Possible Port Towns of Harappan time in Gujarat:
- Rick Doble: Neolithic Fertility Symbolism During the Winter Solstice at the Newgrange Passage Tomb in Ireland: 2015
- Ray Ashoka: Matrikashakti (Beng)

- Sali Dr S A: Excavation at Daimabad: 1983
- Sarkar Amrita: Indian Chalcolithic Culture: Aspects of Craft and technology Article: 2014
- Seignobos Charles: History Of Ancient Civilization
- Sekhar DMR: Indus Religion
- Shaffer J G & Thapar B K: Pre-Indus And Early Indus Cultures Of Pakistan And India
- Sharif M And B. K. Thapar: Food-Producing Communities In Pakistan And Northern India:
- Sharma Dr. Rudranath: Culture and Cililisation as revealed in the Shrautashutras: 1977
- Sharma G R: Excavations at Kaushambi: 1960
- Sharma Shalini, Sanjay Kumar Manjul, Arvin Manjul, Puran Chand Pande, & Anil K Pokharia: Dating Adoption And Intensification Of Food-Crops: Insights From 4msr (Binjor), An Indus (Harappan) Site In Northwestern India: 2020
- Shinde Vasant: The Origin and Development of the Chalcolithic in Central India
- Shinde Vasant And Sengar P B S: Excavations At Karsola Kheda, Jind District, Haryana,2010- 11
- Shinde Vasant, Osada Toshiki, Uesugi Akinori And Kumar Manmohan: Linguistics, Archaeology And The Human Past A Report On Excavations At Farmana 2007-08: 2008
- Sinha B P: Potteries in Ancient India: 1969
- Sonawane V H: Early Farming Communities of Gujarat, India
- Soni Neha: Important Fertility symbols and Rites (Northern India)
- Staal Frits (Edited): Agni The Vedic Ritual Of The Fire Altar Vol I & II: 1983
- Subramanian T.S.: Telltale Furnaces in Frontline: June 23, 2017 (Bijnor 4MSR)
- Sykorova I: Ancient Indian Mathematics: University of Economics, Department of Mathematics, Prague, Czech Republic: 2006
- Sri Aurobindo: Hymns to the Mystic Fire: 1995
- Sankhya -Vedantatirtha Durgacharana: Brihadaranyakopanishad (two volumes): 1371 (Beng)
- Shastri Dakshinaranjan: Prabandha Sanggraha; 1946 (Beng)
- Thapar B K: Kalibangan A Harappan Metropolis Beyond the Indus Valley: 1975
- Thite Ganesh U: Apastamba Srauta Sutras 2 volumes: 213
- Thite G U: Katyayana Srautasutra English Translation 2 Vols

- Teshim Hideki: Variations of the Vedic Unit Prakrama (Step) Applied for Measuring Length at Ritual Sites: 2019
- Trivedi P K: Excavations At Tarkhanewala-Dera And Chak 86 (2003-2004): 2009
- Tsuji N: The Agnicayana Section of the Maitrayani-Samhita with Special Reference to the Manava Srautasutra, in AGNIThe Vedic Ritual Of The Fire Altar, Volume II Ed- Frits Staal
- Tull Herman: Vedic Agni: 2014
- Tarkatirtha Dayalakrishna: Govil Grhya Sutra (Beng)
- Trivedi Ramendrasundar: Veda Katha Yajna Katha: 2017 (Beng)
- Trivedi Ramendrasundara : Ramendra Rachnavali Pancham Khanda: Aitareya Brahmana (Beng)
- Uesugi Akinori: Current Research on Indus Archaeology: 2018
- Vats M S: Excavations at Harappa Vol I & II: 1940
- Wheeler Sir Mortimer: Civilizations of the Indus Valley and beyond: 1966
- Wheeler Sir Mortimer: The Indus Civilization: Supplementary Volume To The Cambridge History Of India: 1968
- Wright Rita P: The Ancient Indus: Urbanism, Economy, and Society: 2009
- www.wisdom.lib.org for Sulvasutras and other important Vedic scriptures.